Cameron McKenzie's

SCJA Certification Guide

SCJA

www.scja.com

Sun Certified Java Associate

The Best Java Certification Site: www.scja.com
Free J2EE Tutorials: www.portorials.com
Just Darned Good Books: www.agoodbookon.com

978-1-59872-902-3

By Cameron McKenzie

Edited by Daniel Thaemar, Kerri Sheehan, Kaydell Leavit & Jim Anderson

Cameron McKenzie's SCJA Certification Guide

By Cameron McKenzie

Edited by Daniel Thaemar, Kerri Sheehan, Kaydell Leavit & Jim Anderson

2nd Edition, First Printing

Good Book Publishing

Notice of Liability

The information in this book is printed and distributed on an "as is" basis, without any warranty or guarantee of accuracy. IBM WebSphere® and J2EE is a huge technology, so any application of the technology, or following of any suggestions in this book, must be tested and retested before any conclusions are to be made about its validity. While every effort and precaution has been taken in the preparation of this book and materials, the author and publisher shall have no liability to any person, company or entity with respect to any loss, damage, problems or conflicts to be caused directly or indirectly by the instructions contained in this book, or by the hardware and software components described in this book. The content of this book is the opinion of the author. It is the responsibility of the reader to use the technology and test the validity of any opinions or assertions made in this document, and come to their own conclusions.

Trademarks

IBM® and IBM Rational® are registered trademark of International Business Machines in the United States, other countries or both.

WebSphere® is a trademark of IBM as well. IBM also owns DB2®, Informix®, SP® VisualAge®, iSeries®, SP2®, Informix®, MQSeries® Rational® and Sametime®, CICS®, QuickPlace®. These are all trademarks in the United States, other countries or both.

Java® J2EE® J2SE® J2ME® and all Java-based trademarks are trademarks of Sun Microsystems®, Inc

Microsoft®, Windows®, .NET® and the Windows logo are trademarks of Microsoft® Corporation.

Oracle® is a registered trademark of Oracle® Inc.
Palm Pilot® is a registered trademark of palmOne
Netscape® is a registered trademark of Netscape Communications Corporation.
Opera® is a registered trademark of Opera Software AS
Unix is a registered trademark of The Open Group in the US and other countries.
These trademarks and registered trademarks are of the US, other countries or both.

We have attempted throughout this book to distinguish proprietary trademarks from descriptive terms by following the capitalization style used by the manufacturer.

We are in no way associated with IBM, Microsoft, Oracle or Sun Microsystems. We just really like their products, and we want you to like them too!

ISBN 978-1-59872-902-3

**Thanks to all the girls at Tim Hortons,
especially that cute brunette on drive-thru. :)**

**Thanks to Kaydell Leavitt, Daniel Thaemar and Jim Anderson
for the great feedback and smart suggestions.**

**No book is perfect, but we try. ☺
For earrattuh, go to http://www.scja.com/errata.html**
(This is the 1st printing of the 2nd edition)

I do short print runs, and am constantly updating & improving the content. If you catch a typo, or have a suggestion, let me know. You'll be amazed at how quickly your suggestions and comments make it into print!

Table of Contents

Part One:
The Wide World of Java

Chapter 1
The Java Split

In The Beginning

A long time ago, in a cubicle far, far away, a really clever dude named Patrick Naughton was working at Sun Microsystems for the summer. He did all sorts of odd jobs around the office, with some of his most annoying and repetitive tasks being answering the same dumb questions, and solving the same dumb programming problems, for a variety of different programming languages, that ran on a variety of different hardware and software platforms.

Like so many young bucks about to leave their summer job, Patrick sent out a snotty little letter to all of his superiors that outlined everything that he thought was moronic about how languages were being developed at Sun, and how things could be done so much better, and so much easier, if they just put the time and effort into improving and consolidating their programming technology. Patrick then ended the letter with some statement about *"the horse you rode in on"* and then looked forward to his next career at a little up and coming company called Netscape. Remember, this all happened around the early 90's.

Well, something strange happened after Patrick sent out his letter. Rather than getting a swift kick in the ass by all the starched shirts at Sun, Mr. Naughton was told that he should come back, work with some of the most brilliant Canadians at Sun Microsystems, and see if they could all come up with something *kewl* and *exciting*. It was out of these mental jam sessions that the cross platform, object-oriented programming language named Oak, later renamed Java because the name Oak was taken, was finally born.

Cross Platform and Network Savvy

Now back in the mid-nineties, people had this crazy idea that one day you'd be able to order pizzas from your TV. Furthermore, people envisioned a future where every appliance in your house would be interconnected, so that your alarm clock would be connected to your coffee machine, and your lawnmower would be connected to your TV, so when you turned off your alarm clock in the morning, your clock would start the coffee maker, and when you finished mowing your lawn in the afternoon, your lawnmower would tell your TV, and your TV would then order you a donair pizza from KOD using that TV-top ordering system that everyone was talking about. Yes, it all seems so silly now, but it seemed like a great idea at the time, so everyone went for it.

When Java was originally released, it was designed to run on toasters, televisions and alarm clocks. Okay, maybe it was actually designed to run on any machine that had a computer processor and a Java Virtual Machine to turn compiled Java code into instructions for a computer. Regardless, Java was designed to run just about anywhere you could stick a computer processor. Furthermore, Java was designed with networking in mind; after all, it was through some kind of networking that Java programs could communicate with each other.

Now, as you've probably figured out, the whole idea of the TV-top ordering system never really panned out. Furthermore, the idea of toasters talking to lawn mowers never really seemed to appeal to kitchenware makers, so that whole networking scenario didn't turn into much of a money maker, either. So, by about 1995, Sun Microsystems had developed a really kewl, cross-platform programming language, but had no place to really showcase it. But, we all know what happened in and around 1995, don't we?

Java and the World Wide Web

In 1995, Tim Berners-Lee's (TimBL) world wide web was really starting to gain steam, as crazy academics from all around the world uploaded the articles that no reputable or dignified journal would ever publish. The problem was, back in 1995, web pages were really just text, with perhaps an image or two, but they weren't really interactive, and it was very difficult to deliver an interactive experience to users through a web page. Back in 1995, the World Wide Web was pretty boring.

So, in 1996, Sun Microsystems unleashed their Java Runtime Environment (JRE) on the unsuspecting world, along with a HotJava browser that allowed dynamic and interactive content to be delivered to end users through little Java programs that would run inside of an html page. These little Java programs were called ***applets.***

You see, the Java programming language was designed to be cross platform, so it was easy to make the JRE run on Macs, OS/2, IBM compatible PCs, and computers running all sorts of operating systems like Windows NT, 98 or Linux. Java was also designed with networking in mind, so being able to write programs that took information from a client, and shot that information back to a server, was fairly easy to do with a Java applet. I actually remember signing up for my MCSE exams way back in 1997 through a nifty little online Java application that was quite impressive, although it did take about five hours to download and initialize.

So, as the Internet took off, so did Java. Java was a kewl and fun language to learn. It was also a kewl and fun language to use. Furthermore, it made often-difficult tasks, such as networking and application distribution, a fairly easy endeavor. Also, Java was designed with a number of best practices in mind, so even though it was only in its infancy, and many improvements were yet to be made, people really enjoyed working with this new, clean, simple and straight forward, object-oriented, programming language.

Moving Beyond Applets

Unfortunately, the Java applet didn't really stand the test of time. Now don't get me wrong – Java applets are still around today; it's just that so many more web based technologies are around today that address the deficiencies of the web that Java addressed so many years ago.

Also, there were problems with delivering applications as applets. Back in 1996, bandwidth was a real problem, so if you had a fairly large JAR file to distribute to clients, which was often the case if you had to package a network enabled, Java database connectivity (*JDBC*) driver, then your clients would be waiting a long, long time for your application to download and initialize. Furthermore, some of the Java environments worked better than others. Surprisingly, the Windows JVM was one of the fastest. Unfortunately, back in 1996, Apple was more concerned with making it to 1997, so their JVM was buggy at best. Linux provided a pretty solid JVM, but it was slow, and that frustrated the open source community. As someone much more clever than me once said, "the Java philosophy of 'write once, run anywhere' turned into a reality of 'write once, *debug everywhere*.'"

Java was the first great technology that made TimBL's Internet baby dynamic, but Java wasn't the only Internet technology to emerge, and pretty soon, technologies such as JavaScript, which is not Java at all, but a little scripting language that has a Java-like syntax, and Flash, were developed. JavaScripting could be used to validate user information on the client side, or even do some simple animations. Flash made it possible to embed highly dynamic and interactive content and movies into an html page. Furthermore, for delivering applications, most vendors decided it was best to simply send html forms back to clients, allow those forms to be validated by JavaScript on the client side, and then have the server take the client information and process it on the server side. This would allow the data sent to the client to be incredibly thin, and allow all of the processing and data control to reside on the server side, where developers and administrators have more control over their data.

So, by the late 90's, server side applications that sent very thin html applications to the client, and performed the vast majority of data processing on the server side, were all the rage. Microsoft's Active Server Pages (ASP) were probably the most dominant server side technology, with technologies such as CGI and ColdFusion coming in as close competitors. Java really wasn't dominant in the server-side application development race, although that would quickly change.

Server Side Java

And though web development had moved to the server-side, where Java had a very minor presence, the fact of the matter was, everyone had fallen in love with the revolutionary spirit of Java, and nobody wanted to give up on this great, new, programming language. So, instead of surrendering to technologies such as ColdFusion or Active Server Pages, the Java community developed a new technology called Servlets and Java Server Pages. Servlets and JSPs would allow simple html pages to be sent to clients, and then have clients send information back to the application server, where it would then be processed by programs written in Java. Java was now becoming the language of choice on the server side.

And server side application development wasn't the only ring in which the Java programming language decided to throw its hat. By the late 90's, hand held devices such as cell phones and PDA's were becoming more and more intelligent. As a result, a lightweight distribution of Java, where MIDlets were created, as opposed to applets or Servlets, emerged. With MIDlets, lightweight Java applications could run on handheld devices that couldn't afford the processing power needed to do things such as validate bytecode and signatures of Java classes.

The Java Split

Now the impression you should be getting is that by the late 90's, Java was being pulled in a number of different directions. To try and get a better handle on things, the Java Gods at Sun Microsystems decided to split the Java world up into three distinct environments. The powers that be broke the Java world into three distinct segments:

- *Java 2 Standard Edition (J2SE™)*
- *Java 2 Micro Edition (J2ME™)*
- *Java 2 Enterprise Edition (J2EE™)*

J2SE – The Standard

The Java 2 ***Standard*** Edition, J2SE, is really just the basic Java development and runtime environment that has been available to developers since day one, although many improvements, such as the addition of the lightweight, javax.swing components, have been made over the years. J2SE is also referred to as, correctly or not, the SDK (Standard Development Kit), JDK (Java Development Kit) or even the JRE (Java Runtime Environment). Regardless of how people refer to it, from a runtime perspective, J2SE provides a basic, Java Runtime Environment for running stand alone, Java applications on a desktop computer, and the plugin required to run the latest version of Java applets inside of a web browser.

java.awt.*: The Heavyweight Champions

When it was first released, Java desktop applications were created using a set of GUI packages known as the ***abstract windowing toolkit*** (awt), which were conveniently packaged together in the java.awt API library. The awt components worked by having the local Java Virtual Machine (JVM) figure out what type of operating system it was running on, and then asking the underlying system to display a button when a button was needed on a graphical user interface (GUI), or have the local operating system render a textfield when a textfield was needed. Delegating the task of rendering components to the operating system allowed Java programs to be cross platform, but it also created some rather *difficult to swallow* restrictions, as the set of graphical components available to Java applications ended up being a *lowest common denominator* conglomeration of graphical components available across all platforms.

javax.swing.* and the J Prefix

When Java 2 arrived, Sun Microsystems swung their GUI ship in a new direction, and made a new, lightweight, set of graphical components available to developers coding desktop applications. These new graphical components are referred to as *swing* components, and are grouped together in a package named java**x**.swing (note the x in the package name.) Swing components are easily identifiable in code, as their class names all start with the letter J. So, a java.awt textfield would be simply called TextField, whereas a swing component would be named **J**TextField.

The awt components are known as ***heavyweight components***, because they simply ask the operating system to do all of the heavy lifting when it comes to rendering graphical components. On the other hand, swing components are known as lightweight components, as they simply ask the local operating system for a java.**awt.**Containter, and then draw themselves on the canvas the OS provides. Because the Java Virtual Machine simply paints a button on the screen for a user, as opposed to asking the native OS to render a GUI component, there is less stress on the OS, and thus, these swing components are referred to as being ***lightweight***.

A Grand Proliferation of J2SE APIs

Of course, the Java 2 Standard Edition is much, much more than just a set of GUI application development tools. In fact, the awt and swing packages make up a very small portion of the entire J2SE API.

A rich set of programming libraries and APIs come packaged with J2SE, making it fun and easy to create applications that connect to databases using JDBC, read and write to the local file system using java.io, connect to resources running on a network, and even connect to and invoke various J2EE components. In fact, you can even use *JNI,* the Java Native Interface, (not to be confused with JNDI, the Java Naming and Directory Interface) if you need to connect a Java application to a non-Java program written in C++ or Visual Basic. While the J2SE is often seen as a desktop development environment, it is certainly possible to access and take advantage of a variety of services and components, potentially even components hosted on a J2EE application server.

Furthermore, Sun Microsystems has integrated Java Web Start Technology into the Java 2 Standard Edition, making it possible to update and deploy J2SE applications over a network, and even ensuring that clients have the latest JVM versions installed for their applications.

It should be stressed that J2SE applications do not define enterprise, J2EE components such as Servlets, EJBs and Java Server Pages (JSPs). You can't run a Servlet or a Java Server Page on the J2SE edition, although you can write code that invokes them. Furthermore, J2SE doesn't provide facilities for developing small, compact applications, that run well on Palm Pilots® or cell phones. The J2SE simply provides an effective environment for developing fully functional desktop applications and applets in a manner consistent with the original Java development environment that was originally released in 1996.

The Micro Edition

J2ME, the Java 2 ***Micro*** Edition, is a special Java runtime and development environment that makes it easy to create applications that can be run on small, handheld devices.

Figure 1-1

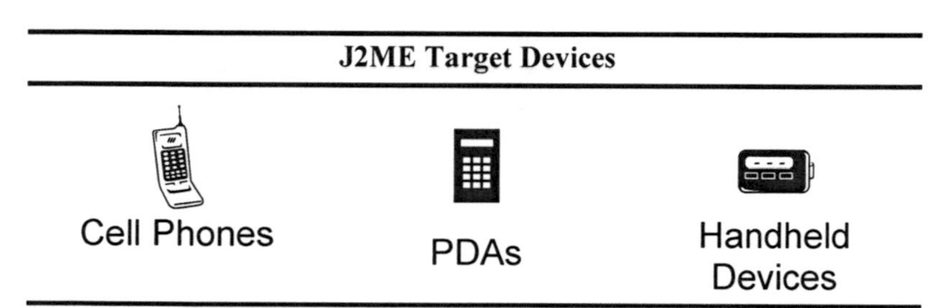

Micro devices have a much smaller amount of memory and processor power at their disposal than do desktop applications, so micro applications must have a much smaller footprint. The Java 2 Micro Edition (J2ME) makes the development of these types of applications possible, while at the same time, leveraging a developer's knowledge of normal Java application development.

Mobile Information Device Applications (MIDlets)

When developers create J2ME applications, they create special components called MIDlets, as opposed to applets or Servlets. Because of the limited processing power of mobile devices, MIDlets have many characteristics that set them apart from typical Java applications, with the main difference being the need to pre-verify a jar file containing MIDlet code. A standard JVM goes through a variety of byte-code verifications before it is run, but handheld devices just don't have the processing cycles to spare to perform these types of activities. As a result, all J2ME jar files must be pre-verified, and sometimes, even signed by the mobile device vendor.

Even access to persistent memory is greatly limited with J2ME applications. You could never store a massive database on a handheld device, although J2ME devices do have access to persistent memory storage, making it possible to save application preferences and settings.

J2ME MIDlet Profiles

The J2ME applications you develop are designed against a *profile*. A profile basically defines the various classes a MIDlet application can access and use. For example, there is an Information Module Profile (IMP) for designing applications that don't typically have normal user interfaces, or user interfaces at all, such as vending machines and security systems (these are horrifically referred to as *headless* applications.). As you could imagine, access to clickable buttons and textfields isn't necessary in a device using the IMP profile.

On the other hand, the Mobile Information Device Profile can be used for small display screens like the ones you would see in cell phones, or even for slightly more complicated user interfaces, such as the ones provided by personal organizers.

It isn't necessary to know all of the intricacies of how mobile applications are developed for the sake of the certification exam, but what is important is understanding that J2ME applications can be built for a variety of different types of micro-devices, and depending upon the type of microdevice being developed, the application will be associated with a specific application profile.

Like normal Java applications, J2ME applications are deployed in JAR files. However, unlike typical Java applications, the code in this JAR file must be pre-verified, and must contain a Java Application Descriptor (JAD) file that describes the micro application.

J2EE - Kirk to Enterprise

Developing enterprise applications is a difficult and daunting task. A typical enterprise application must interact with a variety of complex data systems, including message queues, databases and people management software.

They must also support a variety of different client types, such as stand alone applications that run on a desktop computer, or applications that use an Internet web browser as their user interface.

J2EE is the Java 2 *Enterprise* Edition, and it is designed to help facilitate the development of sturdy, scalable and bulletproof enterprise applications.

☞ *J2EE is a specification.*
☞ *J2EE is a philosophy.*

J2EE is a framework for building and deploying enterprise scale applications.

J2EE is a specification managed by Sun Microsystems, although all of the big players in the Java middle-tier market, such as WebLogic and IBM, contribute to the development and evolution of the spec.

The J2EE specification outlines how a developer should go about developing an enterprise application, and it defines a variety of services that a vendor, such as IBM and BEA, must implement if they want to advertise a J2EE *certified* application server.

The WebSphere Application Server is IBM's certified, J2EE runtime environment. WebLogic is BEA's middle-tier, J2EE certified runtime environment. J2EE is the specification that defines how a Java based, middle tier, application server should behave.

The Importance of the Middle Tier

If you think about it, every time we use the Internet, our interactions are *data driven.* Whether we are checking to see if our electricity bill is past due, or searching for the correct spelling of a word they were throwing around on last nights Charlie Rose, our interaction is *data driven.* We live in the information age, and information is power. Big businesses and domineering governments hold huge stores of information, some of which they want us to see, and some of which they want to secure very tightly.

The terabytes of data companies store in db2 and Oracle databases represents the 'data-tier.' The data-tier, also known as the 'back-end,' is what hackers, crackers, and everyday users want to get their dirty little fingers on.

The middle tear is the one you shed after finding out your solution doesn't work, and before your manager reminds you of how much your non-functional solution has cost.

These users, and the web browsers they use, such as Firefox, Netscape and Opera, represent the 'client tier' in a J2EE environment. The client tier is also known as the 'front end.'

So, if all of our data is stored in databases on the back end, and our clients are surfing the Internet on the front end, then the middle-tier represents the infrastructure needed to bridge the gap between the client-tier and the data-tier. J2EE is all about the middle-tier.

Components that Reside on the Client, Middle and Data Tiers

Client Tier	Middle Tier (J2EE)	Data Tier
Web Browsers	Web Services	Message Queues
PDAs	J2EE Servers	Databases
Cell Phones	.NET Servers	Persistent Data

J2EE is a complex monster, and any attempt to capture what J2EE is must start by breaking it down into its three very distinct parts:

- *The components we create and subsequently deploy to a J2EE Application Server*
- *The services a J2EE certified Application Server will provide to our components*
- *The protocols used by clients to interact with our J2EE components*

The SCJA exam requires a high level knowledge of the differences between J2SE, J2ME and J2EE. However, it also requires a fundamental understanding of the different types of J2EE components, when those J2EE components should be used, and the types of services and protocols available to those components. The various services, components and protocols associated with the J2EE components will be the focus of the next few chapters.

Question

The J2SE component that delivers dynamic content while running within the confines of a web page is:
O a) a Servlet
O b) a JSP
O c) JavaScript
O d) a Java Applet

Question

J2ME developers must be concerned with which of the following J2ME artifacts?
☐ a) Servlets
☐ b) Applets
☐ c) MIDlets
☐ d) Profiles

Question

Which components would you find on the middle tier?
☐ a) MIDlets
☐ b) Applets
☐ c) Servlets
☐ d) EJBs

Question

Application Servers such as WebSphere and WebLogic are focused at delivering what type of solutions?
☐ a) J2EE
☐ b) J2ME
☐ c) J2SE
☐ d) J2IE

Answer

The J2SE component that delivers dynamic content while running within the confines of a web page is:
○ a) a Servlet ○ b) a JSP ○ c) JavaScript ○ d) a Java Applet
Option d) is correct. Java Applets are the cute little components that run within the confines of a web page. Unfortunately, their star has faded in the last decade, as newer client/browser side technologies such as Flash and JavaScripting have provided much of the functionality that was originally delivered by Applets. Nevertheless, there is still a place for Applets in many enterprise architectures that need slightly fatter clients on the browser side.

Answer

J2ME developers must be concerned with which of the following J2ME artifacts?
☐ a) Servlets ☐ b) Applets ☐ c) MIDlets ☐ d) Profiles
Options c) and d) are correct. MIDlets and Profiles are J2ME artifacts. MIDlets are the Java code that gets written and turned into cute micro applications or video games that run on cell phones. The profiles define what types of libraries and capabilities a MIDlet program can leverage on the microdevice to which the application is targeted.

Answer

Which components would you find on the middle tier?
☐ a) MIDlets ☐ b) Applets ☐ c) Servlets ☐ d) EJBs
Options c) and d) are correct. The middle tier is J2EE centric, which means you would find Servlets, JSPs and EJBs, all running on the middle tier. The RDBMS data tier is the third tier, which is usually communicated with through JDBC, the cross platform Java database protocol. The web browser, or handheld device, is often thought of as the client tier.

Answer

Application Servers such as WebSphere and WebLogic are focused at delivering what type of solutions?
O a) J2EE O b) J2ME O c) J2SE O d) J2IE
Option a) is correct. For the most part, your WebSphere Application Servers and WebLogic servers are J2EE application servers that host EJB containers and Web containers. Now having said that, I'm sure IBM and BEA would get real upset if you suggested that their middle tier solution was simply just a J2EE compliant application server. WebSphere and WebLogic servers do a lot more than just host J2EE compliant containers, but when thinking about J2EE, J2SE and J2ME, WebSphere and WebLogic servers are traditionally thought of as J2EE application servers.

Chapter 2
Servlets and JSPs

Strictly speaking, there are two types of components that can be created and deployed to a J2EE application server, although a variety of subtypes do exist, making the J2EE framework appear much more complicated than it really is.

Servlets and EJBs are the J2EE components we create, and then deploy to the J2EE Application Server.

Servlets, and their close cousin, JSPs, are the J2EE components we use to handle and respond to Internet based requests.

An important part of the SCJA exam is understanding ***how and when*** Servlets and JSPs should be used. You do not need in-depth knowledge about how to code or deploy a Servlet or a JSP, but you do need a solid grasp on how Servlets and JSPs can be used, and when it is appropriate to use them.

Stand alone applications and applets, which are J2SE components, can be configured to interact with J2EE components. They can also take advantage of some J2EE services, but only EJBs and Servlets are deployed directly to an Application Server

What exactly are Servlets?

An application server must be capable of handling and responding to requests that come in over the Internet. A Servlet is simply a Java based component that handles web-based requests.

The purpose of a Servlet is to accept and process a web-based request, and subsequently send a response back to the client. Since the client is likely a person surfing the Internet, the response delivered to the client usually takes the form of a web page.

Servlets are popular because they are incredibly easy to code. With only a little bit of a Java background, anyone can code a Servlet and dive head first into that empty pool known as server side development.

Coding a Servlet

There are only two methods you really need to worry about when coding a Servlet:

- *the **doGet** method*
- *the **doPost** method.*

The ***doGet*** method of a Servlet is automatically called when a client invokes your Servlet by clicking on a link, choosing a bookmark from their list of favorites, or typing the name of your Servlet directly into the address bar of a web browser.

Figure 2-1

Typing a URL in the address bar will trigger a Servlet's doGet method

The ***doPost*** method of a Servlet is usually invoked when a user fills out an html form and clicks the submit button.

If a user is going to call your Servlet by clicking on a link, you code the doGet method. If the user will be filling out a form and sending data to the server, you code the doPost method. It's just that easy!

Choosing which of these two methods to code is one of the more difficult parts of Servlet programming. ☺

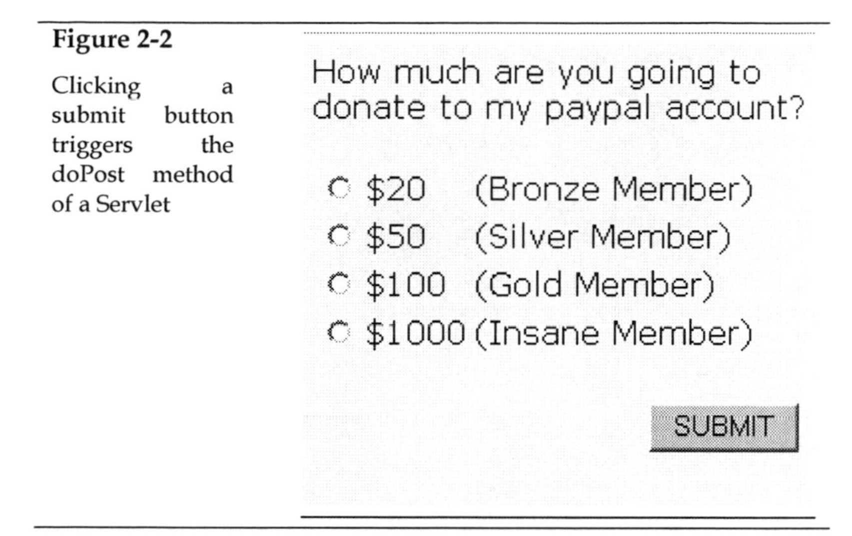

Figure 2-2

Clicking a submit button triggers the doPost method of a Servlet

The Request and Response Objects

The doPost and doGet methods of a Servlet are passed two very important objects:

- *an HttpServlet**Request** object*
- *an HttpServlet**Response** object*

The HttpServletRequest, a.k.a. *request*, and the HttpServletResponse, a.k.a. *response*, make handling web based requests incredibly easy.

Anything you want to know, or for that matter, are allowed to know about the client, comes through the *request* object. **Get it?** The *request* object describes the *request* that has come in from the client.

Anything you want to do to the client can be done through the *response* object. **Get it?** The *response* object allows you to manage the *response* that gets sent back to the client.

Servlet programming really is that easy. Sure, there are a few method calls you have to get familiar with, but with a bit of a Java background, getting up to speed with Servlet programming will be a lead-pipe cinch.

Could you show me a simple Servlet?

We never like to muddy the waters with all sorts of Java code, but in this case, an example is probably a worthwhile venture.

```
public class SampleServlet extends HttpServlet
{

public void doGet(HttpServletRequest request,
                  HttpServletResponse response)
                        throws IOException,
                               ServletException
  {
    PrintWriter out = response.getWriter();
    out.print("<HTML><BODY>");
    if (request.getLocale().equals("en_ca"))
    {
      out.print("Let's go for a Tim's, eh!!!");
    }
    else
    {
       out.print("See ya at Starbucks.");
    }
    out.print("</BODY></HTML>");
  }

}
```

The Notorious JavaBean

Servlets use, and delegate to, JavaBeans. A JavaBean is simply a reusable, logic component written in Java. A JavaBean can perform business logic, interact with backend resources, or simply act as a data transfer object.

JavaBeans are sometimes referred to as POJOs, which stands for Plain Ordinary Java Object.

The following JavaBean is simply a timer. It keeps track of the time somebody invoked the start method, and then can calculate how much time has elapsed when someone invokes the getElapsedTime() method.

```
public class Timer implements Serializable
{
  private long startTime;
  public Timer()
  {
    startTime = 0;
  }
  public void start ()
  {
     startTime = System.currentTimeMillis();
  }
  public long getElapsedTime ()
  {
     return System.currentTimeMillis() - startTime;
  }
}
```

Debriefing the Servlet

In the preceding Servlet, the request object is used to see if the client is Canadian. If the client is indeed a Canuck, well, they probably really love Tim Hortons coffee. If the client is not Canadian, the client probably does not appreciate good coffee, and would likely settle for a Starbucks.

The request object is used to find out information about the client making the request. In this case, the request object is used to determine the user's locale.

Using the response object, some delicious HTML is sent back to the client and subsequently displayed in the client's browser.

Again, Servlet programming is easy. Anything you want to find out about the client and their incoming request is in the HttpServletRequest object. Anything you are allowed to do to the client is done through the HttpServletResponse object.

So, with a little bit of a Java background, coding a Servlet and using the request object to figure out what a user typed into a text field, or finding out which radio button they selected, is relatively straight forward.

Furthermore, displaying text in a client's web browser, or even redirecting a client to a different web page, is accomplished fairly easily through methods in the response object. From that point on, what a developer does with a user's request and the user's response object is only limited by their Java programming skills.

You will notice that the doPost or doGet method of a Servlet throws the IOException.

My bank throws the same exception. They keep calling me up, telling me that I owe them this, and I owe them that.

An Example of a Request-Response Cycle

Let's take a look at a simple example of a request-response cycle that might occur between a web-based client and the J2EE Application Server.

Let's say you, as a developer, wanted to know which browser a client was using. Maybe you were even wondering if the client was using a Palm Pilot or a Nokia cell phone. Maybe you need to know which language the client speaks. Where would you find this information? In the HttpServletRequest object of course!

And say you wanted to plant a cookie on a client machine, or simply send some HTML back to be displayed in the client's browser. How would you do that? Well, you'd call some methods in the HttpServletResponse object, that's how!

For the most part, the primary job of the Servlet is to inspect the incoming request, and then figure out what kind of a response to send back to the client.

Inspecting the Request

From the request, we can find out what a user may have typed into a given text field, what their preferred language is, and even which browser they are using. The Servlet then uses this information to make sure the request being made is indeed a valid request.

If the request is indeed valid, the Servlet will execute the appropriate business logic required to fulfill the request, and then figure out what type of markup language and content should be sent back to the client.

Generating a Response

After handling a request, the Servlet must formulate a response and subsequently send something handsome back to the user. After processing a request, it is very important that we inform the user about the success, failure, or overall status of their interaction with the application server. This is the gist of handling the Servlet request-response cycle.

The Challenge

The challenging part of developing Servlets is deciding what to do between handling the request and formulating a response.

For example, the request object can tell you what a user has typed into a couple of text fields, or which radio buttons a user has selected. What are you going to do with this information?

Perhaps you want to save the input to a database. Maybe you want to place some information about the client's request on a message queue. Maybe you want to interact with an Enterprise Java Bean, which would then require a JNDI lookup and an interaction with the UserTransaction object. Crazy stuff for sure, but you can do it if you want to.

The point I'm trying to make is this: it is easy to get information about a client from the request object, and it is even easier to send a response back to the client using the response object. What you do between handling the request and sending a response back to the client is only limited by your own creativity and the extent of your Java programming skills.

Rendering a View with Java Server Pages

There are only two types of J2EE components we can write: EJBs and Servlets. This may come as a bit of a shock, but a JSP is really just a Servlet, although coded in a slightly different manner.

The SampleServlet coded earlier had an ugly mix of HTML tags and Java. Optimally, markup language and Java code should never be mixed together.

Servlets are intended to acts as controllers, and Java is used to implement this control logic. However, HTML tags get mixed in with the Java code if the Servlet also takes on the responsibility of sending data back to the client.

Mixing Java and HTML within a single component creates a maintainability nightmare, so as much as possible, we try to keep complex Java logic in a Servlet, and have the generation of dynamic HTML factored out into a JSP.

Servlets vs. JSPs

A JSP is just a Servlet that's been turned inside out. ☺ A Servlet is Java code with a little bit of HTML in it. A JSP file is mostly HTML with a little bit of Java inside of it. But there's nothing you can do with a JSP that you can't do with a Servlet.

Looking at a JSP

Here is the previously viewed SampleServlet turned into a JSP:

```
<HTML> <BODY>

<%
      if (request.getLocale().equals("en_ca")) {
%>

Let's go for a Tim's!!!

<%
}
else
{
%>

I guess we have to settle for Starbucks.

<% } %>

</BODY> </HTML>
```

Mixing Java Code and HTML

It is unhandsome when we mix HTML tags and Java code together in our Servlets. It is equally unhandsome when we mix HTML with Java code inside of our JSPs. A separation of responsibilities is definitely in order.

While they are coded differently, at runtime, JSPs and Servlets are two peas in an iPod. JSP files are actually converted into Servlets when they are run on the application server; as a result, all of the tweaking the web container does to make your Servlets run so efficiently is implicitly available to your JSPs as well.

What should I use, a Servlet or a JSP?

To a question like that, there really are no right answers. There are only wrong answers, and all we can do is try not to get a wrong answer.

As a good rule of thumb, a Servlet should be used to initially handle an incoming request and implement some control logic. This might include validating user input and making sure a user is making a reasonable request.

A Java Server Page should be used when you are mostly generating HTML. A JSP should only ever require a minor amount of Java logic. This makes JSP files much easier to maintain.

Generally speaking, most applications have a Servlet handle the incoming request, and then the Servlet forwards to a JSP to generate display and subsequently send HTML back to the client.

Again, anything a Servlet can do a JSP can do, and vice-versa. In fact, the only real difference between the two is how they're coded.

Servlets and JSPs sure don't look the same!

Even though they look different, when a client calls a JSP, the Application Server actually calls on a special Servlet of its own that reads the JSP, and subsequently creates a Java Servlet based on what is coded inside the Java Server Page.

The Application Server then compiles the code that it creates, and then the newly compiled Servlet is loaded and run on the server. All JSP files get turned into a Servlet at runtime.

Since it is usually a Servlet that turns the JSP into a Servlet, I often refer to it as the BorgServlet, although the actual name vendors use is much less creative.

Question

Post and Get invocations are part of which J2EE protocol?
O a) http O b) rmi/iiop O c) rmi O d) JDBC

Question

Handling an incoming http request, and subsequently acting as a controller in an MVC type of architecture, is the responsibility of:
O a) an Enterprise Java Bean (EJB) O b) a Servlet O c) a JSP O d) an HTML page

Question

While designed and developed differently, at runtime, the web container treats JSP pages as:
O a) JavaBeans O b) Servlets O c) EJBs O d) Applets

Question

Which of the following resources can Servlets take advantage of:
☐ a) java.util and java.net packages defined by J2SE ☐ b) J2EE lookup Contexts made available through a JNDI service ☐ c) classes and packages defined in the J2ME runtime ☐ d) classes defined in the java.lang package of the J2SE

Answer

Post and Get invocations are part of which J2EE protocol?
O a) http O b) rmi/iiop O c) rmi O d) JDBC
Option a) is correct. A Servlet has a doPost and a doGet method to handle requests that come in over the http protocol. The RMI/IIOP protocol is used when invoking EJBs, and RMI alone makes object distribution possible with just J2SE. JDBC is a technology used to connect Java programs to a variety of different back end, RDBMS databases.

Answer

Handling an incoming http request, and subsequently acting as a controller in an MVC type of architecture, is the responsibility of:
O a) an Enterprise Java Bean (EJB) O b) a Servlet O c) a JSP O d) an HTML page
Option b) is correct. Now, anything you can do in a Servlet, you can do in a JSP, so technically, a JSP would be a correct answer to this question, if it wasn't for the fact that using JSPs as a controller is completely frowned upon. Servlets are supposed to act as a controller in a J2EE architecture, handling incoming requests, and delegating work to EJBs and JavaBeans. Servlets typically forward to a Java Server Page (JSP) for the generation of markup, such as HTML or WML, which eventually gets delivered back to the client.

Answer

While designed and developed differently, at runtime, the web container treats JSP pages as:
O a) JavaBeans O b) Servlets O c) EJBs O d) Applets
Option b) is correct. Anything you can do with a Servlet, you can do with a JSP, and the reason for that is the fact that when you pull back the covers of the J2EE web container, at runtime, JSPs are actually turned into Servlets and executed with all of the semantics associated with a Servlet.

Answer

Which of the following resources can Servlets take advantage of:
☐ a) java.util and java.net packages defined in J2SE ☐ b) J2EE lookup Contexts made available through a JNDI service ☐ c) Classes and packages defined in the J2ME runtime ☐ d) classes defined in the java.lang package of the J2SE
Options a) b) and d) are correct. A Servlet is a J2EE component, which means all of the resources, services and protocols that are made available through a J2EE server are available to a Servlet. Also, a Servlet can take advantage of all of the classes in the standard edition, so you can use all of the classes in java.util or java.io or java.net if you so please. Of course, java.lang is, by default, available to all J2EE components, so answer d) is correct as well.

Chapter 3
Enterprise Java Beans

Let us establish one undeniable fact: **enterprise programming is hard.**

Sure, Servlets are superb at handling client requests, and Java Server Pages are fabulous at generating markup for a client, but request-response programming is not where Java developers earn their salt. Java developers earn their salt by implementing some seriously complicated business logic. Fiddling with a Servlet's request and response objects all day long won't impress anybody.

Enterprise programming is hard, but EJBs make some of the toughest parts of enterprise programming just a little bit easier.

EJBs and the SCJA Exam

An important part of the SCJA exam is to know what types of EJBs are available to enterprise applications, and when you would chose one type of EJB component over another. In depth knowledge of how to create, package and deploy EJBs is not required to pass the SCJA exam, but you absolutely must know when to use a certain type of EJB, and what type of underlying infrastructure, be it a queue, topic or database, with which a given type of EJB will interact. This chapter will tell you everything you need to know about EJBs to ace the EJB related objectives of the SCJA exam.

The Challenges of Enterprise Programming

Enterprise programming is hard. In an enterprise environment, there are a number of mission critical challenges that must be addressed and implemented properly, otherwise applications will fail. Some of the typical challenges that enterprise developers encounter include:

Database Access:

How do we ensure that data in our application is completely, totally, 100% in sync with what is in the database? This is a requirement of almost every enterprise application, but without an intimate knowledge of how a database works, implementing database synchronization properly is a significant challenge.

Transactional Updates:

If I'm updating three different databases in an 'all or nothing' type of scenario, and one of those database writes fails, how do I roll back writes to the other two databases?

What if one of those databases is in Kalamazoo and two of them are in Tuktoyaktuk? How do you maintain the transactional integrity of your updates? You could use the Java Transaction API (JTA) to access the Java Transaction Service (JTS) programmatically, but that's a heck of alot of work.

Distributed Programming:

I'm in Gun Barrel, Texas, but I want users in Antigonish, Nova Scotia to remotely invoke the methods in my Java components. How do I make a local component accessible to remote applications?

Multithreading:

Multithreading remotely accessible components that must handle a gargantuan load is a difficult and onerous task. How are you going to do it?

Secure Access:

You only want Double Agents to call one method of your JavaBean, and only Secret Agents can call the other method. How ya gonna do it? With a typical Java application, it's almost impossible.

EJBs: Rising Up to the Challenge

Database concurrency, distributed transactions, multithreading, distributed programming and secure accesses are all issues our enterprise applications must deal with.

If we have to deal with these issues alone, we're going to be in an ugly world of hurt. The good news is that EJBs deal with these issues, and by dealing with them, they make enterprise programming much, much easier.

How EJBs Work

There is quite a bit going on inside an EJB.

To take care of things like security and transaction management, EJBs use special XML files called *deployment descriptors*. The deployment descriptor contains information about how the EJB, and its methods, should behave at runtime. When an application server loads an EJB, it reads the associated deployment descriptor and follows the instructions therein.

EJBs also implement a number of common design patterns, such as the proxy, pooling and singleton patterns. EJBs are designed well, and EJBs work well when used properly.

Another interesting thing about an EJB is that unlike a regular Java component, an EJB isn't just one single file on the file system. An EJB is actually a collection of three or more class files that work together to create a single, logical entity.

An EJB, like the TimerEJB, is actually three or more Java files working together to create a single, logical component.

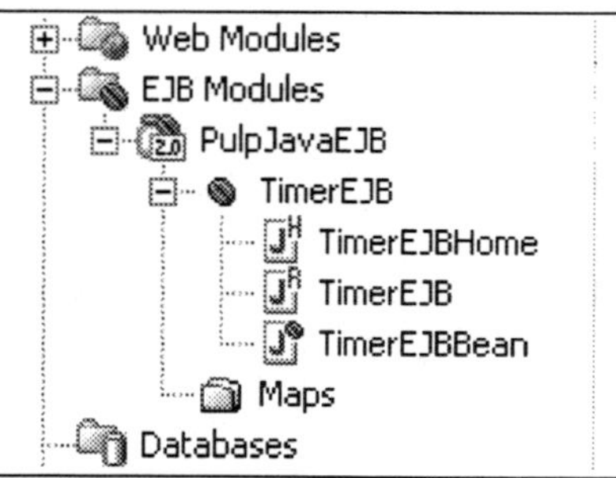

Let there be no mistake about it: EJBs have a learning curve associated with them. Enterprise Java Beans are harder to write than a regular JavaBean or Java component. But don't fret. The payoffs make the learning curve well worth it.

Anyone who has a Java background can pick up EJB technology relatively quickly. A few learning pains will result in a vast array of programming gains.

What types of EJBs (Enterprise Java Beans) are there?

EJBs come in three different flavors:

- *Entity Beans*
- *Message Driven Beans*
- *Session Beans*

Let's take a look at them one at a time.

The Persistently Amusing Entity Bean

Entity Beans represent an object-oriented bridge between your enterprise application and your relational database.

Entity beans are special Java components that represent persistent data. When we say persistent data, we are usually speaking about data stored in a database. Theoretically though, Entity Beans could map to anything from data in a text file, to a serialized JavaBean on the file system. Nevertheless, the vast majority of the time, your persistent data is stored in a database.

An Entity Bean Example

Imagine you have a database containing a table named USER. This USER table has columns that represent a user's name, phone number, password and email address. An entity bean, very creatively named UserEJB, could be created that matches the USER table, and accordingly has properties that match the name and data type of the data contained in that USER table.

Since an entity bean represents data in a database, if a developer called setter methods such as setPassword("xyz123"), the EJB promises to immediately update the underlying data in the database.

An entity bean represents your backend data, and the EJB framework ensures that an entity bean is always 100% completely and totally in sync, at all times, with the data in your database. That is the promise of the EJB spec.

Accessing data is the flipside of updating data, but with an EJB, the promise is the same: 100% synchronicity.

When a developer calls a getter method on an EJB, such as userEJB.getName(), the application would subsequently be given exclusive access to the name field of that particular user in the database.

When you call a getter method on an EJB, the application server absolutely guarantees that the returned information will be completely and totally in sync with what is in the database. Achieving this end on your own by hacking around with regular Java code would be hard, if not darned near impossible. Accomplishing this with an entity bean is incredibly easy.

An entity bean maps to a database table. Properties of the Entity Bean map to columns in the database table.

Enterprise Beans	Tables
PulpJavaEJB	PULPJAVA
User	ADMINISTRATOR.USER
id : java.lang.Integer	ID : INTEGER
name : java.lang.String	NAME : VARCHAR(100)
phone : java.lang.String	PHONE : VARCHAR(100)
email : java.lang.String	EMAIL : VARCHAR(100)
password : java.lang.String	PASSWORD : VARCHAR(100)

Entity Beans and Data Integrity

I often get asked how entity beans ensure the transactional integrity of the data they represent? The answer: I really don't know.

I think it's done through a collection of database locks, method calls, and a little bit of Haitian Voodoo, but I'm not completely sure.

The fact is, I don't know, and I don't need to know. All I have to worry about is writing the EJB.

All the underlying plumbing that makes these EJBs work is implemented by a bunch of clever sausages that know far more about database access and transaction management than I'll ever know. I'll leave the infrastructure stuff up to them. I'll stick to coding these simple little entity beans.

Container Managed Persistence Beans (CMPs)

Entity beans come in two different flavors: Container Managed Persistence (CMP) and Bean Managed Persistence (BMP)

Since most applications need to interact with persistent data, and since most vendors want you to buy their application server, each vendor has implemented a custom mechanism to easily create an entity bean that maps directly to a database table and the subsequent columns contained in that table.

Not only do these vendor-supplied components represent data contained in a database, they have inherent knowledge about how to update the database, retrieve data, and even create new rows in the database table, so long as they are supplied with a unique primary key. These vendor-supplied components are quite amazing, and remove much of the need to compose boring SQL statements or develop data components whose silly setters and getters transactionally interact with a database.

These vendor supplied entity beans are know as CMPs, or Container Managed Persistence beans, because it is the vendor's EJB container that implements the persistence for us.

Entity Bean Mappings

Vendors provide many ways to create Container Managed Persistence beans (CMPs), including:

- *top down*
- *bottom up*
- *meet in the middle*

'Bottoms-up' occurs when you already have a database, and you want to create EJBs based on your database tables.

Top down happens when you first create your EJBs and object model, and want to have database tables created based upon that model.

With a top down mapping, tools such as IBM's Rational Application Developer, will allow you to create EJB components first, and then the tool will generate SQL scripts that will create database tables based upon the components you have coded.

Meet in the middle happens when your database administrators and your application developers just can't agree on how to coordinate the relational model with the object model. The developers go off and create EJBs. The database admins go off and create their database. Then some poor shmuck has to figure out how to bring the two parts together. In other words, the shmuck must meet the relational and object models in the middle.

Meet in the middle allows Java developers to map EJBs that have been created in isolation to database tables that already exist. This is probably the most common type of EJB mapping we see in the industry.

Bean Managed Persistence (BMPs)

A BMP is any entity bean that isn't a CMP. That was easy. ☺

As was discussed earlier, Container Managed Persistence (CMP) beans relieve the developer from having to write SQL code, which Java developers are notoriously bad at doing.

With Bean Managed Persistence (BMP), the developer is burdened with the responsibility of writing all of the SQL code required to update, delete, create and find data in our underlying database tables. Basically, with a BMP, the developer has to do more work, and God forefend, maybe even talk to a database person to help put together some SQL statements.

Reasons for Using a BMP

Creating BMPs is definitely a more involved process than having a development tool create CMPs for you. Nevertheless, compelling reasons to use BMPs do exist.

Your Database Doesn't Support Container Mapping

Depending upon your database, a CMP isn't always an option. For example, IBM's Rational Application Developer only allows you to create CMPs for certain databases, although most major databases are supported. However, you might be in trouble if you're using a special object oriented database, or perhaps a database that doesn't have the same market penetration as Oracle or DB2.

Your Database is Far Too Complicated

Your database might be too complicated for the development tools that make container-managed persistence possible.

If your database is filled with crazy joins, you have an egregious amount of mango to mandarin relationships, and your ERD looks like a map of the North American rail system, then I'm afraid that the conventionally available CMP tools won't be much use to you. In a case like this, you have to write your own crazy SQL code to interact with your crazy database - the development tools simply won't have anything to do with you.

Portability is an Issue

Another thing to think about is portability. Of course, if you're using DB2 and WebSphere, portability isn't an issue, because IBM is the best, and you would never want to leave them. But it is important to note, despite an ongoing effort to standardize EJB development, one vendor's CMPs are a little bit different from that of another vendor. WebSphere CMPs won't necessarily port to a WebLogic server, although the latest incarnation of the CMP spec is indeed bridging that gap.

Assuming the SQL being used within them is fairly standard, BMPs will port from one database to another with ease. Portability is more achievable with a BMP than a CMP.

Performance and Control

Generally, a CMP will perform faster than a BMP, especially if the J2EE server vendor and the database vendor are one in the same, or at least, tightly tied together.

Furthermore, CMPs can take all sorts of shortcuts behind the scenes that we simply don't know about. Vendors compete on who has got the most efficient application server, and efficiently connecting to a backend database is a pretty big sales point. CMPs are generally better at interacting with a database than BMPs.

Combining CMPs and BMPs

Choosing between CMPs and BMPs is not an all or nothing decision. Container and Bean Managed Entity beans can coexist quite efficiently within the same application server.

In fact, a creative use of inheritance and interfaces makes it easy to interchange BMPs and CMPs. This would allow you to quickly create CMPs, but seamlessly switch to BMPs in the future if the need ever arises.

What is better, a CMP or a BMP?

I'm sure some would argue that BMPs, since you code them pretty much from scratch, give you more control, and even though I suggest that CMPs are faster than BMPs, others might argue that by implementing things like a 'dirty bit' pattern and performing some funky SQL magic, you could actually make BMPs more efficient than CMPs. That may be true as well. The ability to control database access in a BMP provides the opportunity for infinite refinement.

Nevertheless, the cost of any application is not how much it costs to create, host, or get it deployed. The biggest cost associated with an enterprise application is ***maintaining it over time***. Maintaining the optimized BMP code, which was written by the in-house, super-genius, after she's left the company to invigilate at MIT, might be insurmountable. CMPs are best if you can use them.

CMPs are much easier to maintain than BMPs. Maintaining a component with no code inside of it is the kind of task for which I'll gladly volunteer.

This brings us to another point – love them or hate them, CMPs do provide a standard framework for mapping Java components to a back end database – making object-oriented, transactional, database access possible. A common framework that is easy to learn, and for that matter, easy to find a new hire that understands it, is a good thing.

Use CMPs if you can. They will make your life easier in the long run.

Message Driven Beans (MDBs)

Anxiously anticipated, and newly introduced with J2EE 1.3, is the Message Driven Bean (MDB).

Messaging is an important part of any enterprise application. Messaging allows an application to put information on a message queue, and be assured the information will be processed at some time in the foreseeable future.

Essentially, message queues allow an application to implement delayed processing. Delayed processing of messages is also known as *asynchronous* messaging.

MDBs Only Support Asynchronous Messaging

Have you ever placed an order over the Internet, been told that your order has been processed, and then you don't get an actual confirmation email for about an hour or two?

When you placed your order, the website grabbed your order information, which likely included your email address and credit card number, and then shoved that information in a message, and plopped that message on a message queue. When the application server got a little bored, or at least when the workload died down a little bit, the application server grabbed your order off the queue and processed it, thus the delay in getting your email confirmation. That is asynchronous messaging in action.

By using a message queue, we can delay processing, while at the same time, ensuring that a particular task will be transactionally performed.

Asynchronous messaging, which occurs when a message is placed on a queue and a client does not need to wait for that message to be processed, is an important part of any enterprise environment. Curiously though, J2EE has been fairly shy when it comes to providing a framework that eases the burden of message-oriented programming.

Well, with J2EE 1.3, we have message driven beans, MDBs, which make reading messages off a queue much, much easier.

Message driven beans are a special type of Enterprise Java Bean (EJB) that are designed to wait for messages to be dropped off on a message queue or topic, and then subsequently read those messages and react to the information contained therein.

On the Topic of Queues and Topics

For the certification exam, you should know that there are two very important, and very different, types of messaging infrastructure you can configure, namely topics and queues. The terms have been used interchangeably so far in this book, but there is a major difference between them.

Using the JMS API (Java Messaging Service), messages can be placed in one of two types of holding places, either a topic or a queue. A queue is associated with a point to point type of messaging infrastructure, and a topic is associated with a publish-subscribe type of architecture. Being able to differentiate between a publish-subscribe and a point to point architecture, and being able to associate these architecture with the corresponding topic and queue, will win you a few points on the exam.

With a queue, a message is produced by a client, it comes in to the server, and it sits on the queue until some resource, perhaps a message driven bean, reads that message off the queue and handles it. With a queue, a message is placed on a queue, and it is not removed from the queue until a single message consumer reads that message, and handles it appropriately. This type of messaging is known as point-to-point messaging.

Alternatively, messages can be placed on a topic, instead of a queue. With a topic, many different message *consumers* can *subscribe* to the topic, and are subsequently informed when a message arrives. With a topic, many consumers receive the message, and many consumers may handle the message in their own unique way. A message on a topic is not considered to be handled until all of the message consumers that subscribe to that topic are aware of the message; thus, the term *publish-subscribe* messaging.

The key certification point is that topics are associated with a publish-subscribe messaging infrastructure, and queues are associated with point to point messaging. Message driven beans support both of these types of infrastructures in an asynchronous manner.

Comparing MDBs to Other EJBs

In use, creation and deployment, a message driven bean is quite a bit different from any other type of EJB. To be honest, I kinda cringe at the fact that this snobbish little messaging component has been included under the sacrosanct heading of EJB. However, I must be remiss and accept the wisdom of those who created and contribute to the J2EE specification.

Messaging is an important part of almost every enterprise environment, and until J2EE 1.3, the developer was responsible for reading messages from a queue, and subsequently processing those messages.

To help standardize the way applications read asynchronous messages off a queue, and to stop the pissing contest between developers who contended they had the best implementation of messaging, J2EE introduced the Message Driven Bean (MDB).

Essentially, an MDB reads messages off a queue or topic, and then executes business logic based on the contents of that message. Quite often, the MDB just converts the message into a plain ordinary Java object (POJO), and then passes that POJO off to a Session Bean for further processing.

The Session Beans

There are three types of Enterprise Java Beans:

☞ *Entity Beans (BMPs and CMPs)*
☞ *Message Driven Beans (MDBs)*
☞ *Session Beans (Stateless and Stateful)*

We have discussed entity and we have discussed message driven beans. A session bean is anything that doesn't fall into the two aforementioned categories. ☺

A tongue in cheek definition for sure, but it is surprisingly accurate. After all, message driven beans are tied to a message queue or topic. An entity bean is bound to persistent data. A session bean is truly a free spirit, entitled to do whatever the heck it wants.

Using Session Beans

Session beans are important J2EE components, but before we dive into the virtues of the session bean, let's rehash the reasons why we would want to use an EJB in the first place. EJBs are great because they provide:

☞ *Remote distribution*
☞ *Transaction management*
☞ *Multithreaded control*
☞ *Secure access down to the method level*

Now imagine we wanted to take advantage of all, or even just some, of these great services, but we weren't interested in persisting data to a database, and we weren't interested in reading messages off of a message queue. What option would we have? Well, we could use a Session bean!

Session beans come in two different flavors:

☞ *Stateful Session Beans*
☞ *Stateless Session Beans*

Stateful Session Beans (SFSB)

A stateful session bean is a session bean that maintains internal data in the form of instance variables. Furthermore, when a user creates a stateful session bean, the internal properties of that bean are tied to the user that created it.

If America was an EJB, it would be a stateful session bean. After all, it has fifty different states, 52 if you include Canada and Mexico.

A simple stateful session bean might be a timer. If a user logs into our website, we could create a stateful timer that stores the time of first contact. The login time would represent the internal state of the session bean.

Using our stateful session bean, any time our user requests a new web page, we could query the stateful session bean and ask how long it has been since the user logged in. Using higher calculus, we could triangulate the elapsed time based on the current time and the time the user first entered our site, which is stored in our TimerEJB. The timer would be a simple, yet perfect, stateful session bean.

Stateless Session Beans (SLSB)

If you make eye contact with a session bean, and it is not a state**ful** session bean, then you are staring deep into the soul of a state**less** session bean.

A stateless session bean is a session bean that doesn't possess any internal state.

From a Java programming standpoint, a stateless session bean doesn't contain any meaningful instance variables.

From a users point of view, one instance of a stateless session bean is identical to any another instance of the same stateless session bean. Since there is no internal state to differentiate one stateless session bean from another, a client cannot tell the difference between one and another.

A stateless session bean does have methods. A stateless session bean 'does stuff,' but it doesn't necessarily keep track of what it has done from one method invocation to another.

You could think of a stateless session bean as a 'task oriented' component that can do something important for us, and when it is done, it is ready to do the same thing again for someone else. A stateless session bean doesn't discriminate.

Using Stateless Session Beans

On the surface, a stateless session bean might appear to be rather useless. After all, it doesn't interact with a database, it doesn't read from a message queue, and it doesn't even possess any internal state; and internal state is what makes typical Java components interesting.

Quire contrary to first impressions, stateless session beans are the most important, most useful, and most exciting Enterprise JavaBeans our developers will create.

Stateless Session beans might not have any internal state, but they do have methods that can invoke any number of objects that do indeed possess internal state, and that is exactly what stateless session beans usually do.

A Stateless Session Bean Scenario

Imagine your application had a requirement that it must be able to update three different databases in an all or nothing type of transaction.

Database One might represent a users savings account, for which the user is transferring out $100.

Database Two represents the users checking account, which the user is transferring in $100. The money being transferred *into* the checking account is equal to the money being transferred *out* of the savings account.

And when the transfer into the checking account is complete, and the transfer out of the savings account is complete, a third database keeps track of the transaction, so that the user can be charged exorbitant banking fees at the end of the month.

How could we coordinate this simultaneous and transactional update of three different databases? How could we ensure that if one database write fails, all three database writes are rolled back? After all, people get upset when money is transferred out of one account, and not subsequently transferred into the other. People are picky that way.

To control the transactional update of three different databases, we could simply create a stateless session bean with a single method that calls on three different entity beans.

We could tell this one method, by configuring its deployment descriptor, to run within the scope of a transaction, so if any database writes fail, all the database writes will be written back.

We could even slap a security attribute on the method as well so that only certain users can call it.

Furthermore, by using an inherently multithreaded EJB, we know that concurrent access won't be a problem. After all, that is what a J2EE compliant application server promises us when we use EJBs.

We can also invoke the session bean's method remotely, since EJBs implicitly implement remote distribution through remotely invocable interfaces.

Stateless session beans become the glue that holds the whole EJB horse together.

When should you use EJBs?

EJBs are incredibly powerful components that allow developers to easily take advantage of the application server's security, transaction, naming and distribution services. However, EJBs are also incredibly resource intensive. If you use EJBs excessively, you've just bought yourself a one-way ticket to performance problemville.

Before committing to using an EJB, ask yourself the following questions:

- ☞ *Do I need to manage some serious database transactions?*

EJBs are great for managing transactions, and if you have a largely transactional system, EJBs just may be your saving grace.

You can always access the Java Transaction Service (JTS) programmatically though the Java Transaction API (JTA), but the declarative security, which EJBs define in an XML file, external to any Java code, is much, much easier to use, configure and maintain.

- ☞ *Do I need object distribution?*
- ☞ *Are users calling my components remotely?*

This is a good case for using EJBs, as EJBs are inherently distributed objects. However, this alone is not a compelling reason to employ an EJB centric solution.

There are many mechanisms for implementing remote distribution including remote method invocation (RMI) and network socket programming, both of which are more efficient than using an EJB.

Needing object distribution is a good reason for using an EJB, but I'd look for another reason or two before committing to an EJB based solution.

It should be noted that prior to J2EE 1.3, all EJBs had remote interfaces, which could be used by any client that could get a connection to the J2EE server and invoke an EJB. However, it was decided that making it possible for any remote client to invoke an EJB probably wasn't such a good idea, so the idea of local interfaces were introduced. Essentially, if an EJB had a remote interface, it could be invoked by *any* client that could get a connection to the server. On the other hand, a local interface could only be used to invoke an EJB that was running on the same server as the client. The use of a local interface greatly restricts, and helps to control, the number of clients that can invoke an EJBs methods.

Typically, session EJBs are given remote interfaces. On the other hand, entity beans, which typically represent important data which needs to be heavily protected, are given local interfaces. It is always a priority to protect application data as much as possible, and, using local interfaces with entity beans is an accepted best practice.

☞ *Do I need security down to the method level?*

EJBs provide the ability to interact with the security service of the application server, and you can lock EJBs right down to the method level. This type of security would be relatively difficult to implement with regular JavaBeans.

Needing this type of security is a good reason to use an EJB, but it shouldn't be a reason on its own.

If security is the problem you need addressed, you could probably avoid using EJBs and lock down your applications by securing Servlets and JSPs instead. The Java Authentication and Authorization Service (JAAS) could also be used to facilitate a secure system without using EJBs, but even JAAS introduces an extra level of complexity.

EJBs do indeed provide secure access right down to the method level, and if this is the type of security you need, EJBs might be a viable solution.

☞ *Do I need to make sure that the data my application receives is completely and totally in sync with the data in the database?*
☞ *Do I need a persistence model?*

CMPs and BMPs address the many difficulties associated with communicating with a database, as they provide a persistent object model that makes sure the data obtained by your application is completely and totally in sync with the database.

Again, if this type of persistence model is what you need, go ahead and use EJBs. However, if your application is largely reading data from a database, and data collisions are rare and not likely to be detrimental when they do happen, I wouldn't use an entity bean framework. In that scenario, I'd look at Java Data Objects (JDO) or Hibernate. Remember, entity beans are incredibly resource intensive. Use them only if you need them.

☞ *Do I need multithreaded access with large workloads*

EJBs are inherently multithreaded, and J2EE application servers are highly scaleable. The need for a soundly multithreaded system is a good peripheral reason for using EJBs, but I wouldn't base my decision on multithreading support alone. After all, you can always synchronize methods in a regular POJO (plain ordinary java object.).

Use EJBs Sparingly

The point is, EJBs are incredibly powerful, but they are also incredibly resource intensive. Use them when they make sense, but use them sparingly.

Unnecessary EJBs will slow down your applications, and performance will quickly become an issue. There is a good reason why many of the J2EE design patterns demonstrate how you can achieve many of the benefits of using EJBs, while minimizing their actual use.

If you choose to use EJBs, choose to use them wisely.

Question

Which of the following EJBs do not provide a remote interface for synchronous interaction with a client:
O a) Stateful Session Bean
O b) Stateless Session Bean
O c) Entity Bean
O d) Message Driven Bean

Question

Which of the following EJBs map directly to persistent data?
O a) Stateful Session Beans
O b) Stateless Session Beans
O c) Entity Beans
O d) Message Driven Beans

Question

An entity bean, where all of the JDBC is coded by the developer, is known as a:
O a) Bean Managed Persistence Entity Bean
O b) Container Managed Persistence Entity Bean
O c) User Managed Persistence Entity Bean
O d) EJB Managed Persistence Entity Bean

Question

A message driven bean can be configured to read messages off of:
☐ a) databases
☐ b) topics
☐ c) queues
☐ d) file systems

Answer

Which of the following EJBs do not provide a remote interface for synchronous interaction with a client:
O a) Stateful Session Bean O b) Stateless Session Bean O c) Entity Bean O d) Message Driven Bean
MDBs, as we like to call them, do not provide a remote interface that clients can invoke synchronously. Instead, clients place messages on a queue or topic, and when an MDB feels like it, it reads the message off the queue. The interaction is asynchronous, which implies that the client places a message on a topic or queue, but does not wait for the message to be processed.

Answer

Which of the following EJBs map directly to persistent data?
O a) Stateful Session Beans O b) Stateless Session Beans O c) Entity Beans O d) Message Driven Beans
Session beans are worker beans, and MDBs read messages asynchronously off of a queue or topic. Entity beans, which come in two flavors, CMPs and BMPs, map to persistent data, which is typically represented by data in a database.

Answer

An entity bean, where all of the JDBC is coded by the developer, is known as a:
O a) Bean Managed Persistence Entity Bean O b) Container Managed Persistence Entity Bean O c) User Managed Persistence Entity Bean O d) EJB Managed Persistence Entity Bean
BMPs, or Bean Managed Persistence Entity Beans, require the developer to code all of the database interactions. This is more work than using a container managed persistence bean, but it does allow the developer a bit more flexibility when implementing a solution.

Answer

A message driven bean can be configured to read messages off of:
☐ a) databases ☐ b) topics ☐ c) queues ☐ d) file systems

Topics and queues are the two places MDBs can be configured to read messages. A queue is associated with a *point to point* type of messaging infrastructure, whereas a topic conforms to a *publish-subscribe* type of architecture.

Seeing there's some extra space on this page, here's a little more on messaging from the Wikipedia. Enjoy:

"The JMS API supports two models: **point-to-point or queuing** model and the **publish and subscribe** model.

In the point-to-point or queuing model, a *producer* posts messages to a particular queue and a *consumer* reads messages from the queue. Here, the producer knows the destination of the message and posts the message directly to the consumer's queue. It is characterized by following:

Only one consumer will get the message

The producer does not have to be running at the time the receiver consumes the message, nor does the receiver need to be running at the time the message is sent

Every message successfully processed is acknowledged by the receiver

The publish/subscribe model supports publishing messages to a particular message topic. Zero or more *subscribers* may register interest in receiving messages on a particular message topic. In this model, neither the *publisher* nor the subscriber know about each other. A good metaphor for it is anonymous bulletin board. The following are characteristics of this model:

Multiple consumers can get the message

There is a timing dependency between publishers and subscribers. Publisher has to create a subscription in order for clients to be able to subscribe. Subscriber has to remain continuously active to receive messages, unless it has established a durable subscription. In that case, messages published while the subscriber is not connected will be redistributed whenever it will reconnect."

Retrieved from Wikipedia, May 14th, 2006 http://en.wikipedia.org/wiki/Java_Message_Service

Chapter 4
J2EE Protocols and Services

J2EE components by themselves are pretty boring. What makes J2EE components interesting, far more interesting than anything you could write using the Standard Java Development Kit (SDK), are the various J2EE ***services*** they can access.

What services are we talking about?

To name a few:

- *A Transaction Service*
- *A Session Management Service*
- *A Naming Service*
- *A Messaging Service*
- *A Security Service*

A J2EE application server implements a variety of application programming interfaces (APIs) that provide EJB and Servlet developers access to the important J2EE services.

Using various J2EE APIs, a developer can access the security service, and do sexy things with it, such as finding out the name with which a user has logged in.

It was mentioned earlier that EJBs can easily manage distributed transactions. Well, it's not the EJB that manages the transaction, it's the J2EE application server vendor that does it. The underlying transaction service handles the distributed transaction. As developers, we simply edit a little deployment descriptor that tells the J2EE application server how our EJB will participate in that transaction that the application server will handle.

The HttpSession of the Servlet and JSP API

A session, or more accurately, an HttpSession, is probably the most important object in the entire Servlet API. Its importance cannot be understated.

First of all, an HttpSession object has nothing to do with a Session EJB, so let's get that association out of your mind right away. It is a completely different monster. An HttpSession is a server-managed component completely independent of the EJB spec.

The Session Issue

Here's the issue: the http protocol, the mechanism we use to surf the Internet and browse websites, is stateless. Once a Web server is done handling a client request, the web server completely forgets about what it just did, kinda like that fish in *Finding Nemo.*

The http protocol treats every request as a brand spanking new, unassociated request, regardless of how many client-server interactions may have happened with a particular client in the past.

A web server, using the http protocol, doesn't maintain any meaningful state with a client.

The Impact of a Stateless Protocol

A stateless protocol, such as http, causes all sorts of problems for our web-based applications. For example, if a user surfs to our site and sees a product they want to buy, we want to keep track of that information until the user decides to check out.

Or perhaps a user is taking an online exam: we would want to keep track of every answer the user has provided. The http protocol provides no mechanism for keeping track of a user's actions from one invocation to the other. That's where the Servlet API, and more specifically, the HttpSession, comes in.

Canada and the http protocol have one thing in common: they are both stateless. Canada has ten provinces and three relatively empty territories, but no states. Of course, they have been eyeing Michigan for a while.

The Purpose of the HttpSession

The HttpSession object, with the help of the HttpSession *service*, adds state to a stateless, web based, interaction with a server. When a client makes a call to an application server, a Servlet developer can programmatically create and associate an HttpSession with that client. The session can then be used to keep track of all sorts of information about the user.

If the user tells us their favorite color, we can store that information in their session. If the user gives us their address and phone number, we can store that in their session. If they're taking an online exam, we can put the answer to every question they've been given into the session as well. We can then go back into that session object, at any point in time, and pull that information out.

So when a user is done taking an online exam, we can go into their session and find out which questions they got correct, and which questions they got wrong. If the client is picking out books, or other products they want to purchase, when they click 'check out,' we can go into their session, process their order, and tell them how much their purchase will be. HttpSessions add state to a stateless protocol, and they are pivotal in making online applications work.

Java Naming and Directory Interface (JNDI)

JNDI, the Java Naming and Directory Interface, is one of the most important J2EE services your applications will employ.

J2EE components are interesting and powerful because the can take advantage of a variety of features and services that are implemented and managed by the J2EE application server; However, most of these services and features are created, initialized, maintained and exist outside of the Java code our developers write.

Applications must be capable of accessing these server managed J2EE resources and services. The first step towards gaining access to these resources is looking them up through a directory naming service.

JNDI vs. JNI: Just to Throw You Off

As just a bit of a *heads up* for the SCJA exam, you should know that ***JNI*** is the **J**ava **N**ative **I**nterface, which is different from ***JNDI***. JNI makes it possible for Java programs to invoke methods on code libraries written in C++, Smalltalk, Turbo Pascal, or any other non-Java programming language. JNI is not listed on the exam objectives, but Sun may throw it in as a question option, just to throw you off.

Common Victims of JNDI Lookups

A short list of the elusive enterprise objects initially accessed though a naming service includes:

- *Remote Enterprise JavaBeans*
- *DataSources (Database Connection Pools)*
- *Transaction Objects*
- *Custom Services*
- *Message Queues*
- *Local Enterprise JavaBeans*
- *Mail Servers*

All enterprise environments, be it CORBA or .Net, use the facilities of a naming service. In a J2EE environment, the Java Naming and Directory Interface (JNDI) provides our components access to the underlying naming service implemented by the Application Server.

The Naming Service at Runtime

When an application server boots, a variety of resources are initialized and subsequently bound to the naming service.

The first step in accessing a JNDI bound resource, such as an EJB, is to look up the resource according to its JNDI bound name. The naming service will then return to the client a reference to the object of interest.

Assigning JNDI Names to Resources

When resources, such as DataSources and message queues are created and configured by the administrator, the JNDI name is one of the configurable properties. For the most part, the application server administrator has the final say over the name a resource will use when binding itself to JNDI.

The JNDI Context, or InitialContext

A naming service uses a directory, or folder structure, to keep track of objects and their corresponding names.

For example, EJBs usually go under a sub-directory named *ejb*, and database related objects usually go under a subdirectory named *jdbc*. An InitialContext is a connection to the *root* or *base* directory of the naming service, off of which all folders or subdirectories branch.

To use an analogy, if the Windows operating system was a directory server, the InitialContext would be the root, C:\, since all folders and subdirectories sprout from there.

When looking up an object bound to a JNDI server, we reference the name of the object relative to the root of the directory, or as we say in developerspeak, we reference the InitialContext.

A Conversation Between JNDI and an EJB at Start-Up

EJB:Hey, JNDI, do you know who I am?

***JNDI**:Ya, you're a really important EJB.*

EJB:That's right, and people are going to be coming around these parts asking for me.

***JNDI**: What's your name?*

EJB: "ejb/com/pulpjava/session/Timer"

***JNDI**:Great. And when someone asks, where should I send them?*

EJB:Point them to my home. It's the big mansion on the corner.

***JNDI**:Will do! After all, binding names to objects is what I do best!*

JNDI and Distributed Programming

To obtain a reference to an EJB running on a remote server, we must first connect to the naming service on that server. Once we have a connection to the remote naming service, we provide the JNDI name of the desired EJB. If we provide the correct name, the naming service will return a reference to the EJB in question.

Objects are bound to the naming directory in a tree like manner.

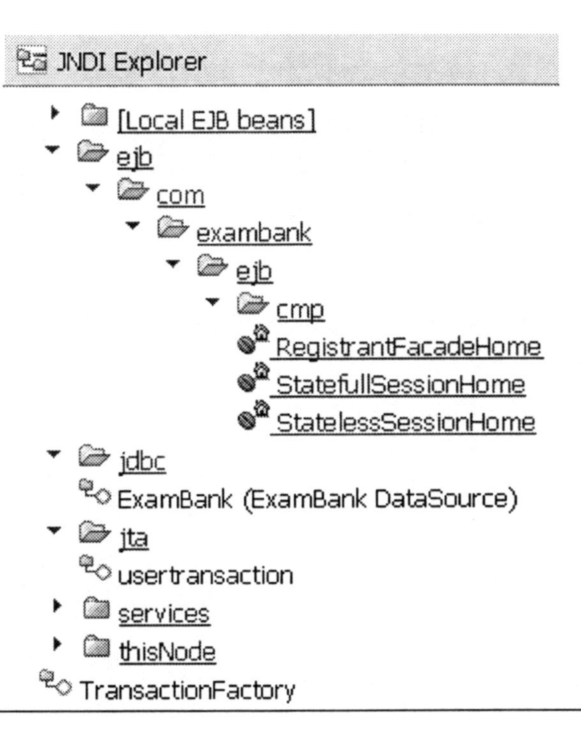

Looking Up JNDI Addressable Resource

When a database connection pool (aka *DataSource*) is created, or an EJB is deployed, those resources are configured with a JNDI name.

A DataSource might be bound to the naming service with the name jdbc/pulpds, or an EJB might be bound with the name ejb/com/pulpjava/session/Timer.

To lookup a JNDI addressable resource in your application, your Java code would look something like this:

```
//connect to the root of the JNDI server
InitialContext jndi = new InitialContext();
//lookup a datasource
jndi.lookup("jdbc/pulpds");
//lookup the Timer EJB
jndi.lookup("ejb/com/pulpjava/session/Timer");
```

Connecting to a Database: JDBC

All enterprise applications require database connectivity, so it probably comes as no surprise to find out that a database connection service is an integral part of any J2EE application server.

Now the tough challenge with connecting to a database from a cross-platform programming language like Java is the fact that there are an innumerable number of different databases on the market. To create a cross-platform database programming environment, Java provides a standard set of APIs defined in the java.sql and javax.sql packages. To address the fact that every database is implemented differently, the Java world asks each of the database vendors to provide a set of drivers that makes their database work with Java's DataBase Connection architecture (JDBC).

Vendors are actually allowed to implement their own drivers in any way they see fit, so long as they work properly when accessed through the JDBC API. Some vendors choose to provide a *type 4 driver* that is itself written entirely in Java. Other vendors provide type 2 drivers, which are written in a language other than Java. With DB2, IBM actually provides both a net (type 4) and an app (type 2) driver. And to connect to a MS Access database, Sun Microsystems even provides a flimsy, *I mean functional*, JDBC-ODBC bridge.

Database efficiency and transactional integrity is a huge competition point, so allowing vendors to implement their JDBC drivers in the best possible way, ends up benefiting everyone.

Web Services: What are they?

Imagine an Estonian and a Cree *Indian* (North American Indigenous) were doing business together. Communication would be an issue, after all, not many Cree Indians speak Estonian, and not many Estonians speak Cree. For the two to communicate, they would be best to try and learn a common language that both could agree on. If they were perhaps to be conducting business in the US, they might agree to use the common language of America – Spanish.

So the Cree Indian learns Spanish, and the Estonian learns Spanish, and the two can communicate with each other. Furthermore, if anyone else wants to jump into the conversation, all they have to do is learn Spanish, and they can contribute as well. Spanish becomes the common language for doing business.

In the enterprise world of application development, J2EE isn't the only middleware solution, although it is definitely the best. A variety of standard and proprietary middleware implementations exist, from new .NET implementations, to legacy CORBA infrastructures. In fact, as companies merge and grow, these diverse sets of systems often exist within the same company. Getting these different middleware solutions to communicate is a problem, after all, they don't speak the same language – Web Services address this very issue.

Working with Web Services

Once they are discovered, potentially through UDDI, the universal discovery mechanism, web services work by communicating with each other through text marked up in XML format. These XML text messages are transported across a network on a standard protocol called SOAP (Simple Object Access Protocol), which runs over http, the transport protocol of the Internet.

A Web Service describes itself in a Web Services Definition Language file (WSDL). The WSDL file describes what a web service can do, and how text messages should be formatted when a client wants to invoke a Web Service.

For example, a credit card verification Web Service would have a WSDL file that would say something like this:

"Hey, I'm a Web Service named CreditCardChecker. If you want me to verify a credit card date and number, send me an XML message formatted like this:

```
<number>### ### ### ###</number>
<date>MM-DD-YY</date>
```

"If you give me an XML message marked up like that, I'll give you response in XML format that looks like this:

<valid>true || false</valid>

"You can just parse the XML for *true* or *false* to find out if the credit card is valid or not.

That's it! I'm looking forward to hearing from you!!!"

Of course, this whole WSDL definition is in a structured, XML format, but you get the idea.

So, in order to create or use a Web Service, a component really only needs to be able to understand XML, and send a message over a network using the SOAP protocol. Supporting Web Services is a bit of work for sure, but no more than teaching a Cree Indian and an Estonian to speak Spanish. ☺

And in fact, the Java API for XML based Remote Procedure Calls (JAX-RPC) makes creating web services out of existing Java components such as Servlet and JSPs incredibly easy. With JAX-RPC, already existing Servlet and EJB applications can be easily converted into web services.

But regardless of whether you're using JAX-RPC or not, reading a WSDL file, and parsing an XML message, isn't a lot to ask, considering that the payoff is the ability to communicate with any available Web Service on the Internet, regardless of its 'behind the scenes' implementation. Web services are truly a gift from God.

Drawbacks to Web Services

Web Services are slow.

Imagine a Cree Indian and an Estonian speaking Spanish to each other. The Cree Indian is translating all Spanish words back into Cree in order to understand the Estonian. When the Cree Indian wants to say something back to the Estonian, she figures out what she wants to say in Cree, and then translates it into Spanish, sending a Spanish translation to the Estonian. These translations would really slow down the whole process.

Of course, the Estonian is new to Spanish as well, so the same type of translations between Estonian and Spanish must take place as well. It would be very interesting being a fly on the wall when this conversation is going on – assuming you're a fly that speaks Spanish that is.

Web Services are equally slow – after all, XML must be parsed and reconstructed on both sides of the Web Services equation. Furthermore,

Web Services will be passing text-based messages across a network, which is always a potential application bottleneck.

Of course, the benefit is the fact that the Web Services are more effective than any other solution on the market for gluing together diverse architectures and implementations. If your problem is making a .NET application talk to you Enterprise JavaBeans, Web Services will solve your problems, and the performance issue will seem rather insignificant when compared to the overall benefits.

J2EE Protocols

As interesting as your Servlets and EJBs might be, nobody cares about them if they can't interact with them, which brings us to the third prong of the J2EE spork: protocols.

When it comes to J2EE, there are four basic protocols we will encounter:

- *RMI (remote method invocation)*
- *IIOP (Internet inter-orb protocol)*
- *http (hypertext transport protocol)*
- *https (secure http)*

Http and Https

Http is the protocol of the Internet. When someone requests an html file, opens up a pdf, or downloads a zip file, they're using the Hyper Text Transfer Protocol. When a client calls on a JSP or a Servlet, they invoke it using the http protocol.

Of course, some people don't like the idea of their requests, which includes anything they may have typed into a textfield or an online form, shooting across the Internet in plain text.

To address the security concerns associated with transferring data across the Internet, Netscape created https, the Hyper Text Transfer Protocol with *secure sockets*, also known as "secure http."

Https basically piggybacks on top of http, encrypting and securing a request and response so that nobody can view it, and no unscrupulous individual can tamper with the request or response midstream.

Http and https are the protocols we use to access web-based components, which from a J2EE perspective, means Servlets and JSPs.

Remote Method Invocation (RMI)

RMI stands for Remote Method Invocation, and it is actually a technology that was released with Java 1.1 to make it possible for one JVM to invoke methods on objects running on JVMs outside of the local, physical machine. RMI makes JVM to JVM, remote, distributed, *procedure* calls possible. RMI is part of the standard edition, although J2EE components such as EJBs rely heavily on the RMI protocol when speaking with each other, or being spoken to by Servlets and JSPs.

RMI technology is implemented using a number of standard design patterns, such as the proxy pattern, to make remote method calls possible. Part of the implementation of an RMI system is the requirement that Java components, wishing to be remotely accessible, register themselves with a special RMI registry, that is similar in many respects to a JNDI server. RMI is a very robust and scalable mechanism for implementing object distribution. It's no wonder that EJBs build heavily upon RMI technology for their implementation of object distribution.

Using the RMI Protocol When Invoking EJBs

Invoking EJBs is quite a bit different from invoking a Servlet or a JSP. EJBs use *RMI over IIOP* to handle EJB requests, and to send back a response to the invoking client. Regardless of whether it is a Servlet or a stand-alone Java application that might be invoking an EJB, RMI over IIOP is the protocol being used.

JavaMail and SMTP

While it doesn't get nearly the exposure of the http protocol running on port 80, or the https protocol running on port 443, the Simple Mail ***Transfer*** Protocol, SMTP, is a pretty integral part of any enterprise environment, whether it is a .NET or a J2EE environment. SMTP is the standard protocol used to send and receive emails.

Together, JavaMail and SMTP are like two peas in an iPod. JavaMail is the Java API that provides a "platform independent and protocol independent" means for writing Java applications that can send and receive email. Of course, if you want to send email, you need a transport mechanism. SMTP has been around since 1982, and is a reliable, and widely accepted protocol for sending and receiving email messages. JavaMail can work with a variety of different email protocols, but SMTP is the de facto standard, and is in use in most enterprise environments. SMTP, along with RMI and http, is another important J2EE protocol.

What J2EE is All About

J2EE is all about the various components a developer can write when developing an enterprise application, namely EJBs and Servlets.

J2EE is all about the various services that are implemented by an application server vendor, and subsequently accessed by the J2EE components we write.

And finally, J2EE is all about the various protocols that can be used to interact with our J2EE components, namely:

- *http*
- *https*
- *rmi*
- *iiop*

And when we talk about J2EE protocols, we probably shouldn't neglect the Simple Mail Transfer Protocol, SMTP. Email is catching on, and pretty soon, every corporation will use it. ☺

Question

Which J2EE service creates a stateful experience for users using the stateless http protocol?

- O a) http service
- O b) web container service
- O c) HttpSession service
- O d) JNDI Naming Service

Question

Objects that are created and managed by the application server, and have scope beyond any normal developer created resource are first accessed by:

- O a) interacting with the web container service
- O b) interacting with the J2EE container service
- O c) performing a lookup against a naming and directory service
- O d) accessing the J2EE transaction service

Question

To allow a Microsoft .net application to interact with functionality implemented through an Enterprise JavaBean, which technology would be most appropriate?

- O a) A Servlet
- O b) A JSP
- O c) A Web Service
- O d) A Database Connection service

Question

Which of the following technologies are tightly associated with web service implementations?

- ☐ a) databases
- ☐ b) UDDI
- ☐ c) SOAP
- ☐ d) WSDL

Answer

Which J2EE service creates a stateful experience for users using the stateless http protocol?

O a) http service

O b) web container service

O c) HttpSession service

O d) JNDI Naming Service

Option c) is correct.

The http protocol provides for client-server interactions, with no memory of past communications; However, server side applications must keep track of the various web page transitions made by an end user, not to mention remembering information that a client may have provided to a server. T0 overcome the stateless nature of the http protocol, the Servlet and JSP API defines an HttpSession object that can be used to statefully tie an end user with subsequent http requests.

"HTTP can occasionally pose problems for Web developers (Web Applications), because HTTP is stateless. The advantage of a stateless protocol is that hosts don't need to retain information about users between requests, but this forces the use of alternative methods for maintaining users' state, for example, when a host would like to customize content for a user who has visited before. The common method for solving this problem involves the use of sending and requesting cookies."

Retrieved from the Wikipedia, May 14th, 2006
http://en.wikipedia.org/wiki/Hypertext_Transfer_Protocol

Answer

Objects that are created and managed by the application server, and have scope beyond any normal developer created resource are first accessed by:
O a) interacting with the web container service O b) interacting with the J2EE container service O c) performing a lookup against a naming and directory service O d) accessing the J2EE transaction service
Option c) is correct. The application server creates and initializes a number of different objects, including connection pools, aka DataSources, EJBs and Transaction objects. To access these objects, a developer must request the object by name, or potentially object type, from a JNDI server. The Java Naming and Directory service is one of the most commonly relied upon services in a J2EE application.

Answer

To allow a Microsoft .net application to interact with functionality implemented through an Enterprise JavaBean, which technology would be most appropriate?
O a) A Servlet O b) A JSP O c) A Web Service O d) A Database Connection service
Option c) is correct. Microsoft .net technologies and J2EE technologies don't inherently communicate with each other. However, both technologies can be wrapped up as a web service, and web services should be able to communicate with other web services, regardless of the vendor or the underlying implementation. For communicating between technologies that don't usually talk to each other, web services is the right answer.

Answer

Which of the following technologies are tightly associated with web service implementations?
☐ a) databases ☐ b) UDDI ☐ c) SOAP ☐ d) WSDL
Options b) c) and d) are correct. While web services often pull data from a database, or store data to a database, a web service doesn't require the services of a database system. UDDI is a mechanism for publishing information about a web service, so that applications can find or discover web services at either design time, or at runtime. SOAP is an XML based, envelope format, for passing information between web services, over a bound protocol such as http or, to a lesser extent, smtp. A WSDL file describes the web service interface, explaining what types of parameters can be passed, and what type of data will be returned from the web service. You can expect a very high level question about one of these three technologies, UDDI, SOAP or WSDL, on the SCJA exam. Understand their basic function, as described in this answer, and you'll be one question closer to achieving your SCJA certification.

Chapter 5 Java and J2EE at Runtime

Let's look at a typical web based interaction with a J2EE application server at runtime.

Let's use a typical scenario where the request is coming in from an Internet browser, such as Internet Explorer, Mozilla Firefox, Netscape Navigator or Opera. We'll just focus on a typical web based interaction between a web based client and our application server, although it should be noted that a handheld device, such as a J2ME application, or even a stand-alone J2SE application, may indeed invoke a Servlet or a JSP.

From Client to Web Server

When dealing with web based requests, before tunneling through to our application server, a web-based client will hit a web server first. The application server does not completely replace the need for a web server. A web server remains as pivotal a part of the architecture as ever.

Web servers are great at doing one thing: serving up files. A web server takes requests from clients, maps that request to a file on the file system, and then sends that file back to the client.

A web server responds to a request for static content.

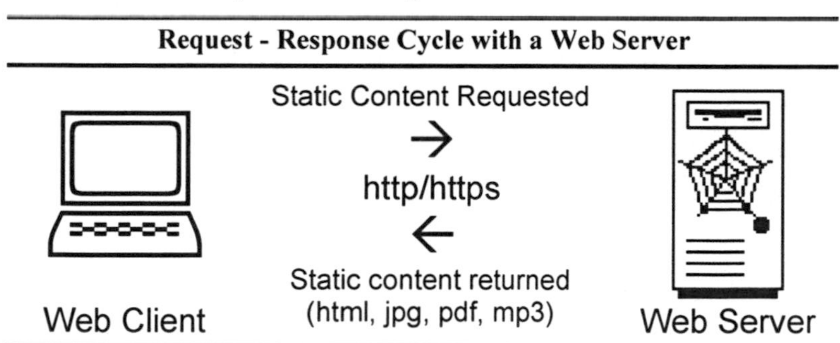

If you want an html file, a web server can efficiently and reliably find that file and send it back to you. If you need an image, a web server can serve it up to you as well. You want to download a zip file or a pdf file quickly and efficiently? A web server can make that happen.

Unfortunately though, your web server is about as intelligent as a male model. A web server can serve up static files until the cows come home, but ask your web server to add 'one plus one' and you'll be waiting there for a very, very long time.

If our applications use any images, HTML, pdf or zip files, we like to keep all of those static files on the web server. If we need some logic or dynamic content in our applications, we will delegate to our Servlets, JSPs, EJBs and JavaBeans that are running on our Application Server.

Now here is the dilemma. Our application server contains all of our Servlets and JSPs, but all of the requests go through the web server, and the web server, not being a very clever machine, tries to handle *all* requests, regardless of whether the request is for an image, html file, or to our detriment, a Servlet or a JSP.

How do you stop a web server from trying to handle requests for our Servlets and JSPs?

The key to stopping a web server from trying to serve up JSPs or Servlets, is to install some type of plug-in on the web server.

The general idea, although not a hard and fast rule, is that before you install a middle tier application server, you should first install your web server.

Web servers forward all request for JSPs or Servlets to the J2EE server. This all occurs over http/https.

Forwarding Servlet Requests to a J2EE Web Container

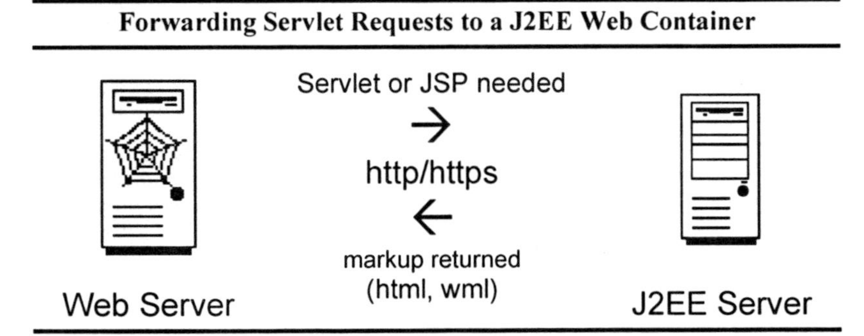

As was stated earlier, the web server tries to handle every single request that it receives. However, when an J2EE complaint application server comes onto the scene, it introduces itself to the web server and has a conversation that goes something like this:

Application Server: Hey, WebServer?

Web Server: Ya, what's up.

Application Server: Hey, not much.

Web Server: What can I do for you?

Application Server: Well, I know that you're really great at serving up static files and all, but you're going to get some crazy requests for JSPs and Servlets that won't be able to find on your file system.

Web Server: Really? What am I going to do? I won't be able to find any of these JSPs and Servlets, and I'll end up sending a bunch of 404 errors back to clients, and the clients will be pissed!

Application Server: Hey, calm down. Here's what you do: just take those requests and send them to me. I'll handle the request, generate some HTML, give that HTML back to you, and you can send the HTML back to the client.

Web Server: Kewl. You do the work, but the client thinks it's me handling the request? I like this arrangement already. How do I know what files to send to you though?

Application Server: Don't worry. I'll make a thorough list and write it all down in a special file. Just read that file every once in a while and keep up to date on which requests you need to send back to me.

Web Server: Great. But when I do get a request for an item on the list, how will I know where to send it.

Application Server: Hey, don't worry. I've got it all covered. I've got a list of JSPs and Servlets that might be requested, and a list of the IP addresses and port combinations to send them if you do get them.

Web Server: Kewl. I think this is going to be a great relationship.

Application Server: I think so too. It usually is.

From Web Server to Application Server

When a client makes a request for a JSP or a Servlet, the request initially goes to the web server. The web server reads a special file listing and realizes that the request that came in should be sent to the application server for processing.

This special file also provides the ipaddress/port combination of listening application servers. The web server, using the http protocol, or the https protocol, then sends the request to the application server JVM listening on the appropriate port (usually port 80 for http, and port 443 for https). That JVM listening on the appropriate port represents our J2EE application server, and the port the JVM listens on can be configured through that JVM's web container.

The web server handles the incoming request, and matches that request to the application server set up to handle the given Servlet or JSP.

Inside the Web Container

If the Servlet hasn't been called before, the JVM loads the Servlet and then generates a thread to handle the request.

Servlets are shy little creatures. They sit on the hard drive just minding their own business, and don't bother anyone if they've never been invoked. However, feed a few drinks to those Servlets and get them *loaded*, and they remain resident in memory until the party ends, which happens when someone pulls the plug on the application server.

So, the request gets sent from the client, to the web server, and the web server passes the request to the Application Server, who in turn invokes and threads the appropriate Servlet.

What exactly does a Servlet do?

Well, the Servlet can do pretty much anything the developer wants it to do. When programming Servlets, a developer is only limited by their creativity, and more likely, their Java programming skills.

Typically, a Servlet implements some control logic. For example, a Servlet might figure out what a user typed into some textfields in a web-based form. It might then take that information and save it to a database.

Servlets are intended to be controllers. While Servlets can interact directly with a database, they're not really supposed to. Instead, Servlets are supposed to delegate to a JavaBean or an EJB to do such things. Let's say, for the sake of argument, our Servlet calls an EJB to perform some synchronized, transactionally aware, distributed process.

How does a Servlet Invoke an EJB?

To call an EJB, especially one residing on an application server in a galaxy far, far away, we must first connect to the naming service of that remote application server.

The naming service is like a gatekeeper for objects running on a server. If someone wants access to a remote EJB, they call on the gatekeeper and ask if an EJB named "com/examscam/UserEJB" is around. If there is indeed an EJB with that name running around the server, then you're in. If not, you get an exception.

So, to call our EJB, we first connect to the EJB's naming service and ask if it's Home. If it is, we get a handle to that EJB and can call its methods, just as though it were a regular JavaBean.

So, what will we do with this remote EJB? Well, we'll probably tell it what the user typed into the textfields that appeared on the users web page. The EJB can then shove that information on a message queue, or if it is an Entity Bean, the data might even get saved to a database. The world is your oyster when you're using EJBs.

Switching Protocols

Now you may not have noticed the little slight of hand that was played on you there, but there was a switch of protocols when you weren't looking.

When the client request is routed from the client to the web server, http/https is the protocol. When the web server forwards to the web container of the application server, the protocol remains http/https.

Web servers forward all request for JSPs or Servlets to the J2EE server. This all occurs over http/https.

Servlet Invoking an EJB

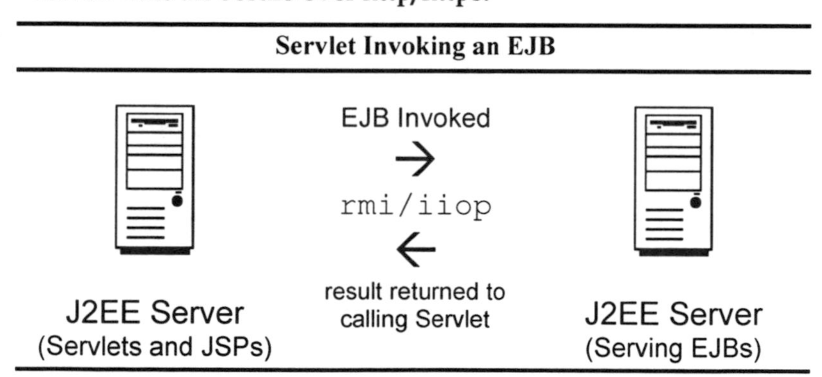

However, when a request is made from the Servlet engine to the EJB container, the protocol switches from http to RMI/IIOP (Remote Method Invocation over the Internet Inter Orb Protocol).

Don't worry, the whole protocol switch happens behind the scenes, so we don't have to worry about it in our code, but it is empowering to know what is going on under the covers.

From the Web Container, Back to the Web Server

Once the Servlet is done interacting with the EJBs, JavaBeans or other Java components that might help the Servlet implement control logic, it then figures that it has to send some response back to the client. After all, the client always likes to see a web page that lets them know that everything is working the way it should.

Servlets themselves don't generate HTML to display to the client. Well, they can, but again, they're not supposed to. Instead, they forward to a JSP.

The JSP then runs, and when it's done running, it forwards all of the HTML it has generated back to the web server. The Web server then forwards the html back to the client along with any images or other files the html page might need to display properly.

And that's it, a simple round trip for our J2EE application.

Workload Managing the Web Server

The above scenario assumes all of your requests are routed through a single web server. Of course, your site might just be so popular that one web server isn't enough. If that's the case, you'll need to set up two or more web servers, and then get a third machine that will work as an IP sprayer. An IP sprayer handles all incoming requests, and then sprays those requests across your various HTTP servers. They also usually provide a variety of caching mechanisms as well.

What happens when you turn on security?

When you turn security on, the J2EE Security Service will challenge the client for a username and password as soon as a secured resource is requested. The client then provides the appropriate credentials, and the J2EE application server will validate those credentials against a user registry, most likely an LDAP server.

If your credentials check out, and you are indeed authorized to view the Servlet you selected, the application server will invoke that Servlet, and your credentials will even be passed onto any EJBs or JSPs that your Servlet subsequently invokes.

When content is returned to your browser, the application server will go so far as to place a little token in a cookie it plants on your machine. The cookie keeps getting sent back to the server on subsequent requests, and the token tells the application server that it can trust you and that it doesn't need to ask you for your username and password again.

Can you access the application server directly?

Typical client requests go through a web server, and couple of firewalls, and eventually end up at the web container or the application server, but an external web server isn't a required part of the mix. A J2EE compliant application server has what is known as an 'embedded http server' as part of the web container that manages Servlets and JSPs. A client can make requests directly to this embedded web server, although this server doesn't typically run on the standard http port of 80.

Clients can also directly invoke EJBs as well, without going through a Servlet or JSP. In fact, a J2EE client doesn't even have to be a web based browser. J2SE provides plenty of facilities to create standalone applications that communicate directly with a Servlet or an EJB. Furthermore, you can even create a handheld devices using J2ME, and have that device communicate directly with a Servlet or a JSP. In this type of scenario, you wouldn't have a J2SE client in the mix at all!

Question

Http based client requests are typically handled first by a:
O a) web server
O b) J2EE web container
O c) J2EE EJB container
O d) Servlet

Question

Secure, web based interactions occur:
O a) over the http protocol on port 80
O b) over the https protocol on port 443
O c) over the http protocol using secure SOAP envelopes, on random ports
O d) Using secure html on random ports

Question

A Servlet typically forwards to which view rendering component for dynamic markup generation?
O a) JavaBeans
O b) Java Server Pages (JSPs)
O c) Session EJBs
O d) Entity EJBs

Question

Which of the following is true:
☐ a) EJBs can directly invoke other EJBs
☐ b) J2ME applications can interact with J2EE components
☐ c) Swing based applications can invoke EJBs
☐ d) JSP pages can invoke EJBs

Answer

Http based client requests are typically handled first by a:
O a) web server O b) J2EE web container O c) J2EE EJB container O d) Servlet
Option a) is correct. Web based request typically go through a web server first, which then forwards the request, often through a firewall, to a J2EE application server, where a Servlet or JSP handles the request.

Answer

Secure, web based interactions occur:
O a) over the http protocol on port 80 O b) over the https protocol on port 443 O c) over the http protocol using secure SOAP envelopes, on random ports O d) Using secure html on random ports
Option b) is correct. Secure web based connections use the https protocol, which typically runs on port 443. *"**https** is a URI scheme which is syntactically identical to the* `http:` *scheme normally used for accessing resources using HTTP. Using an* `https:` *URL indicates that HTTP is to be used, but with a different default port and an additional encryption/authentication layer between HTTP and TCP. This system was developed by Netscape Communications Corporation to provide authentication and encrypted communication and is widely used on the World Wide Web for security-sensitive communication, such as payment transactions. "* *Retrieved from the Wikipedia, May 14th, 2006* *http://en.wikipedia.org/wiki/Https*

Answer

A Servlet typically forwards to which view rendering component for dynamic markup generation?
○ a) JavaBeans ○ b) Java Server Pages (JSPs) ○ c) Session EJBs ○ d) Entity EJBs
Option b) is correct. Servlets act as controllers, handling incoming requests, and figuring out which model components, such as JavaBeans or EJBs, should be invoked to perform business logic. Once all of the model components have completed executing their business logic, a Servlet calls on a JSP to render dynamic markup, such as HTML, which eventually gets sent back to the client.

Answer

Which of the following is true (trick question):
☐ a) EJBs can directly invoke other EJBs ☐ b) J2ME applications can interact with J2EE components ☐ c) Swing based applications can invoke EJBs ☐ d) JSP pages can invoke EJBs
Options a) b) c) and d) are correct. Well, this is a trick question, as all of the components named here can interact with an EJB. That's the great thing about Java applications; they are built upon the same basic foundation, and interactions between them, while sometimes complex, is always possible.

Fifteen Questions: Java Technologies

Question1

Headless, micro-device applications, are associated with which profile?

- O a) MIDP
- O b) J2ME
- O c) PMI
- O d) IMP

Question 2

Which of the following is true about J2EE development:

- ☐ a) all of the J2SE APIs are available to J2EE applications
- ☐ b) J2EE applications cannot reference the J2SE swing packages
- ☐ c) J2EE can be said to build upon the J2SE platform
- ☐ d) J2EE applications run on the client side

Question 3

Which of the following would be considered to be typical, J2EE application design best practices?

- ☐ a) HTML forms should be handled by Servlets
- ☐ b) Servlets should interact directly with databases using JDBC
- ☐ c) Entity beans should have remote interfaces, while session EJBs should have local interfaces
- ☐ d) Java Server Pages should contain a minimal amount of Java code

Question 4

Database types, such as a ResultSet and PooledConnection, can be found in which of the following two packages?

- ☐ a) java.jdbc
- ☐ b) javax.jdbc
- ☐ c) java.sql
- ☐ d) javax.sql

Question 5

JNDI is used to:
O a) connect clients to a database
O b) allow local JavaBeans to invoke methods on JavaBeans running on remote JVMs
O c) provide a naming service to J2EE components
O d) allow native programs running on a computer to invoke components running on a JVM

Question 6

When implementing a solution that leverages Message Oriented Middleware (MOM), what types of destinations can be configured for JMS messages?
☐ a) publication
☐ b) topic
☐ c) queue
☐ d) port

Question 7

Which of the following are true about RMI:
☐ a) RMI allows Java calls to remote JVMs
☐ b) RMI accessible objects register themselves in an rmiregistry
☐ c) RMI allows native applications to call Java components
☐ d) RMI is part of the J2SE platform

Question 8

Which of the following are part of J2ME's appeal?
☐ a) a large programmer base
☐ b) offline functionality
☐ c) persistent memory
☐ d) J2ME builds upon the J2SE APIs

Question 9

Which of the following pieces of information is a Java applet allowed to know about the client?
☐ a) Java version of the installed plug-in
☐ b) Operating system name and version
☐ c) User name
☐ d) Users home directory

Question 10

Swing components:
☐ a) are more consistent in appearance than awt components
☐ b) appear like any other visual component on a native system
☐ c) are considered to be lightweight
☐ d) essentially draw their look onto the visual screen

Question 11

Which of the following statements are **not** true about HTML? (Choose 2)
☐ a) all web browsers are capable of rendering HTML
☐ b) HTML is based on XML
☐ c) applets are rendered within HTML pages
☐ d) HTML poses a security risk to clients

Question12

Which of the following are true of awt components?

O a) they are prefixed with the letter J, as in JApplet

O b) they are found in the javax.awt package

O c) they use native components for GUI display rendering

O d) they essentially draw their components on heavyweight components

Question 13

The job of a Servlet typically involves:

☐ a) handling incoming HTTP requests

☐ b) interacting with JDBC databases

☐ c) delegating business logic to JavaBeans and model components

☐ d) validating user input before business processing

Question 14

A stateless session bean is typically used to:

☐ a) coordinate complex business operations

☐ b) manage the transactional integrity of multiple entity beans working on a business scenario

☐ c) directly connect to and update a database

☐ d) manage session state for a web based client

Question 15

Which of the following execute within a J2EE container?

☐ a) MIDlets

☐ b) Servlets

☐ c) JSPs

☐ d) EJBs

Answer 1

Option d), IMP, is correct.

The IMP, Information Module Profile, is associated with *headless* J2ME applications, such as vending machines and security systems, that don't have a typical user interface, and have limited network connectivity. Option a), MIDP, or Mobile Information Device Profile, is associated with J2ME micro-device application development when the targeted applications have typical user interfaces, such as a cell phone. J2ME is the overall edition name given to the environment for developing micro-applications. Option c), PMI, is meaningless, and was only thrown in to throw you off.

Answer 2

Options a) and c) are correct.

J2EE applications run on the server side, on a J2EE compliant application server. The J2EE APIs build upon the J2SE APIs, meaning J2EE applications can access all of those delicious collection classes and networking components found in the java.util and java.net packages of the SDK. J2EE applications can even access the swing and awt packages, although you'll rarely see a Servlet or EJB doing so.

Answer 3

Options a) c) and d) are all correct.

Servlets are intended to act as controllers in a web based architecture, and part of being a controller is to handle incoming requests from the client. HTML forms will typically invoke servlets to perform request handling.

EJBs can have either remote or local interfaces, and in fact, they can even have both. Entity beans typically have local interfaces, in order to provide a greater level of security over the data they represent. Session EJBs typically have remote interfaces in order to support remote distribution and client access.

JSP pages are intended as view components, and as such, should contain mostly markup, such as HTML tags, and a limited amount of Java. The logic that requires Java coding should reside in the Servlet as much as possible.

It is a poor design to have a servlet use JDBC to interact directly with a database. Instead, client request should be handled by a servlet, and the servlet should delegate any database interactions to database components or Data Access Objects (DAOs). This creates for a more manageable and flexible design, as if the database ever changes, only the database interaction objects need to be updated.

Answer 4

Options c) and d) are correct.

The core JDBC classes, and the JDBC extension classes that provide J2SE client access to server side data sources (aka connection pools) are provided through the java.sql and javax.sql packages respectively.

The question mentions the PooledConnection and ResultSet object types. The SCJA exam won't be quizzing you on all of the objects associated with JDBC, but it is important to know the names of the packages in which the standard JDBC components can be found.

From Wikipedia, to fill out the rest of the page:

JDBC has been part of the Java Standard Edition since the release of JDK 1.1. The JDBC classes are contained in the Java package `java.sql`. *Starting with version 3.0, JDBC has been developed under the Java Community Process. JSR 54 specifies JDBC 3.0 (included in J2SE 1.4), JSR 114 specifies the JDBC Rowset additions, and JSR 221 is the specification of JDBC 4.0 (included in Java SE 6).*

JDBC allows multiple implementations to exist and be used by the same application. The API provides a mechanism for dynamically loading the correct Java packages and registering them with the JDBC Driver Manager. The Driver Manager is used as a connection factory for creating JDBC connections.

JDBC connections support creating and executing statements. These statements may be update statements such as SQL CREATE, INSERT, UPDATE and DELETE or they may be query statements using the SELECT statement. Additionally, stored procedures may be invoked through a statement. Statements are one of the following types:

`Statement` *– the statement is sent to the database server each and every time.*

`PreparedStatement` *– the statement is cached and then the execution path is pre determined on the database server allowing it to be executed multiple times in an efficient manner.*

`CallableStatement` *– used for executing stored procedures on the database.*

Update statements such as INSERT, UPDATE and DELETE return an update count that indicates how many rows were affected in the database. These statements do not return any other information.

Query statements return a JDBC row result set. The row result set is used to walk over the result set. Individual columns in a row are retrieved either by name or by column number. There may be any number of rows in the result set. The row result set has metadata that describes the names of the columns and their types.

There is an extension to the basic JDBC API in the `javax.sql` *package that allows for scrollable result sets and cursor support among other things.*

-http://en.wikipedia.org/wiki/JDBC

Answer 5

Option c) is correct.

JNDI is the Java Naming and Directory Interface, and it is used to provide a naming service to J2EE applications. Many J2EE components are created, managed and maintained outside of the applications developers create. In order to access these components that are managed by the application server, the first step in garnering access, is often performing a JNDI lookup.

JDBC is the technology used by Java applications to connect to a database, and RMI, Remote Method Invocation, is the technology used to allow local Java components to invoke Java components running on remote JVMs.

Option d), refers to JNI, the Java Native Interface, that allows Java non-Java programs to interact with programs and components running on a standard JVM.

You are ***not*** expected to know JNI for the test, but Sun is well within their rights to make incorrect answers anything they want them to be. Sometimes Sun will try to throw you off by mentioning something that isn't directly referenced by the exam objectives in an incorrect answer. Don't let Sun Microsystems throw you off!

Answer 6

Options b) and c), topics and queues, are the correct answers.

JSM messages can be placed on topics, which are associated with a publish and subscribe type messaging solution, or on a queue. The term **MOM**, message oriented middleware, was thrown in to catch you off guard.

Answer 7

RMI, Remote Method Invocation, allows local JavaBeans to connect to an rmiregistry running on a remote machine, look up RMI accessible objects through the rmiregistry, and then invoke their methods. RMI is an important part of the J2SE platform, as it is the J2SE standard for doing remote method invocation. **Options a) b) and d) are correct.** JNI, a different Java technology, is used to allow native programs to interact with components running on a JVM.

Answer 8

Options a) b) and c) are correct. There are millions of developers that make up the J2ME community, which is great when you need help from a message board or user group. Of course, J2ME is Java, so it uses the basic syntax used by J2SE and J2EE applications. However, because J2ME devices are so small and limited, J2ME does not have access to all of the libraries of J2SE, as J2EE does. This is the biggest hurdle for many Java developers switching to J2ME development.

J2ME applications also have access to persistent storage, if the device profile allows it, that is. Some small persistent space to store information is considered an essential part of J2ME profiles, and being able to store user preferences and device settings locally is a big J2ME benefit.

Answer 9

Options a) and b) are correct.

Okay, I admit, this one was a bit of a curve ball, but there are a few things you need to know about an applet, and some of the information an applet can find out about the client is one of them.

Java applets run in somewhat of a security sandbox that makes it impossible for the applet to access local resources. As you can imagine, having a computer program, downloaded off the internet, running in a web browser, accessing information from the local user's file system would be a huge security hole. Applets have great restrictions on them as far as what they can know and access with regards to the local environment.

There are a number of system properties that a Java applet can read to get information about the client, including: file.separator, java.version, os.arch, and os.name. However, some properties are forbidden, due to security restrictions, such as user.home and user.name.

For the most part, applets can take input from the user, and send that information back only to the server from which the applet originated.

Answer 10

Options a) c) and d) are correct. Many computer programs work by having the local, or native, operating system render GUI components when there is a need for a textfield or a radio button. When a native operating system renders the various GUI controls for a computer program, the GUI components are considered to be heavyweight components. However, this creates all sorts of problems with cross platform Java, because different systems render components in different ways. A Windows button doesn't look like a Unix button.

Swing components don't rely on the native operating system for GUI component rendering. Instead, Swing components grab a canvas, and draw their components on that canvas. Since Swing components just draw their canvas on a native java.awt.Component, or similar canvas, the Swing GUI components are more consistent in appearance than native java.awt components from one platform to the other.

Answer 11

Options b) and d) are the correct answers, as HTML is not based on XML, and HTML does not pose any real security risks.

Answer 12

Which of the following are true of awt components?

O c) they use **native** components for GUI display rendering

Only option c) is correct.

J is a prefix for swing components, such as JApplet and JOptionPane. The awt GUI components do not use the letter J as a prefix. Also, awt components are in a package named java.awt, not javax.awt. The swing components reside in the javax.swing package. Finally the swing components, which are considered lightweight components, simply draw themselves on the screen of the operating system in which they render. Of course, they must draw themselves on an OS specific canvas or component, and the OS specific component is referred to as being a heavyweight component. **Lightweight Swing components** get drawn on heavyweight components. That's how Swings works, but just because Swing components draw themselves on a heavyweight component doesn't mean they're heavyweight as well. Swing components are as lightweight as they come.

On the other hand, awt components completely depend upon the native OS components for their rendering, regardless of whether it's a Button or a Frame. **This is why the java.awt components are referred to as being heavyweight components.**

Answer 13

Options a) c) and d) are all correct answers to this question.

The job of an HttpServlet, in a well designed MVC application, is to act as a controller. The Servlet will handle incoming client requests, perform some input validation, and then, once the Servlet has figured out what the client is doing, the Servlet will delegate to JavaBeans or even EJBs to perform business and data logic. Servlets will not typically interact with a database. In fact, having a Servlet interact with a database, which is by all means possible, is certainly frowned upon. Instead, Servlets should delegate to other Java components to do database interactions.

Answer 14

Options a) and b) are correct.

While capable of making JDBC calls, a stateless session EJB should not typically update a database, making option c) incorrect.

Also, stateless session beans do not manage state for HTTP clients; that is the responsibility of the HttpSession object, which is part of the Servlet and JSP specification, not the EJB spec. Stateless session beans should be like the script in a play, organizing the various entity beans, which are like the actors. A stateless session bean, through a session façade, coordinates the activities of entity beans and other business objects, making sure database updates happen in a transactional and coordinated manner, making options a) and b) correct.

Answer 15

Options b) c) and d) are correct.

Servlets, JSPs and EJBs are all server side J2EE components that have their lifecycles managed by a J2EE container. MIDlets run on Java microdevices, and while they can interact with a J2EE server, they are not server side components, and are not part of the J2EE specification.

Part Two: Object Oriented Analysis and Design

Chapter 6
FUNdamental Data Types

Java is a Programming Language.

In its most vulgar form, Java is just another computer programming language. That's all Java is: a programming language. But what does it really mean to be a ***'programming language?'***

Well, in its most basic terms, a programming language is simply a mechanism for consuming input, manipulating that input, and then generating some form of output. Whether a program is calculating sales tax on a retail purchase, or encrypting a given text String, a computer program simply ingests, manipulates, and spits out data.

Note: The word String will be always be given an upper case first letter, except for the accidental time when it is not. ☺

The Basic Java Data Types

Within the confines of a Java program, there are eight basic types of data you can manipulate: byte, short, int, long, float, double, boolean and char.

Of course, Java is an *object oriented programming language,* which means that developers can create all sorts of handsome assortments of these data types, and organize them in a logical and easy to manage objects, but nevertheless, even the most complex components in Java can be broken down into these eight, fundamental data types. In fact, since these eight variable types are the most fundamental data structures used in a Java program, they are given the special moniker of ***"primitive data types."***

- Java is an object-oriented, computer programming language.
- Computer programs manipulate data.
- Java has eight basic types of data that it can manipulate.
- The eight basic data types are known as primitive types
- Primitive types are not objects, but objects are built from the primitive types

Java is an 'Object-Oriented' Language.

Everything in Java is an object, with the exception of the few things in Java that are not objects.☺ Primitive types are one of the few things in the Java programming language that are ***not*** objects. They are, however, the building blocks of objects, and without them, objects simply wouldn't exist.

Java and Strong Type-ing

Java is referred to as a ***'strongly typed'*** language. If you want to use a chunk of data in your Java program, you must first tell the Java gods the ***'type category'*** into which that data falls.

```
/*Java is STRONGLY TYPED. For the five variables,
named lie, me, flag, age and eresting, you should be
able to tell what type of data they represent.*/


char lie = '1';            // lie is of type char
byte me = 99;              // me is of type byte
boolean flag = false;      // flag is of type boolean
int eresting = 8888;       // eresting is of type int
long age = 29;             // age is of type long

/*Notice that every Java statement ends with a semi-
colon. This conforms to Immutable Rule #16*/
```

So, if you want to use a variable called *age*, you must first tell the Java gods if age is a float, double, int, long or String. If you want to use a true/false flag named *open*, you must tell the Java gods that your flag is of the boolean type.

Data Can't Change Type on the Fly

Furthermore, once a variable is associated with a given data type, that variable will remain a variable of that type forever. If a variable named 'age' is of type byte, it cannot be used in your program as though it were a float or a char. Once a variable is declared as being a particular type, it remains that type forever.

So, every variable in Java must be associated with one, and only one, data type. And secondly, once a variable is associated with a particular type, the variable is associated with that type forever. These two truisms are the essence of ***strong typing*** in Java.

Java Floating Types (Decimal Numbers)

Case Sensitive Name	Range
double (the big one)	4.940658412465 e -324d to 1.7976313486231570 e + 308d
float (the smaller one)	1.40129846432481708 e -45 to 3.40282346638528860 c +38

This page defines seven of the eight primitive types. The remaining type can theoretically consume one, tiny bit of memory. What is it?

Java Integer Types (Whole Numbers)

Case Sensitive Name	Range
long	+9,223,372,036,854,775,807 to -9,223,372,036,854,775,807
int	+2,147,483,647 to -2,147,483,647
short	32,767 to -32,768
byte	-128 to 127
char*	0 to 65,535

**The char is also known as the messed up primitive type. While typically thought of as representing a character or symbol, a char can actually behave as an integer type, if the number is positive (unsigned) and less than 65,536.*

Typing, Naming and Initializing

Within the confines of a Java program, before it is used, a variable must be ***'typed,' 'named', and 'initialized.'*** And when we say ***'typed,'*** we're not talking about tapping keys on a qwerty keyboard.

Once a variable has been named and typed, it can then be initialized. Initialization is simply the process of assigning a value to a variable. All variables declared within the confines of a method, or flow control block, must be assigned a value, aka initialized, before being used in a Java program.

Variable Initialization

Variables are often initialized as soon as they are declared, but they need not be. For example, it is common to declare a variable, providing a name and type, at the beginning of a block of code, and then initialize the variable a little later. The rule you must obey is that a variable must be declared (aka named and typed) before it is initialized, and a variable must be initialized before it is used in code.

```
/*These variables are typed, named and initialized,
all at the same time.*/

int i=0;                  // i is initialized to zero
char ming = 'x';          // ming is initialized to 'x'
float myBoat = 54.22f;// myBoat is initialized to 54.22

/*The following variable is declared in one
statement, and initialized later in a second
statement*/

String subtleSuggestion;
subleSuggestion = "Buy More ExamScam Books!!!";

/*Notice how every statement ends with a semi-colon*/
```

Vowels Don't Cost $500

Well thought out variable names make Java programs easier to read, and easier to maintain. Good names can even make Java programming fun.

When consulting, I often have to remind developers that developing a Java program isn't an episode of Wheel of Fortune – you don't have to spin for a letter, and you don't have to pay $500 for a vowel. I often see garbled code, where variable names have vowels arbitrarily stripped out of them, or the last few letters of a word curiously removed. Smaller variable names don't translate into better code, and the length of a variable name doesn't have any impact on runtime performance – it only impacts readability and maintainability, and long-term maintainability is the most important aspect of any computer program.

Variable Naming Conventions Don't Vary

When naming a variable in Java, the variable name should always startWith a lowerCaseLetter; thenForEverySubsequentWord in the variableName, theFirstLetterOfThatWord shouldBeUpperCased. The same rules go for choosing methodNamesAsWell.

Of course, this is only a convention. A variable that starts off with an upper case letter will not stop a program from compiling. A program that has variable names beginning with upper case letters will run just as well as a program written with variable names leading with lower case letters. However, from a professional standpoint, variable names that start with an upper case letter are completely *unacceptable*. If you create variables with leading upper case letters, you've just labeled yourself as an inexperienced amateur to the rest of the team.

```
/* Dropping vowels or abbreviating important words
does not make for good variable names. Compare the
readability of the following two lines of code, and
choose which application you'd rather be tasked with
maintaining. */


double myNewIncome = myIncome * 2;    /*easy to read*/

double i2 = i1*2;                     /*difficult to read*/
```

In Java, the casing of your code conveys an incredible amount of information. An experienced programmer can gain an instant understanding of a Java source file based on how various words are cased, and to a lesser extent, spelled. Methods and variables should always start with a leading lower case letter, while the name of a class should always start with an upper case letter. Remember though, these are just conventions, and if you violate them, the compiler won't complain. The compiler only flags compile errors – it doesn't complain to you about poorly written code.

The Term *Literal*

You'll often hear the term *Java Literal* bandied about. A literal is simply a value expressed explicitly in code. So, variable assignments often go in the order: type declaration, variable name, assignment operator, literal value, and then semi-colon, as with **int x = 10;** With the initialization and declaration of int x = 10; the number 10 would be a literal value, as it is hard-coded into the program.

```
/*the following are literals, because their values
are assigned directly.*/

String ess = "Sharon"; // "Sharon" is the literal
int x = 10; // 10 is a literal value
int y = 20; // 20 is a literal value
```

As a bit of Java trivia, it's interesting to note that null, true and false, are actually considered literal values as well. The values null, true and false are so integral to Java that most people think of them as keywords, but strictly speaking, they are not. The values of null, true and false are literal values, that like keywords, cannot be used as variable identifiers in Java programs.

"A literal is the source code representation of a fixed value; literals are represented directly in your code without requiring computation."

-http://java.sun.com/docs/books/tutorial/java/nutsandbolts/datatypes.html

Question

Which of the following lines of code will compile:

- O a) boolean b = 'false';
- O b) char broiled = a;
- O c) int j = 10.2
- O d) double d = 99.99;

Question

Which of the following statements are correct?

- ☐ a) Java has eight primitive types
- ☐ b) String is a primitive type in Java
- ☐ c) Variable names can start with upper case letters
- ☐ d) Local variables must be initialized before they are used

Question

What is the result of running the following code:

```
/*System.out.println( ) prints the contents of the brackets to an output window*/
byte b = 12;
System.out.println(b*b);
```

- O a) Code will compile and print 144
- O b) Code will not compile
- O c) Code will compile but will not run
- O d) Code will generate unexpected results

Question

When declaring and initializing a variable in a single line of code, what is the correct order?

- O a) variable name, assignment, type, semi-colon;
- O b) assignment, variable name, type, semi-colon;
- O c) type, assignment, variable name, semi-colon;
- O d) type, variable name, assignment, semi-colon;

Answer

Which of the following lines of code will compile:

- O a) boolean b = 'false';
- O b) char broiled = a;
- O c) int j = 10.2
- O d) double d = 99.99;

Only the line **double d = 99.99;** will compile. The keyword 'false' ***should not*** have single quotes around it, while a char literal ***should***, such as char broiled = 'a'; An int is not a floating point number, meaning it cannot have a decimal, so int j = 10.2; will cause all sorts of problems, not to mention the missing semi-colon at the end.

Answer

Which of the following statements are correct?

- ☐ a) Java has eight primitive types
- ☐ b) String is a primitive type in Java
- ☐ c) Variable names can start with upper case letters
- ☐ d) Local variables must be initialized before they are used

String is not a primitive type in Java, making selection b) incorrect. However, all the other statements are true: there are eight primitive types, local variables must be initialized before they are used, and finally, variable names can start with an upper case letter, although they shouldn't, and if you name variables with leading upper case letters, you're labeling yourself as a Java neophyte – don't do it!

Answer

What is the result of running the following code:

```
/*System.out.println( ) prints the contents of the brackets to an output window*/
byte b = 12;
System.out.println(b*b);
```

- O a) Code will compile and print 144
- O b) Code will not compile
- O c) Code will compile but will not run
- O d) Code will generate unexpected results

Answer a) is correct, as the output is 144. However, you may over think this question, seeing that 127 is the upper limit of a byte. If you wrote the code **byte b2 = b*b;** and then tried to print out b2, you'd really have some problems. Try it and see what happens.

Answer

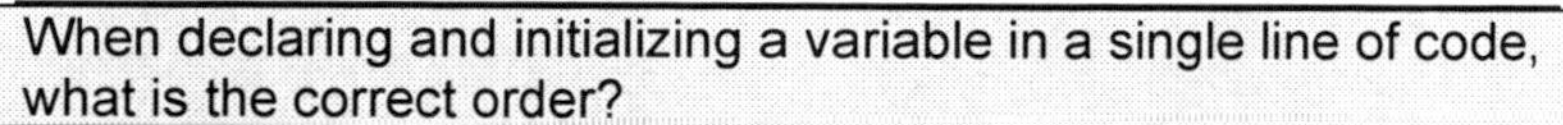
When declaring and initializing a variable in a single line of code, what is the correct order?

- O a) variable name, assignment, type, semi-colon;
- O b) assignment, variable name, type, semi-colon;
- O c) type, assignment, variable name, semi-colon;
- O d) type, variable name, assignment, semi-colon;

Option d) is correct.

Just think **int x = 10;** and you'll remember the order: type, variable name and then assignment, all followed by a semi-colon.

Chapter 7
An Introduction to Object Oriented Programming

Computer programs manipulate data. They manage data in memory, they manipulate data, and then they do something with the data once they're finished manipulating it. That's what computer programs do. Have I pounded that into your head enough, yet?

Now typical programs deal with alot of data; *huge* amounts of data; *massive* amounts of data; *gargantuan* amounts of data, *brobdingnagian* amounts of data; and organizing this data is difficult.

Now imagine you've got a banking application. You've got customers, customers have names, customers have a gender, customers have an income, and customers have an age. How do you organize all of this data? Well, here's one ***very*** non-object-oriented, way to do it:

```
String brothersName = "Marcus";
char brothersGender = 'M';
double brothersIncome = 70000.00;
int brothersAge = 29;


String myName = "Cameron";
char myGender = 'M';
double myIncome = 2500000.00;
int myAge = 29;

String sisterName = "Amanda";
char sisterGender = 'F';
double sisterIncome = 30000.00;
int sistersAge = 24;
```

Now, that's alot of data; well, actually it isn't, but let's pretend it is.

Good variable names make it easy to read, but still, it's all fairly disorganized. Now, a computer program doesn't care how organized or disorganized the data is. A computer can manipulate data in any which way you tell it. But humans care about organization. Organization is very important to humans, and it's very important when it comes to computer programming as well.

Organizing Logically Related Data

From the example, you can see that each grouping of variables describes a Customer. Each set of variables describes a Customer's name, gender, income and age. In Java, rather than scattering variables all across the screen, we like to organize logically related variables into ***objects***, or ***classes***. This example is just begging for a Customer class, where every Customer has a name, gender, income, and an age property. Coding a Customer class in Java would look something like this:

```
/*upper case C for customer*/

public class Customer {
  String name;
  char gender;
  double income;
  int age;
}

/*To the right is a UML class
diagram for the Customer class.*/
```

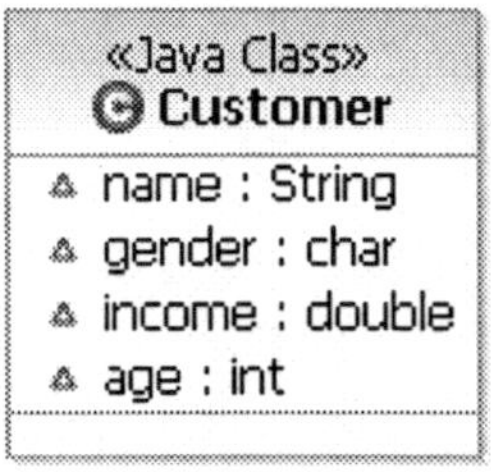

«Java Class»
Customer
name : String
gender : char
income : double
age : int

The Java code for the Customer class, which is accompanied by a UML class diagram, indicates that we are going to be working with a custom coded Java object called ***Customer***, and each customer object has four properties: a name, gender, income and age. Notice that there's no mention of a brother or sister or cousin, as there was in the variable names at the beginning. Class declarations are very generic. A name, or identifier, is provided later, when a reference to the class is declared.

Objects vs. Primitive Types

Objects are different from primitive types in a number of ways, with one of the most significant differences having to do with how objects are initialized. As you know, a primitive type maps directly to a certain number of bits in memory. When you create an int, that int will be stored at a certain memory location, and regardless of how that primitive type is initialized, 32 bits of data will be consumed by that int. Objects however, are a little bit different.

When the JVM creates and initializes a ***new*** object, the JVM has to look at the various data types that the object uses, and from that, figure out how much memory needs to be set aside. This isn't an easy task. For our Customer object, with every new instance that is created, the

JVM must put aside enough memory for a char (gender), double (income), int (age) and a String (name).

Actually, Strings are objects themselves, which means the JVM doesn't know how big the String is actually going to be when it sets memory aside for the Customer, so instead, the JVM just puts in a blank pointer that will be used to point to the actual name String later on, when the String is provided by the program. Putting aside enough memory to store all of the primitive types, and object pointers, that a new object needs, is by no means a simple task.

We don't really have to worry about the intricacies of what goes on with the JVM, but it's good to have an appreciation for just how much work is going on behind the scenes. Suffice to say, the process of initializing a complex object is much different, and much more stressful on the JVM, than simply initializing a primitive. As a result, we need to provide a bit of warning to the JVM when we are about to create, and have the JVM set enough memory aside, for a *new* object.

Creating New Objects: The new Keyword

As I said, managing objects is a fair bit of work, and lots of stuff has to be configured in memory when an object is initialized, so whenever we need the JVM to put aside enough memory and pointer space for a new object, we have to use the special keyword ***new***. So, to create an instance of a blank, Customer object, here's how we'd do it:

```
Customer me = new Customer();
Customer myBrother = new Customer();
Customer mySister = new Customer();
```

The front part, the type declaration and variable naming, is very similar to the type-ing and naming of a regular primitive type: you always need to identify the type, and then you need to provide a variable name.

```
/*Both when initializing a primitive type, and
initializing an object, you need to specify the type,
and provide a variable name.*/

int i = 10;
Customer p = new Customer();
```

Casing the Joint

One major difference between primitive types and objects is how their names are *cased.* Notice how the name of a class, Customer in this case, starts with a capital letter. Primitive types, such as int and float, are named with lower case letters. In Java, class names should always be spelled with a leading Upper Case Letter; and let's stress, we're talking about the class name, *Customer,* not the variable name associated with an instance, such as *myBrother.*

The right hand side of the object initialization, **= new Customer();** is completely whack. Essentially, this half of the equation tells the Java virtual machine (JVM) to put aside enough memory to manage all of the properties associated with a customer object. A method that has the same name as the class, such as Customer( ) in this case, is a special method known as a constructor. When no arguments are passed to the constructor, the constructor is known as the ***default constructor***, or ***zero argument constructor.***

Initializing the Properties of an Object

As kewl as it may look, object declaration and initialization with a default constructor does little more than set aside enough memory to store data for the object of interest. Properties of the object that are primitive types are initialized to zero, and objects are initialized to nulls. To make your Java classes really useful, you want to initialize all of that blank data, which in the case of the Customer class would be the name, gender, income and age of an instance. Property initialization is done by using the name of the instance, then a 'dot' notation to specify the name of the property you are initializing. The equals sign is used to assign a value to a property.

```
Customer myBrother = new Customer();
myBrother.gender = 'M';
myBrother.income = 70000.00;
myBrother.name = "Marcus";
myBrother.age = 29;
```

Notice that the variable types need not be declared for the properties of the Customer object after the constructor has been called. The variables gender, income, name and age have already been *typed* in the Customer class definition. From the class definition, the JVM knows that gender is of type char, and income is of type double, as that is how they are declared in the class definition.

Using.Dot.Notation

Dot notation is used to reference the properties of an instance. So, take the scenario where the instance of the Customer class is named myBrother, and the properties of myBrother are name, gender, income, and age. Using dot notation, the properties would be referenced by myBrother.name, myBrother.gender, myBrother.income and finally, myBrother.age.

```
/*use dot notation to print out my brothers name*/
System.out.println("My brothers name is: "+myBrother.name);
/*use dot notation to give my brother a 15% raise*/
myBrother.income = myBrother.income * 1.15;
/*use dot notation to give my brother an operation*/
myBrother.gender = 'F';

Customer me = new Customer();
me.name = "Cameron";
me.gender = 'M';
me.income = 2500000.00; /*wishful thinking*/
me.age = 29;

Customer mySister = new Customer();
mySister.name = "Amanda";
mySister.gender = 'F';
mySister.income = 30000.00;
mySister.age = 24;
```

Now, you'll notice with all of these Customer objects, that as soon as we call the no-argument constructor using the keyword new, *new Customer(),* we immediately code and initialize all of the instance variables, aka properties, of the Customer. This is so often the case, that most Java classes contain non-default constructors that allow the JVM to both create a new object, and initialize the instance variables, all at the same time.

The Non-Default Constructor

A non-default constructor is simply a constructor, which means it is a method with the same name as the class and no return type, that takes at least one argument. For our Customer class, we should have a constructor that takes four arguments: a String name, char gender, double income and an int age.

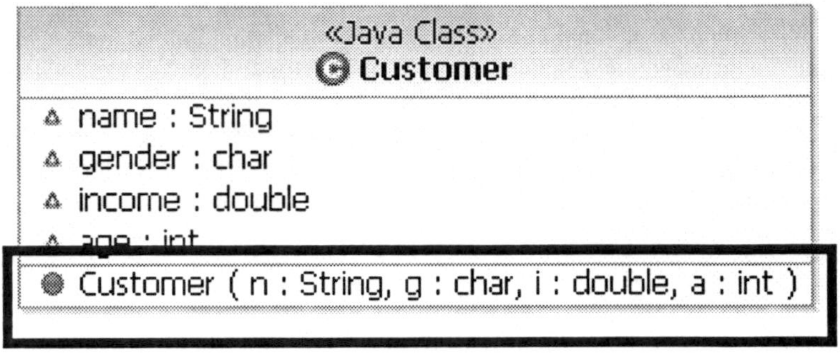

«Java Class»
Customer

- name : String
- gender : char
- income : double
- age : int

- Customer (n : String, g : char, i : double, a : int)

Notice how the number of arguments to be passed to the non-default constructor matches the number of properties, or instance variables, defined by the class. For simple to moderately complex objects, the number of arguments passed to a constructor usually matches the number of instance variables defined in the class.

```
public class Customer extends Object {

/*instance variables*/
  String name;
  char gender;
  double income;
  int age;

  public Customer(String n, char g, double i, int a){

/*make the Customers name equal to the value n passed into
the method*/
    name = n;
/*make the Customers gender equal to the value g passed
into the method*/
    gender = g;
/*make the Customers income equal to the value i passed
into the method*/
    income = i;
/*make the Customers age equal to the value a passed into
the method*/
    age = a;

  }
}
```

Using the Non-Default Constructor

To use the Customer class with the non-default constructor, our code would look like this:

```
Customer me = new Customer("Cameron", 'M', 2500000.00, 29);
Customer myBrother
            = new Customer("Marcus",'M',70000.00, 29);
Customer mySister
            = new Customer("Amanda",'F', 35000.00, 24);

/*Yes, my brother and I have both been 29 for a number of
years now.*/
```

Comparing Data Manipulation Mechanisms

Let's take a look at the following three blocks of code. The following three blocks of code do exactly the same thing, from the standpoint of initializing four Java variables.

All three code blocks declare four variables, including a String, char, double and int; All three code blocks use the same amount of memory to store these pieces of data; And all three code blocks initialize data that will be manipulated by a computer program at some time in the future. The only difference between these three blocks of code, is the way in which the code is organized, and/or the way in which the code is written.

The First Code Block – Poor OO

```
{
/*This first code block initializes four,
disorganized variables*/
String brothersName = "Marcus";
char brothersGender = 'M';
double brothersIncome = 70000.00;
int brothersAge = 29;
}
```

The first code block simply declares and initializes four variables, but notice how there is nothing linking those variables together, other than some good variable names. The compiler, or JVM, has no idea that these separate variables are logically associated with each other. The first code block is not object oriented at all.

The Second Code Block

```
{

/*This block initializes four variables, organized
into a Customer object*/

Customer myBrother = new Customer();
myBrother.gender = 'M';
myBrother.income = 70000.00;
myBrother.name = "Marcus";
myBrother.age = 29;

}
```

In the second code block, a default constructor is called to tell the JVM to set enough memory aside to store four related properties of type char, double, String and int. After calling the default constructor, each of the properties of the Customer instance are initialized.

Notice how the various properties are linked together through the variable named myBrother. Unlike the first code block, where variables just dangled independently, we now have four variables all associated with each other through a common ***reference***, myBrother. This is the idea behind object-oriented programming: to be able to create objects that have logically related and associated properties.

The Third Code Block

```
{
/*This block does the same thing as the previous
block, but it does it all in one, sexy, easy to read,
line of code.*/

Customer myBrother
      = new Customer("Marcus", 'M', 70000.00, 29);
}
```

The third code block accomplishes the same end as the second code block, but uses the non-default constructor. Again, this is very object oriented, as all of the properties are being associated with a common, Customer instance. But the code is also much cleaner, as the constructor minimizes the number of code lines required to initialize all of the properties of the object.

Question

According to the JavaBean naming convention, a class name:
O a) should always start with a lower case letter
O b) should always start with an upper case letter
O c) should start with a number
O d) should start with an underscore

Question

The number of arguments in a constructor typically matches the number of:
O a) methods in a class
O b) properties of a class
O c) return types of the constructor
O d) instances the class will create

Question

Memory is set aside for an object when the compiler encounters which Java keyword?
O a) continue
O b) create
O c) new
O d) break

Question

A class named Account has an instance property called balance. Given an instance named account, how would you reference the property?
O a) Account.balance
O b) account.balance
O c) account:balance
O d) account::balance

Answer

According to the JavaBean naming convention, a class name:
O a) should always start with a lower case letter O b) should always start with an upper case letter O c) should start with a number O d) should start with an underscore
Option b) is correct. Naming conventions are extremely important, not only in your Java code, but on the associates exam as well. All class names should start with an upper case letter, with each new word having an upper case letter as well, such as a class named **A**bstract**S**hape or **G**arage**D**oor.

Answer

The number of arguments in a constructor typically matches the number of:
O a) methods in a class O b) properties of a class O c) return types of the constructor O d) instances the class will create
Option b) is correct. The purpose of a constructor is to create a new instance of a class by placing enough memory aside to store all of the data associated with the instance. As a result, when you call a constructor, you usually want to assign meaningful values to the instance variables of the class. This isn't a hard and fast rule, but generally, the number of instance variables in a class will map pretty closely to the number of arguments passed to a non-default constructor.

Answer

Memory is set aside for an object when the compiler encounters which Java keyword?
○ a) continue ○ b) create ○ c) new ○ d) break
Option c) is correct. With the exception of the freak objects like String, if you want to create a new instance of an object, you must use the new keyword and call the class' constructor. The new keyword informs the JVM to be prepared to put some memory aside to store data about the instance you wish to create.

Answer

A class named Account has an instance property called balance. Given an instance named account, how would you reference the property?
○ a) Account.balance ○ b) account.balance ○ c) account:balance ○ d) account::balance
Option b) is correct. Java uses a dot notation, so to have an instance reference one of its properties, you use dot notation, such as **account.balance** It should be noted that for the most part, instance variables should not be accessed directly, but instead, should be accessed through public setters and getters, so for a property named balance, there would be an associated method in the class called getBalance(). Calling getters is generally preferred over direct variable access. But even with a method call, dot notation is used to call the method on the instance. Using the getter method, account.getBalance() would return the same result as account.balance, if the getter existed.

Chapter 8
Object Associations

Imagine you had a *problem domain* in which you had to keep track of where your customers were living. Not only would you need to keep track of the name, age, gender and income of your customers, but you would need to keep track of where they lived, including their street address, city, state and country.

There are a couple of ways you could approach creating an object model, with one approach being the monolithic object with everything inside of it.

The Monolithic Customer

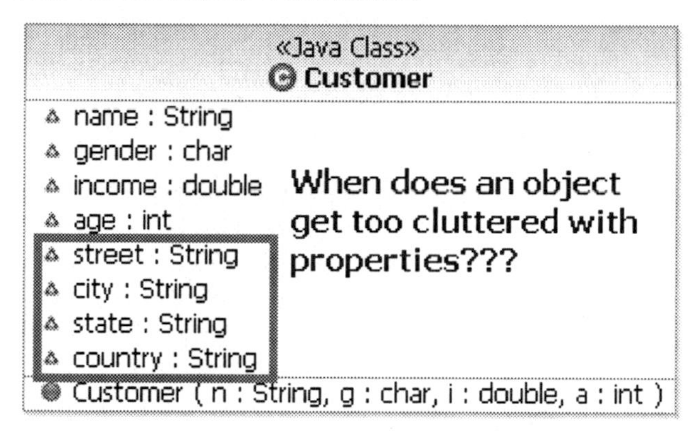

Now, looking at the monolithic Customer class, one thing that should jump out right away is the fact that only name, age, income and gender are really *customer specific*. A Customer has an age, a Customer has a name, a Customer has a gender, and a Customer has an income. Those are true properties of a customer; but a customer can move from one state to another pretty easily, so city, state, street and country are not really direct properties of a Customer. These properties should really be factored out into another class that we could ***associate*** with the Customer. This associated class would quite simply be called the ***Address*** class.

Factoring Out Associated Objects

We never want our objects to become overly complex. When we see a class taking control of properties or attributes that really don't directly apply, we should think about factoring the related properties out into a second, associated class. With our Customer class, properties such as street, city, state and country should be factored out into a completely separate, yet associated, Java class.

Could address related properties be factored out of the Customer class, into a separate, stand alone class? Of course it could - and it should!

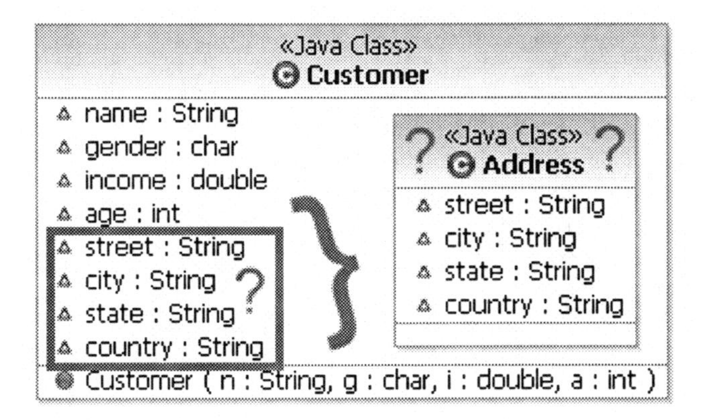

Note that a class diagram inside of a class diagram, such as this, would only be valid UML in a Bizarro World, where the sky is pink and women are nice to me.

Object Associations

So, as we develop our object model, we could say that this *problem domain* involves two associated objects, a Customer object, and an Address object. We could even model this association in UML, with a single line connecting the Customer class and the Address class, and a number indicating the cardinality between the Customer and the associated Address.

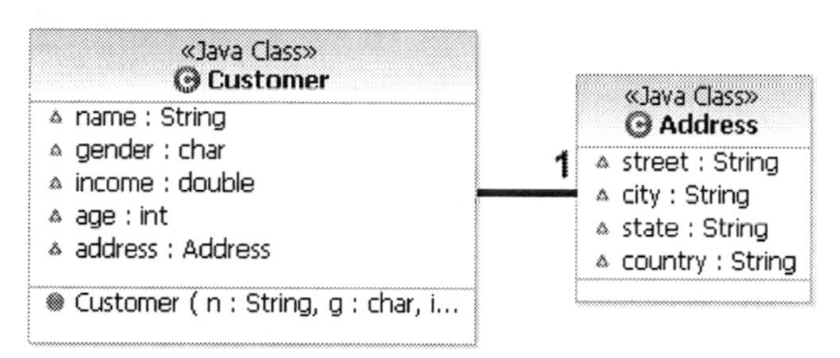

The link reads: "a customer is associated with a single (one) address."

Manifesting UML in Code

So, how does the association between a Customer and an Address object manifest itself in code? Well, we simply say that the Customer class has an instance variable of type Address. A Customer is linked to an Address property through an instance variable.

```
public class Customer extends Object {
  String name;
  int age;
  char gender;
  double income;

  /*The Customer has an address*/
  Address address;

}
```

Navigable Properties

Also, since the Customer has the address as a property, we can say that the Customer class *knows* about their associated address. If the Customer class provided a getAddress() method, we could say that the address was *navigable* through the Customer object. Essentially, saying that a property is navigable simply implies that you could call a getter method, such as getAddress(), and be returned the associated property in which you were interested, which in this case, would be the Customer's address.

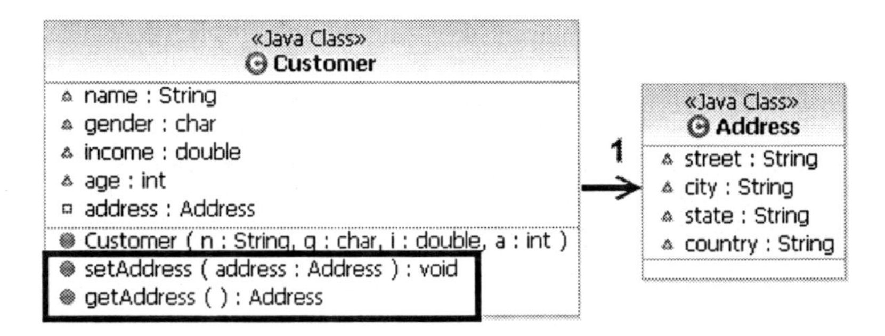

The arrow pointing towards the Address object in the UML diagram indicates that the address object is *navigable* through the Customer. Notice how the realization of this navigable association requires, at the very least, the addition of a getAddress() method in the Customer class.

```
public class Customer extends Object {
  String name;
  int age;
  char gender;
  double income;
  Address address;

/*Through the Customer's getAddress() method, you can
navigate to, and get, the associated address.*/
  public Address getAddress() {
    return this.address;
  }
}
```

Unidirectional vs. Bi-Directional Relationships

Now, does an address know anything about its associated Customer? Probably not.

An address object probably doesn't need to know who its associated Customer is, or for that matter, how many customers with which it might be associated. Now an address object *might* want to allow navigation to its related customers; you could make a Customer a property of an address, and make it possible to ask an address object all of the Customer's with which it is associated, but in our case, this functionality isn't needed. Furthermore, it might lead us into the world of spaghetti code. For our problem domain, this functionality isn't needed, and we will say that ***the Customer class is not navigable through the Address class.***

Always avoid scope creep. In our application, the only required navigability is from the Customer to the Address. We need the Customer to tell us their address, but the Address object doesn't require the ability to tell us about its associated Customer.

Cardinality and Multiplicity

Now when it comes to associations, there is always a multiplicity associated with them. The multiplicity can be anything from zero to one, or one to infinity. With an association, there is always a multiplicity.

If our Customer was associated with one, and always one, Address object, the association would quite logically be *one* (one customer object is associated with one address object). Since our Customer object has only one instance variable to represent an address, the multiplicity of this association is definitely one.

But what if our Customer had potentially two addresses, one for their home and one for their office? How would we implement that in code, or represent that association on a UML diagram? Well, one way would be to simply have two Address properties, with one property being named ***homeAddress***, and the other called ***officeAddress***.

```
public class Customer extends Object {
  String name;
  int age;
  char gender;
  double income;
  Address homeAddress;
  Address officeAddress;
}
```

In this case, we would have a multiplicity of one to two; one, single Customer can have up to, or be associated with, as many as two address objects. Because the UML diagram uses the notation 1..2, we also know that a Customer must be associated with *at least one* address object, and can be associated with *as many as two* address objects.

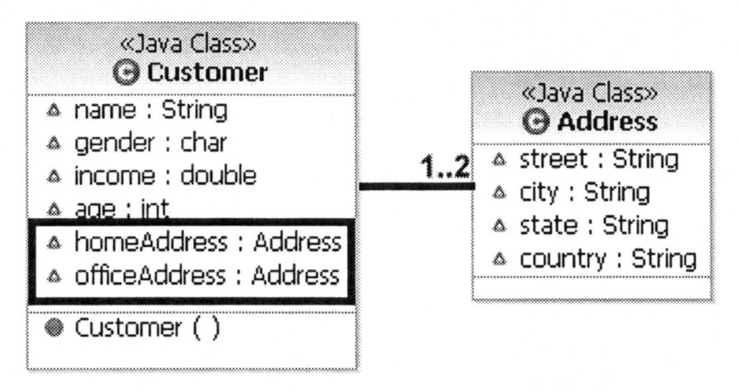

A Customer is associated with at least one, and as many as two, Address objects.

Exploring the Shortcomings of our Object Model

Now, we're actually going to run into a couple of problems here if we keep going with this object model. One problem we will soon run into is the fact that the Customer object is starting to know an awful lot about the address objects with which it is associated. Objects should know everything about themselves, but right now, our Address objects don't know if they're a home address, or an office address. An address object should maintain a String property that indicates what type they are, such as: home, office, mistress, cottage, previous and other.

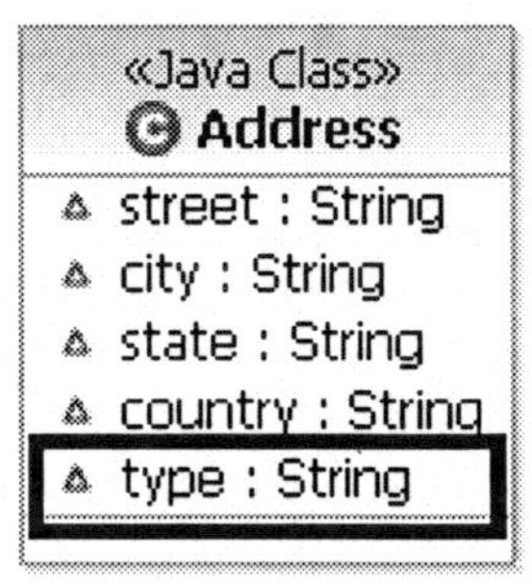

Now, the other problem we run into is "what if a customer has more than two addresses?" For example, they could have a home, office and cottage address. Furthermore, an application would probably need to keep track of past addresses as well, so depending upon how much of a transient your Customer is, he or she might have ten or twelve addresses. How could we manage that?

Well, in UML, we represent a multiplicity of zero to many with the splat, or asterix, *, symbol. A one to many relationship is noted by using the notation 1..*

But how do we represent a multiplicity of one to many in code? Well, there are many ways, the simplest of which is to use a Vector or an array; personally, I like Vectors.

A Vector is a special collection class, found in java.util package, that can hold objects. A vector is very much like an array, with the exception of the fact that it can expand or contract, depending upon how many objects you want to stuff into it. I believe that it starts out with enough room to store ten objects comfortably, but once you put in that tenth, the Vector expands to capacity of twenty, and when you put in the twentieth, the Vector expands its capacity to forty, and so on and so forth.

The Implementation of Multiplicity

If we are going to say that a Customer can be associated with many address objects, we need to use a collection class. A java.util.Vector is very flexible, and very easy to use. It's the collection class that I suggest we use here, although an array would be valid as well.

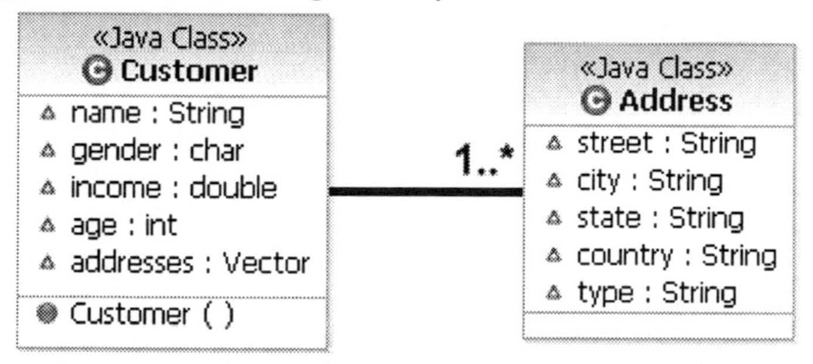

A Customer has at least one, but can potentially be related to many, (1..*) Address objects.

The preceding diagram visually demonstrates how a ***one-to-many*** relationship between the Customer and the Address can be expressed in UML. In code, the association would be implemented in the class by using a Vector, or an array.

```
public class Customer extends Object {
  String name; int age;  char gender;  double income;
  java.util.Vector addresses;
  /*or Address[] addresses; if you used an array*/
}
```

Also notice that when we use the Vector, the descriptive name such as homeAddress and officeAddress go away. This isn't a bad thing, as we can always pull an address out of the Vector, and query the Address in the Vector as to what type of address it is. Objects should know intimate details about themselves, not other objects. Our address object knows what type of address it is. Furthermore, we can always navigate to an address object through a Customer, and find out the address type.

Cardinality/Multiplicity

The association relationship indicates that (at least) one of the two related classes makes reference to the other. In contrast with the generalization relationship, this is most easily understood through the phrase 'A has a B' (a mother cat has kittens, kittens have a mother cat).

The UML representation of an association is a line with an optional arrowhead indicating the role *of the object(s) in the relationship, and an optional notation at each end indicating the* multiplicity *of instances of that entity (the number of objects that participate in the association). The association relationship known as the* "has a" *relationship.*

Common multiplicities are:

0..1	*No instances, or one instance*	**0..*** or *	*Zero or more instances*
1	*Exactly one instance*	**1..***	*One or more instances*

Cardinality/Multiplicity section retrieved from Wikipedia, May 14th, 2006
http://en.wikipedia.org/wiki/Class_diagram

Association vs. Composition

In our example, we said that a Customer was associated with an Address object. An association implies that if the two objects, a Customer and an Address, were no longer associated with each other, they could still logically exist on their own. So, when two objects are associated with each other, a disassociation of the two objects doesn't necessarily destroy or render both objects meaningless. Can we say this is true of our Customer and Address objects?

In my problem domain, I feel comfortable saying that a Customer and an Address object are associated with each other. Robert Pulson could live in the fight club house, and Tyler Durden could live in the fight club house. If Tyler Durden moves out, that doesn't mean Robert Pulson doesn't live there anymore, right? For me, an Address object can be associated with any number of Customer objects, and exist on its own, without a Customer object associated with it.

On the other hand, some database driven applications might say that an address has no meaning without a related Customer; in that type of problem domain, Addresses must be created and destroyed through a Customer object, and when a Customer is deleted, all associated Address data should be deleted as well. If one object is responsible for the lifecycle, such as creation, updating and destruction, of another object, than the relationship is more powerful than a simple association. *When one object is responsible for the lifecycle management of another object, we call this relationship a composition.*

An Exam and its Related Questions

Think about implementing the Sun Certified Java Associate exam as a Java program. You'd probably create an Exam object, and the Exam object would contain Question objects. A Question object really doesn't have any meaning if it isn't part of an exam. Furthermore, the Exam object probably has methods such as addQuestion() or removeQuestion() or updateQuestion(), to manage the various questions that are contained in the exam. Finally, when an Exam object is destroyed, all of the contained Question objects would be removed from memory, since it was agreed, a Question object doesn't really have much meaning in this problem domain if it is not associated with an Exam.

In this problem domain, the Exam is ***composed*** of different Question objects. The relationship between an Exam and the Questions it contains is more than a simple association, and to express this relationship, we use the term composition, which is represented in UML with a **solid diamond** starting with the composing object, in this case, our Exam, followed by a line pointing to the composed objects, which in our scenario, would be the Question objects.

Composition and association both represent a *'has-a'* type of relationship. An Exam *has-a* set of Question objects, and a Customer *has-an* address object. The difference between composition and association is the extent of the influence the containing object maintains over the lifecycle of the contained object.

Composition and UML

In UML, the notation of composition is slightly different than the notation for association. With composition, a line connects the containing and the contained classes, although the line starts with a solid diamond shape *at the containing class*, which in our example, would be the Exam, and would *end with the contained class.*

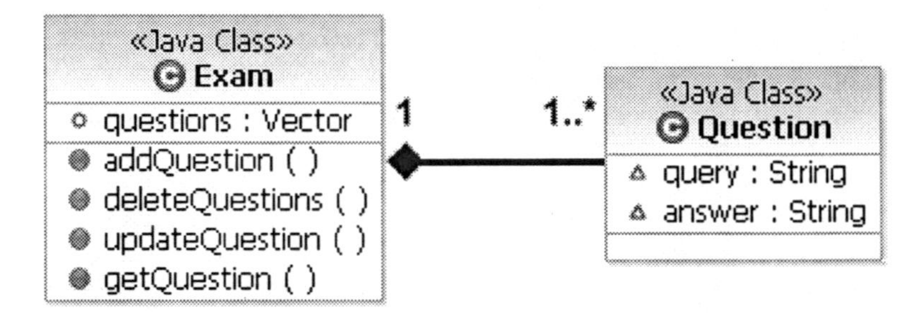

Notice how the UML diagram for the Exam and Question class has multiplicities on both sides of the composition line; this is completely valid. These multiplicities represent the fact that ***an Exam object will have one to many Questions***, whereas ***any given question will only be associated with one, single Exam.*** However, multiplicities are rarely stated on the composing side, as a composed object is only ever associated with one composing object.

You should also notice the lifecycle methods in the Exam class that are responsible for adding Questions, deleting Questions, updating questions, and even getting questions. The Exam object controls the lifecycle of the Question objects, indicating a strong composition relationship.

Question

Which of the following terms represent an is-a relationship between objects?

- O a) aggravation
- O b) inheritance
- O c) aggregation
- O d) association

Question

Which of the following are valid multiplicities?

- ☐ a) 1..0
- ☐ b) 0..1
- ☐ c) *
- ☐ d) 2..*

Question

In a relationship where ObjectA is responsible for the lifecycle of ObjectB, we could say that:

- O a) ObjectA has an association with ObjectB
- O b) ObjectB has an association with ObjectA
- O c) ObjectA is composed of ObjectB
- O d) ObjectB is composed of ObjectA

Question

An association between two classes is implemented in code by:

- O a) extending a parent class
- O b) implementing an interface
- O c) defining an instance variable
- O d) creating getters and setters

Answer

Which of the following terms represent an is-a relationship between objects?
O a) aggravation O b) inheritance O c) aggregation O d) association
Option b) is correct. Inheritance, which happens when one class extends a parent class, represents an ***is-a*** relationship. An is-a relationship can also be expressed in Java when one class implements an interface. With an interface, the sub-type that implements has an ***is-a*** relationship with the interface.

Answer

Which of the following are valid multiplicities?
☐ a) 1..0 ☐ b) 0..1 ☐ c) * ☐ d) 2..*
Options b) c) and d) are correct. 1..0 is not a valid multiplicity. Multiplicities go from the lowest number of objects allowed in the association, to the highest number, such as b) and d), which are 0..1 and 2..*, respectively. * is a valid multiplicity, meaning zero to many.

Answer

In a relationship where ObjectA is responsible for the lifecycle of ObjectB, we could say that:
O a) ObjectA has an association with ObjectB O b) ObjectB has an association with ObjectA O c) ObjectA is composed of ObjectB O d) ObjectB is composed of ObjectA
Option c) is the correct answer. Is this some seriously awkward wording, or what? If one object is responsible for the lifecycle of another object, and there are strong lifecycle ties between the two, then the relationship is a composition relationship, which is what we have here between ObjectA and ObjectB. Perhaps a better wording would be ObjectA is composed of ObjectBs, but regardless of how it's worded, the relationship is one of composition.

Answer

An association between two classes is implemented in code by:
O a) extending a parent class O b) implementing an interface O c) defining an instance variable O d) creating getters and setters
Option c) is the correct answer. The best answer here is c), defining an instance variable. Implementing an interface or extending a parent class creates an ***'is-a'*** relationship, as opposed to the has-a relationship represented by an association. Creating setters and getters for an instance variable provides ***navigability*** for the instance variable, but creating setters and getters does not in and of itself represent an association between objects. Creating an instance variable of a particular object type creates a ***'has-a'*** relationship between the class and the instance variable, which is known in polite circles, as an association.

Chapter 9
Object Abstraction

Learning Java isn't just about learning a programming language. Learning Java is about adopting a whole new philosophy about how we perceive the world around us.

One of the wonderful things about Java is the elegant manner in which it allows us to model the world. Programming in Java is as much about philosophy as it is about coding an implementation

Computer programs are all about manipulating data. That's all they do: they manipulate data. Whether it's as simple as subtracting a withdraw from a bank balance, to the complexity of violently splattering pixilated blood across a computer screen in the latest computer game, computer programs are simply about manipulating data. At that level, every computer program is boring.

Java programs are no different in their fundamental, banal purpose. The purpose of every Java program is simply to manipulate the data it is given. But while the purpose may remain fairly offensive, the implementation of the language itself is very elegant, and few constructs of the Java programming language exemplify that elegance better than the ideas behind inheritance and abstraction.

The Elegance of Abstraction

Imagine I told you that I was heading out tonight with one of my wives to purchase some art. What type of art would you envision? What type of store do you see me walking into, and with what type of art am I going to walk out? Am I purchasing a sculpture? Am I purchasing a painting? Am I purchasing an Elvis Commemorative plate? What you envision is probably heavily impacted by your own personal experience, but there's no denying that the word ***art*** conjures up a number of different ideas.

The same idea applies if I told you I was going to head out and buy a computer or a car. Would I be buying a Mac or a PC? Would I be buying a laptop or a desktop? Would I be buying a used car from some guy who dresses like Herb Tarlek, or leasing an expensive new one from a guy wearing a nice Roberto suit, bought two-for-one from Korry's Clothiers, at 569, Danforth Avenue?

When we speak and communicate with each other, we use many abstract terms that, despite being abstract, convey an inordinate amount of information and meaning.

Abstraction is a hugely important part of both the Java programming language, and the Java certification exam. Abstraction is a concept with which you'll definitely want to familiarize yourself.

Now for the Overworked Cookie Cutter Analogy

In Java, the classes we write represent the cookie cutters from which object instances are created. We can have a Java class called Customer that has properties such as name, age and income, and we could create an instance of that Customer class called myBrother that has the properties of Marcus, 29, and $60,000. In this case, the Customer class is a concrete class, because concrete instances, such as myBrother, can be created from it.

A Customer, or an Address, or even a Button or a Textfield object, are all fairly straightforward concepts to pick up on. A customer has a name and an age. A textfield has a size and background-color associated with it. But what if I threw out the idea of a shape? You know what a shape is, and I know what a shape is, but the idea itself is very abstract. All shapes have common attributes, right? They all have a size. They all have a height and a width. They all have a name. But the term Shape is just an abstract idea. There is really no such thing as a shape, only sub-types of the idea of a shape, such as squares and lines and circles.

The Shape of Things to Come

Imagine we had to design an application that calculated and compared the area of a variety of two-dimensional shapes. We would need to look at, and compare, lines, points, squares, circles, rectangles, and perhaps, if we get really crazy, *even a rhombus*. To begin designing an application like this, we would first try and factor out any properties or behaviors that were common to all shapes, into an abstract class. We'll keep things simple, and call our abstract class *Shape.*

Now, what are some properties, features or functionalities that all shapes have in common, especially with regards to our problem domain? Think about it for a minute, while keeping the problem domain in mind: we need to easily calculate and compare the area of each of these aforementioned types of shapes.

Analyzing the Problem Domain

Well, let's start off by saying that each of our shapes has a height. Do you agree with that?

Most people give me a little bit of static on this point with regards to a circle. Everyone complains that a circle doesn't have a height, but instead, it has a radius. That's true, but what is the radius? I'd say the radius of a circle is really just one half of its height. So, even a circle has a height, although it's not the standard parlance when chatting about things that are round. Even points have a height, although for a point, it's always zero.

And we could also say that all of our shapes have a width. A circle has a width. A square has a width. A rhombus has a width. The same argument goes for a circle, as its width is the same as its radius times two. Even a line and a point have a width, although for both of these shapes, the width is zero.

So, we can say, at a very high and abstract level, all of the shapes in our problem domain have a width, and all of the shapes in our problem domain have a height.

Now let's turn that philosophy into code.

```
/*We have an abstract class called Shape, and every
shape has two properties, a height and a width.*/

public abstract class Shape
{

 double height;
 double width;

}
```

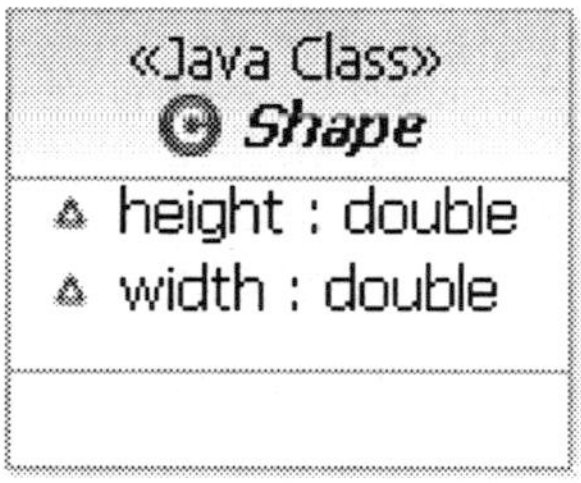

«Java Class»
Shape
height : double
width : double

```
/*In UML, abstract classes and interfaces have their
names italicized. Unfortunately, class diagrams are
often very small and convoluted, and the italicized
class name is often overlooked. Look out for an
italicized class name on the Associates exam,
indicating that a class is abstract.*/
```

Factoring Out Common Behavior

Now, is there any behavior that is common to *all* shapes? Remember, the term ***behavior*** translates into Java code by means of a method. So, another way to ask for common behavior, is to ask if there is a method that might be common to all of the various shapes? Keep the problem domain in mind!

Well, the common behavior we *need* from all of our shapes is the ability of a shape to calculate, and subsequently tell us, its area. We need to know the area of a square. We need to know the area of a rectangle. We need to know the area of a point. Finding the area of each shape is a required commonality, so we could say that every shape in our problem domain must have a **calculateArea** method that returns a double, representing the calculated area.

Implementing Common Behavior

We could be really bold with our calculateArea method in the Shape class, and actually code an implementation. For the most part, for our shapes, area could be calculated by *height * width;*

Think about it: ***height * width*** will return the correct area for a square, for a rectangle, and even for a line and a point. Both a line and a point have a height of 0, so for these objects, the calculation of height times width will correctly return an area of zero.

Of course, circles and triangles will need to override this inherited behavior. Circles are completely whack, so they'll need a completely different implementation for calculating their area. Triangles though, are just height times width divided by two, so we could still use the parent implementation, aka Shape implementation, but cut the calculation in half before returning the result to the calling program.

So, we could add behavior to our abstract class and code the calculateArea method in our *Shape* class as follows:

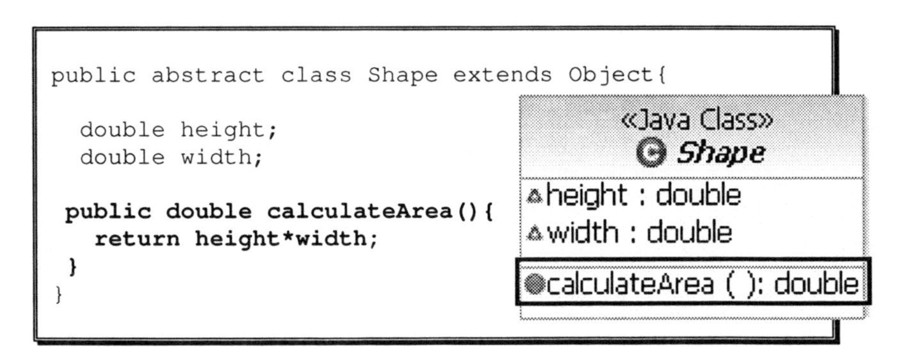

```
public abstract class Shape extends Object{

  double height;
  double width;

 public double calculateArea(){
   return height*width;
 }
}
```

```
/*With UML, a class diagram specifies the name in the
top tier, instance variables in the middle tier, and
methods in the third tier. Notice that the UML syntax
is not Java syntax.*/
```

The Power and Excitement of Inheritance

Now the Shape class, by itself, doesn't seem overly efficacious. The place that you start to really see how powerful and exciting inheritance can be, is when you start ***extending***, or inheriting from, a parent class.

The Shape class will be the parent of our rectangle class. To express inheritance, you use the keyword *extends*, and then the name of the class you are extending; this all goes in the class declaration, as follows:

```
public class Rectangle extends Shape {

  /*all good JavaBeans have a default constructor.*/

  public Rectangle() {
    height = 0;
    width = 0;
  }

 /*custom constructor for initializing instance variables*/

  public Rectangle(double h, double w){
    height = h;
    width = w;
  }

}
```

UML and Inheritance

In UML, inheritance is expressed with a closed headed arrow pointing from the inheriting class, to the parent class. In our Shapes example, the abstract class *Shape* is the parent class, or superclass, and the Rectangle is the child class.

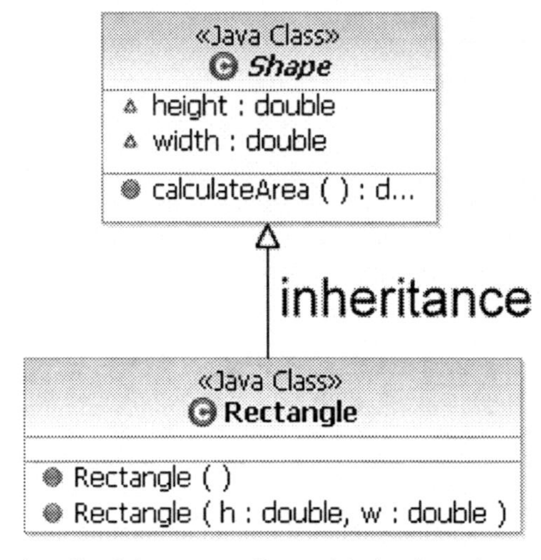

Looking at the UML diagram for the Shape and the Rectangle, we can say that the Rectangle class inherits all of the instance variables and methods that are defined in the Shape class. The Rectangle class inherits all of the properties and behavior of the Shape class.

Rectangle inherits from Shape

Method and Property Inheritance

Notice how this class doesn't declare height and width as instance variables. Instead, since the Square inherits from Shape, it positively inherits the height and width properties. This is how inheritance is so powerful. Common properties and behavior can be coded into a parent, or an ancestor class, and all sub-classes will inherit the behavior described by the parent.

To use the Rectangle in our code, we create instances using the non-default constructor, and call the inherited methods on the instance, as follows:

```
Rectangle r1 = new Rectangle(4,5);
System.out.println(r1.calculateArea());
```

The line of code, **Rectangle r1 = new Rectangle (4, 5);** tells the JVM to point the reference name **r1** to a memory location that stores information about the height and width of the rectangle; the Rectangle r1 has a height of 4, and a width of 5.

When the **calculateArea()** method is invoked on our rectangle, r1, the implementation coded in the parent class is executed, and the number 20 is returned. The number 20 is subsequently printed out to the console through our println statement.

Inheritance and the *Is-A* Relationship

If we really wanted to be hotdogs, we could take inheritance in our object model one step further by defining a class called **Square** that **inherits** from **Rectangle**.

Inheritance represents an ***is-a*** relationship. A sub-type, or sub-class, should have an *'is-a'* relationship with the parent; but in fact, inheritance should go deeper than just ***'is-a'***. A sub-class should also have an ***'is a special-type-of'*** relationship with the parent as well.

So, does our Square pass our **'is-a'** and **'a special type of'** test for inheritance? Sure it does. A square *is-a* type of rectangle, but it is also a *special type of* rectangle, namely, a rectangle that has all sides equal. This distinction is exemplified by the constructor that takes only one argument, **Square (double h) { ... }**

```
/*A Square is a special type of Rectangle.*/
public class Square extends Rectangle {

  public Square (){
    height = 0;
    width = 0;
  }

  /*Why does this constructor take only one argument?*/
  public Square (double h){
    height = h;
    width =h;
  }
}
```

Constructors and Inheritance

Notice how the Square defines a constructor that only takes one parameter? This makes sense, after all, if we know the height of a square, then we know the width of the square as well. A square really only needs one non-default constructor that takes a double as an argument.

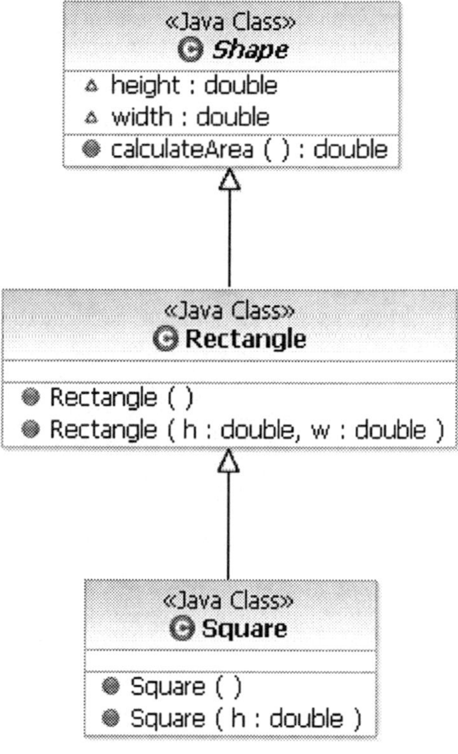

Of course, the Rectangle class defines a constructor that takes two parameters. If a child inherits all the properties and behavior of a parent, does the Square class have access to the constructor of the Rectangle class that takes two parameters? For example, could someone ruin our logic by saying:

Sqaure s = new Square(2,3);

No, they couldn't. While a child inherits all the properties and methods of a parent, a child does not, *repeat, does not*, inherit constructors. Constructors of a parent class can only be called from within the constructor of a child by using the special method super(), but constructors themselves are not inherited from a parent to a child. ***Constructors must be uniquely defined for every class.***

Creating Instances of the Sub Class

So a Square can now be created using the following code:

```
Square s1 = new Square(5);
System.out.println(s1.calculateArea()); /*prints out 25*/
```

Overriding Inherited Behavior (aka Methods)

Now our Square and Rectangle classes cleanly inherit from Shape, although our Square does inherit somewhat indirectly through Rectangle, but a Triangle isn't going to be quite as simple; after all, a Triangle can't just return an area as height times width, since the area of a triangle is ***half*** of the height times the width. So, how do we create a Triangle class that inherits all the properties of the Shape class, but overrides the calculateArea() method with its own implementation? Well, it's relatively easy: we just extend Shape, and code our own calculateArea method, matching exactly the name, return type, and the method signature of the inherited calculateArea( ) method:

```
public class Triangle extends Shape{

 public Triangle(double h, double w) {
  this.height=h;
  this.width=w;
 }

 public double calculateArea(){

  double area = (height * width) / 2;
  return area;
 }
}
```

Again, notice that we need to provide a custom constructor. The custom, non-default constructor initializes the instance variables inherited from the Shape class.

Also notice that we have our own, custom, triangle implementation of the calcluateArea method. When someone creates a Triangle, and subsequently asks for the area, the method in the defining class will be used, not the implementation in the parent class. When figuring out which method to call on an object, the JVM starts at the bottom of the inheritance chain of the object, and works its way up the chain until a matching method name and signature is found.

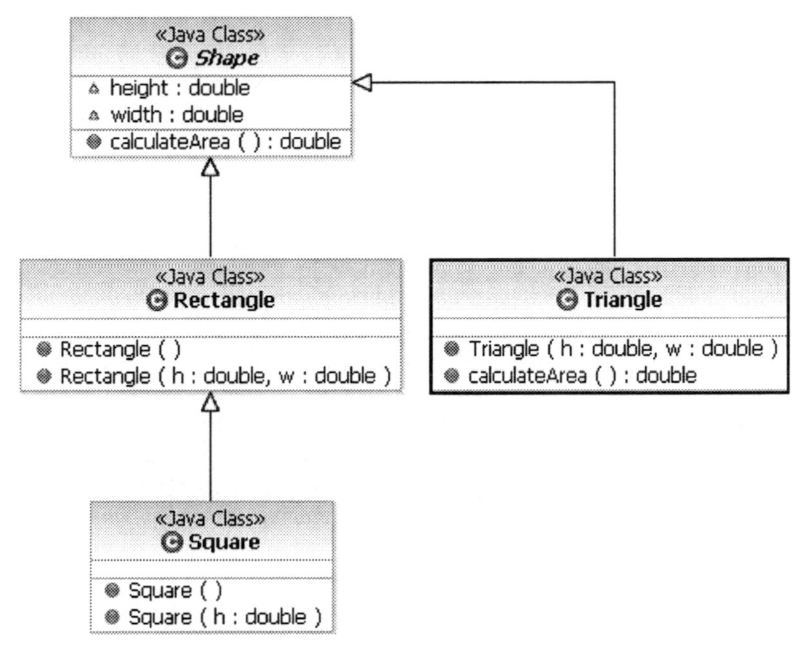

Calling the Right Method in the Hierarchy

When a method is called on an object, the JVM starts at the bottom of the class' hierarchy chain, and looks for an implementation. If an implementation is not found, the JVM will keep jumping up a level in the class hierarchy until it finds an implementation. If two or more implementations of a method exist on a class hierarchy, the concrete implementation *closest* to the object in its hierarchy chain, starting at the bottom and working its way up, will always be chosen.

Overriding Methods

```
Triangle tri = new Triangle(11,12);
System.out.println(tri.calculateArea());
```

Similarly, our Circle class will need to override the implementation of calculateArea. Furthermore, our Circle will provide a custom constructor that takes a radius. Using the radius, we'll initialize the inherited height and width.

The Circle Class

Once the Circle class is defined, we can create an instance of a Circle, and correctly calculate the area using the overriding method:

```
Circle j = new Circle(10);
System.out.println(j.calculateArea());
```

Rule: when a method is defined at several points in the hierarchy chain, the method closest to the defined object, starting from the bottom of the hierarchy and working up, will always be used.

Using the Static Class java.lang.Math

Check out the code for the Circle class on the next page.

Notice how the overridden calculateArea() method in the Circle class uses a call to Math.PI. The Math class is often referred to as a static class, because it only contains constants and static methods, but no instance methods or instance variables. All of the methods and variables are invoked by simply using the name of the class, Math, and then the method name or variable name of interest.

```
Math.PI;
Math.E;

Math.random();
Math.sqrt(25);
Math.pow(11,5);
```

The Circle Class: Extending and Overriding

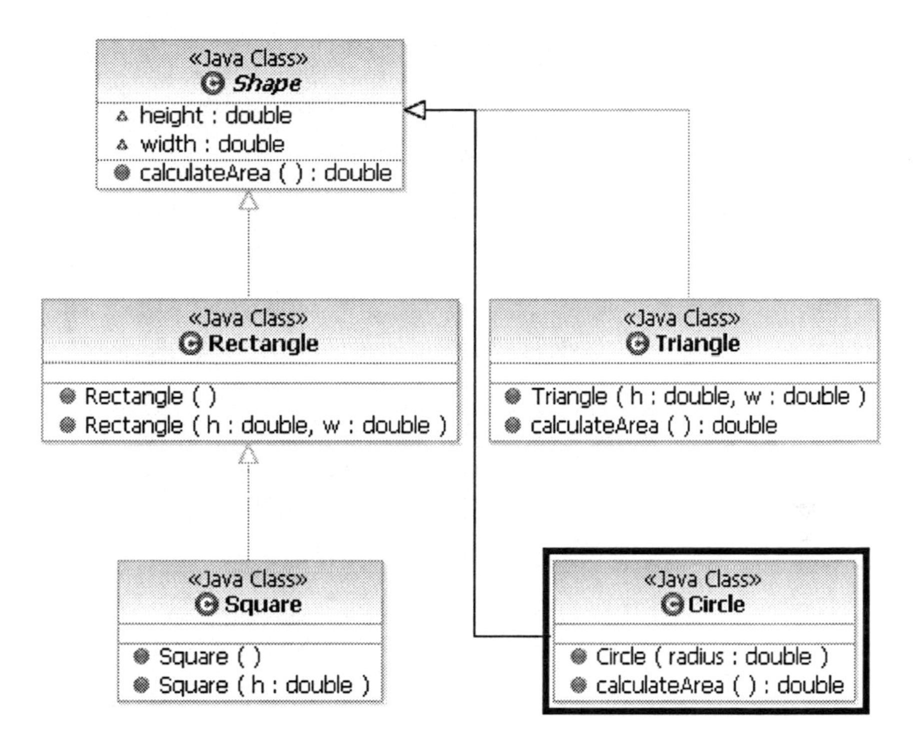


```
public class Circle extends Shape {

  public Circle(double radius) {
    height = radius * 2;
    width = radius * 2;
  }

  public double calculateArea() {

    double radius = height / 2;
    double area = Math.PI * radius * radius;
    return area;
    /* or Math.PI * Math.pow(radius, 2); */
  }

}
```

The Line and the Point:

There are two more shapes we really want to look at, namely the Line and the Point. Let's start off with the Point.

Should our Point class inherit from Shape? Does a Point have an ***'is-a'*** relationship with Shape? Does a Point have a ***'special kind of' relationship'*** with Shape? Yes, I think it does.

```
public class Point extends Shape{

}
```

With inheritance, sub-classes represent special types of objects. Moving down a class hierarchy, we see specialization, whereas moving up a class hierarchy, we see generalization. A Point is definitely a special type of Shape. But in which ways is a Point special?

Sub-Classes are Specialized Classes

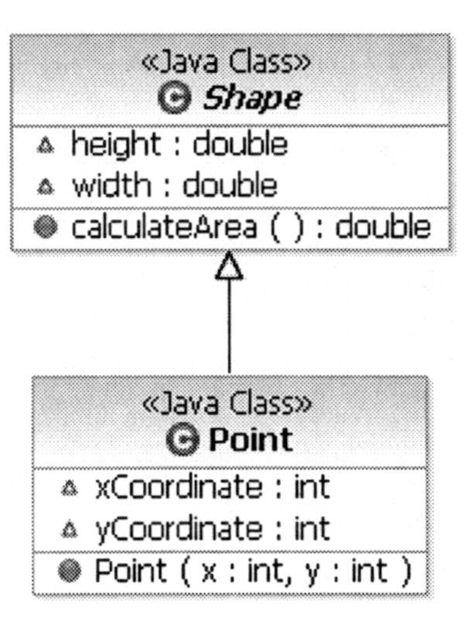

Well, when anyone thinks of a Point, they think of a Cartesian coordinate system with an x and y axis. A Point on a two dimensional Cartesian plane is defined by an x and y value.

Okay, that last paragraph was just a complex way of saying that a point should have two additional properties: an x coordinate and a y coordinate. To define specialized properties, we add those properties as new instance variables, and we also provide a customized, non-default constructor that is capable of initializing those properties.

Getting to the Point

```
public class Point extends Shape {

  int xCoordinate;
  int yCoordinate;

/*non-default constructor to initialize properties*/
  public Point(int x, int y) {
    this.xCoordinate = x;
    this.yCoordinate = y;
    this.height = 0;  this.width = 0;
  }
}
```

So, now when we create a Point, we don't specify a height and a width, but instead, we provide an x and a y value. Earlier it was stated that non-default constructors should typically have a method signature that allows for the initialization of every instance variable. We sensibly break this rule with the Point class, as we don't need to be told by someone calling the constructor that the height and width of the Point is going to be zero.

Here's how we might use the Point class in an application:

```
Point origin = new Point(0,0);
Point pelee = new Point(47,50);

System.out.println(origin.xCoordinate);
System.out.println(pelee.yCoordinate);

/*will return 0*/
System.out.println(origin.calculateArea());

/*will return 0*/
System.out.println(pelee.calculateArea());
```

So, our point is a Shape, and it is a very special type of shape, with extra properties that give the concept of a Point object more meaning.

Drawing The Line

We have one last object in our problem domain to implement: The Line.

Now, should a line inherit from Shape? Is a line ***'a special type of'*** shape? Does a Line share common behavior with a shape, insomuch as the calculation of the area as defined in the Shape class? I think our Line and Point classes clearly push the envelope for using inheritance, but I'm going to go with it. Our Line class will also inherit from Shape.

```
public class Line extends Shape{

}
```

Specialization Happens Down The Hierarchy Tree

Now, one temptation for Java newbies is to think that perhaps Line should extend Point. I can certainly understand why someone might start thinking in that direction; after all, a Line and a Point really are two peas in an iPod. Think about it: what is a line? A line is a collection of Points. Or more correctly, a Line is a collection of all of the Points between a start point, A, and an end point, B. So, when we talk about Lines and Points, there certainly is an *association* between the two.

But a Line is not a "special type" of Point. A Line is certainly a special type of Shape, but it is *not* a special type of Point. Instead, though, a Line is ***associated*** with Points. **A line, really, is defined by two properties: its start point and its end point.** So, when we define the Line class, we should define it as having two properties, pointA and pointB.

```
public class Line extends Shape {
  Point pointA;
  Point pointB;

  public Line(Point a, Point b){

    this.pointA = a;
    this.pointB = b;

  }
}
```

Further Exploration of the *static* Math Class

Furthermore, a line isn't really defined by its height and width, but instead, by its length, which is calculated through the Pythagorean theorem. Now skip this section if your stomach gets queasy when you encounter geometry, but here's how we should provide for the ability to calculate the length of a line.

```
/*  Length of a line = ((x2-x1)² + (y2-y1)²)½  */

public double getLength(){

  height = (this.pointA.xCoordinate -
                              this.pointB.xCoordinate);

  width = (this.pointA.yCoordinate -
                              this.pointB.yCoordinate);

  double length = Math.sqrt((Math.pow(height,2) +
                                      Math.pow(width,2)));

  return length;

}

public double calculateArea() {

  return 0;

}
```

Increasingly Complex Class Diagrams

When the Line, Point and Shape classes are placed together on a single class diagram, you begin to see how effective a class diagram can be at visually providing important pieces of information.

First of all, the closed-headed arrow that points towards the abstract Shape class from the Line and the Point expresses the fact that both Lines and Points are special types of Shapes. Lines and Points share a special “is-a” relationship with the Shape class.

Furthermore, an association line has been created between the Line and the Point class, indicating that a Line is actually associated with Points, or more specifically, as we can read from the class diagram, a Line is defined by two Points.

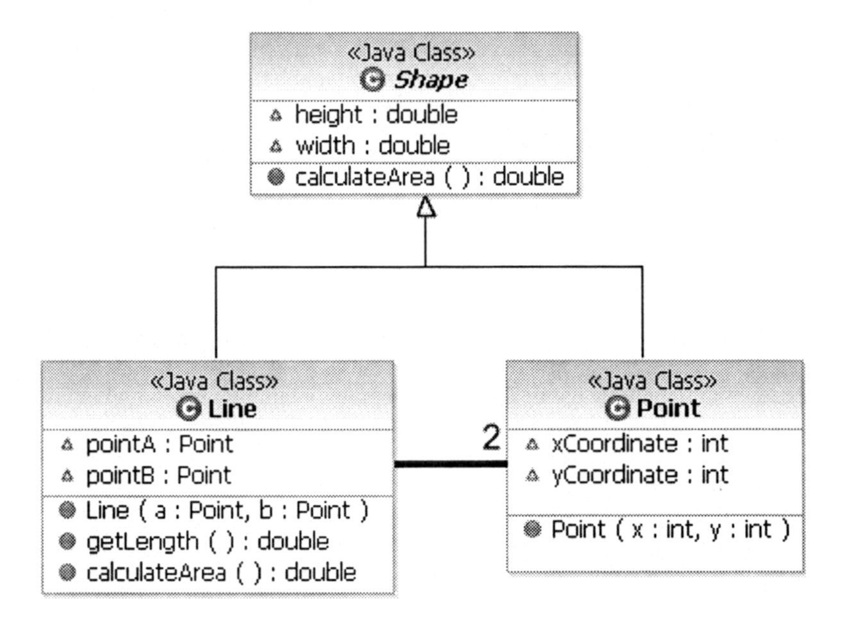

Note how you read the class diagram: The Line class has two Points, where the number two is closest to the Point class, not the Line class. Some people find that nuance a little non-intuitive, although you'll get used to it the more you work with class diagrams.

The Full Shapes Class Diagram

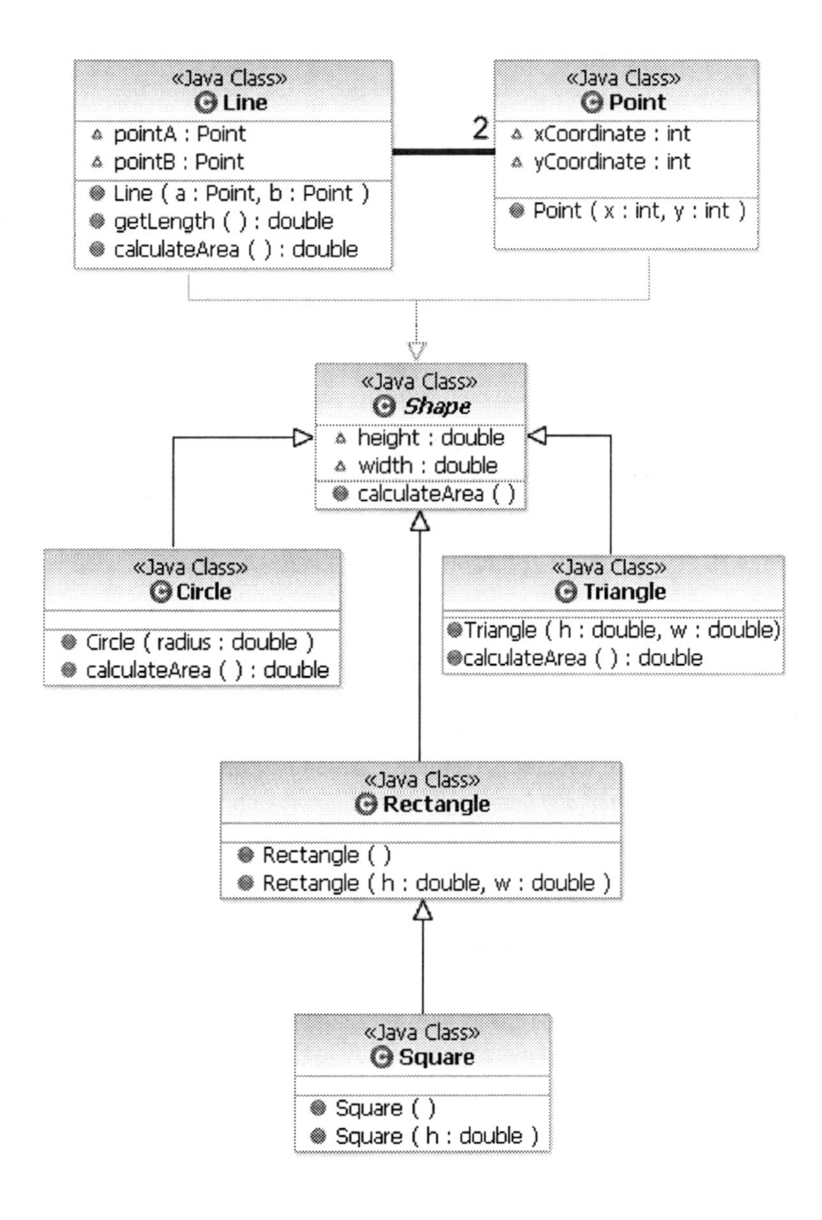

Question

When one object depends upon another for its existence, this is known as:
O a) composition O b) abstraction O c) association O d) inheritance

Question

In Java, single inheritance means:
O a) a class can have only one parent, but many ancestors O b) a class can have many parents, but only one ancestor O c) all classes are related to each other O d) a class can inherit properties from only one other class

Question

Sub classes:
☐ a) are more specialized than their ancestors ☐ b) are more general than their ancestors ☐ c) should be used as method parameters over ancestor classes ☐ d) should not be used as method parameters when an ancestor class will suffice

Question

Inheritance should not be used:
☐ a) when the inheriting class is a special type of the parent class ☐ b) when the subclass needs to override many inherited methods ☐ c) when inherited properties do not make sense in the child ☐ d) when the subclass does not need to make changes to inherited methods

Answer

When one object depends upon another for its existence, this is known as:
O a) composition O b) abstraction O c) association O d) inheritance
Composition is a special type of relationship between objects that involves a 'has-a' relationship, along with strong lifecycle maintenance over the 'had' object. Composition is not a manifestation of inheritance, or the extending of a parent class. Inheritance represents an is-a relationship, which is quite different from the has-a relationship of composition and association.

Answer

In Java, single inheritance means:
O a) a class can have only one parent, but many ancestors O b) a class can have many parents, but only one ancestor O c) all classes are related to each other O d) a class can inherit properties from only one other class
This question seems more like a word game than a Java question. Answer a) is definitely the most correct answer, but the alternate answers certainly have some validity, depending on how you interpret the phrasing. A class can only extend one other class. The class that is extended is known as the parent class. However, the parent class may extend from another class, and so on and so on, and so on. All of the classes above a given class in the hierarchy chain are known as ancestors, so a class can have only one parent, but many ancestors. All classes share one common ancestor in Java, which is the java.lang.Object class. Since all classes in Java share Object as an ancestor, then technically, c) is a correct statement, although it isn't correct with regards to single inheritance, so it isn't really an accurate answer for this given question. Since a class inherits all of the properties from every class on its hierarchy, a class is inheriting properties and methods from potentially many classes. Of course, the parent of a class would have inherited all of these properties as well, so this answer might technically be correct.

Answer

Sub classes:
☐ a) are more specialized than their ancestors ☐ b) are more general than their ancestors ☐ c) should be used as method parameters over ancestor classes ☐ d) should not be used as method parameters when an ancestor class will suffice
Answers a) and d) are correct. Sub classes represent specialization over the class from which they inherit. A Square is a special type of Rectangle. A Triangle is a special type of Shape. Also, when programming, to ensure a high degree of pluggability in your code, you should always program to the most general or abstract class that will provide required functionality. When choosing method parameters, interfaces are better than abstract classes, and parent classes are better than subclasses. Sub classes are specialized classes, but when creating methods or declaring properties of a class, using the most general and non-specific type that is available will always make your code more flexible.

Answer

Inheritance should ***not*** be used:
☐ a) when the inheriting class is a special type of the parent class ☐ b) when the subclass needs to override many inherited methods ☐ c) when inherited properties do not make sense in the child ☐ d) when the subclass does not need to make changes to inherited methods
If an inheriting class is overriding inherited behavior, or simply not using instance variables that have been inherited, then inheritance is not being used properly. Another rule with inheritance is not to define ***roles*** with inheritance, but instead, to use an interface. So, while a manager and a secretary both might logically extend from the employee class, manager and secretary are roles that employees play. The problem occurs when the secretary goes on vacation, and the manager must temporarily assume the duties of a secretary. Single inheritance in Java makes this difficult. However, interfaces, which are about to be explored, alleviate the problem of not implementing specialized roles through inheritance.

Chapter 10
Implementing Interfaces

One of the most powerful constructs of the Java programming language is the concept of inheritance, but as the very best object modelers in the world will tell you, using inheritance should be the exception, never the rule, when designing an object model.

Inheritance is powerful, but it is often *too* powerful. New programmers are anxious to demonstrate their command of object orientation, and tend to see inheritance where instead they should simply see commonality and generalization.

Absolute Inheritance Corrupts Absolutely

Our Shapes example started off with the best of intentions, but it ended up abusing the concept of inheritance. We shouldn't have created an abstract class called Shape, but should have used a common interface instead. Creating an abstract class called Shape was a bad idea.

Inheritance can be a *very, very* bad idea, especially when:

- inherited properties are not being used, or are not being used in the spirit of the inherited class
- inherited methods are continually being overridden with specialized behavior

Rethinking the Shapes Example

From our shapes example, our Rectangle and Square classes made good use of inheritance, but both our Triangle and Circle classes had to override the core behavior inherited from Shape, namely the ability to calculate an area by multiplying *height* times *width*. Furthermore, the properties of height and width were meaningless for the point class, and while height and width had meaning for the line, those properties had more to do with the triangulation of the length of the line, and in the end, storing values for the height and width of a line ended up messing up the calculation of the area of a line - the calculateArea method of a line ended up being overridden to simply return 0 – what a waste.

Defining Common Behavior

With the abstract class Shape, we defined functionality in a method called calculateArea, but in the end, many classes, such as the circle and the Triangle, ended up overriding the implementation of the calculateArea method. When an abstract class wants to define behavior, through a method, that all subclasses must implement, but at the same time, the abstract class does not want to actually code an implementation to the method, then the abstract class can mark the method as being ***abstract***.

«Java Class»
Shape
height : double
width : double
calculateArea ( ): double

```
public abstract class Shape{

  double height;
  double width;

 public abstract double calculateArea();
/* Notice how there is no method body for an abstract
method. Not even {} after the method declaration */

}
/*In the UML diagram, both the class name, Shape, and
the method name, calculateArea, are italicized, to
indicate that they are abstract. */
```

All concrete subclasses of an abstract class must provide an implementation of the abstract methods defined in the parent, or they themselves must also be declared as being abstract. For our Shapes example, the abstract class Shape could have simply declared the calculateArea method as being abstract, and each subclass would then be forced to code a custom implementation.

With abstract methods, there are a few rules you need to remember:

- any class with an abstract method must itself be declared as being abstract
- an abstract class does not necessarily need to have any abstract methods
- abstract methods cannot be declared as being private, as they are intended to be overridden by subclasses
- if a class extends a abstract class, and does not provide implementations to all abstract methods defined in the abstract parent class, that extending class must also be defined as being abstract
- abstract methods can never have a method implementation. Even empty, curly braces after the definition of an abstract method, { }, will cause a compile error.

The great thing about abstract classes is the fact that they can define abstract methods, while at the same time, providing some concrete method implementations, and defining instance variables as well. However, with the abstract class Shape, even the definition of instance variables, such as height and width, don't always make sense, as a Circle is really defined by a radius, and a Point doesn't really have a height and width at all. There are definitely times when abstract classes are the correct Java artifact to use, but I'm afraid that with our Shapes example, we're going to have to use something even more powerful and flexible than an abstract class – we're going to have to use an ***interface***.

An Introduction to Interfaces

There is certainly commonality between all of the Shapes in our example, and all Shapes do indeed need a calculateArea method to fulfill the requirements of our problem domain, but each shape is different enough to make inheriting from a common abstract class a very, very bad idea. Instead of extending parent objects, Java provides a much more powerful artifact for expressing commonality between objects. The most powerful artifact in the Java programming language is the interface.

The Java programming language provides a special construct called an ***interface***. An ***interface*** is simply a collection of non-implemented methods. Any set of classes that ***implement*** a common interface are said to share a common behavior, as they will all have the same set of methods. When a class implements an interface, the implementing class is said to have an 'is-a' relationship with the interface.

```
/*Notice that there are no instance variables or
method implementations in an interface*/

public interface IShape {
  public double calculateArea();
}
```

«Java Interface»
IShape
calculateArea ( ) : double

```
/*Interface names are italicized in UML.*/
```

Interfaces do not have instance variables associated with them. Interfaces can define *static final* variables, although this practice isn't overly common. And while an interface can contain static final variables, conversely, the *methods* in an interface can***not*** be declared as being static or final.

> **<u>Immutable Rule of Java:</u> Everything in Java is an object, except for the things that are not objects.**
> *Supposedly, everything in Java is an object, but primitive types are not objects, and interfaces aren't objects either. A better term than object or class is type. An interface does not define a particular Java class, but it does define a type. A class that implements Serializable can be said to be a serializable type. A class that extends Shape can be said to be of type shape. When talking about objects, it's better to talk about what type of object they are, as opposed to what class from which the object inherits from. The term type applies globally to both the class hierarchy of an object, and the interfaces from which that object inherits.*

Competing Naming Conventions for Interfaces

When naming interfaces, the convention is to either end the name of the interface with *-able,* such as Serializ***able*** or Break***able***, or, to start the name of the interface with the letter I. Since the term Shapeable doesn't really make much sense, I've named the interface for our shapes example ***IShape.***

Like inheritance, a class that implements an interface shares an ***is-a*** relationship with that interface. So, every class that implements the Serializable interface ***is-a*** serializable object. Every class that implements an interface called Breakable is-a breakable object. Every object that implements the IShape interface is a ***type*** of IShape object.

The UML Representation of Java Interfaces

Since implementing an interface represents a different way of expressing an ***'is-a'*** relationship, the UML description is similar to inheritance. Whereas inheritance is represented by a closed arrow and a solid line, with the child pointing at the parent, a class that implements an interface points to the interface with a closed headed arrow, but a dashed, not a solid, line.

The Power of Interfaces

A class can only inherit from one parent class. A class can implement any number of interfaces. This is the power of the interface.

The idea behind interfaces is that they express commonality, without forcing a set of common properties or concrete method implementations upon implementing classes.

Take for example, a Boeing 747 and an Airbus 320. There are similarities, right? If you were modeling them, you might have them inherit from a parent class called plane.

What about adding in a helicopter? Should we create an abstract class, but make it more general? Perhaps call it MechanicalFlyingMachines? Perhaps.

What if we add in birds? Are there any properties that are common between a bird, a plane, and a helicopter? Probably not many. But what if we wanted to deliver a letter from Holland to England? Could you use an airbus? Sure; A plane? Sure. A boat? Sure. A bird, like they did in Operation Market-Garden during WWI? Sure.

Factor Out Commonality into a Common Interface

So, a Homing Pigeon, an airplane, a helicopter and a boat all share the common behavior that they can be used to deliver letters. And birds, planes and helicopters all share the common behavior that they can fly (boats can't fly.) Perhaps we could have two interfaces to express this commonality: Flyable and IDeliveryVehicle

```
public interface Flyable {
  public void takeOff();
  public void land();
}
```

Notice the methods in an interface end with a semi-colon, and have no chicken lips or squiggly braces after them. This emphasizes the fact that in an interface, there is no method implementation at all. Even just putting in empty braces would cause a compile error. In fact, to emphasize the idea that the methods in an interface are to be implemented in a subclass, and not in the interface, you will often see the ***abstract*** keyword in the method declaration.

```
public interface IDeliveryVehicle {
  public abstract void send();
  public abstract void receive();
}
```

The great thing about abstraction is that when you generalize in your code, or code to an interface, client applications could creatively and flexibly use options that you may never have anticipated when you developed your original application. For example you may design an application that delivers packages, and you probably anticipate the use of cars or planes to implement the delivery process. But if you make your methods *so general* that they only need an implementing interface, a client could create a homing pigeon class that implements your delivery interface, and send your important messages using a bird! A solution that uses interfaces is an incredibly flexible solution.

```
/*Always try to program to an interface. Using interfaces
as method parameters provides for the most flexible and
pluggable solutions.*/

public void sendDocument(IDeliveryVehicle vehicle)
```

```
public abstract class Bird {
  int numberOfFeathers;
  /*other properties and methods would go here*/
}

public class HomingPigeon extends Bird implements Flyable,
                                          IDeliveryVehicle{
 public void takeOff(){/*Method implementation here*/}
 public void land(){/*Method implementation here*/}
 public void send(){/*Method implementation here*/}
 public void receive(){/*Method implementation here*/}

}

public class Helicopter implements Flyable,
                                       IDeliveryVehicle{
 public void takeOff(){/*Method implementation here*/}
 public void land(){/*Method implementation here*/}
 public void send(){/*Method implementation here*/}
 public void receive(){/*Method implementation here*/}
}

public class Boat implements IDeliveryVehicle {
 public void send(){/*Method implementation here*/}
 public void receive(){/*Method implementation here*/}
}
```

Interfaces and Our Shapes Example

A better solution for our shapes example, as opposed to creating an abstract class called Shape, would be to create a single interface called IShape, that simply defines the calculateArea method. An interface allows implementing classes to define their own method implementations, and while we will have to define instance variables for sub-classes, this frees us from having to force objects like the Line and the Point class to needlessly inherit properties such as height and width, which would just end up getting initialized to zero and taking up precious bits of memory on the JVM.

Using an interface frees up your Java code. Implementing classes are free to implement their behavior in any way they see fit, using whatever resources are necessary. Using interfaces is always a great option. An important step after creating any class model or object diagram is to iterate over the solution and see if it's possible to factor out any interfaces.

Redesigning our application to use interfaces, we would eliminate the abstract class Shape, and simply use the IShape interface to express commonality.

```
/*Notice that there are no instance variables or
method implementations in an interface*/

public interface IShape {
  public double calculateArea();
}

/*Interface names are italicized in UML.*/
```

«Java Interface»
IShape

calculateArea ( ) : double

Revisiting the Rectangle Class

The Square and Rectangle classes benefited the most from inheritance, as they inherited the properties of height and width, not to mention a correct implementation for the calculateArea method. Nevertheless, we can still take advantage of inheritance by defining the height and width properties in the Rectangle class, implement the appropriate method, and use inheritance by making a Square a subclass of Rectangle. In this case, we take advantage of both inheritance and interfaces.

```
public class Rectangle implements IShape {

 /* we must define instance variables, since they are no
 longer inherited from the abstract class. */

 double height;
 double width;

/*The constructors have not changed when compared to the
Rectangle class that extended abstract Shape.*/

 public Rectangle() {
  height = 0;
  width = 0;
 }

 public Rectangle(double h, double w) {
  height = h;
  width = w;
 }

/*by implementing the IShape interface, we have committed
to implementing the calculateArea() method*/

 public double calculateArea() {
  return height*width;
 }

}
```

Interfaces and UML Notation

In a UML diagram, an interface is named in italics, and classes that implement the interface point to the interface with a dotted line ending with a closed headed arrow.

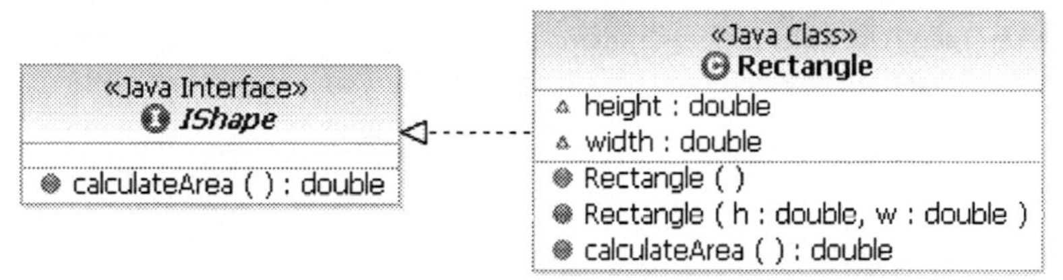

One thing that should strike you about the UML notation for implementing an interface is how closely it resembles the UML notation for class inheritance: they are essentially the same, with the only difference being the dotted line for interface implementation, as opposed to the solid line for inheritance; both lines lead to a closed headed arrow.

The similarity in notations is not coincidental. Both inheritance and the implementation of an interface represent an ***'is-a'*** relationship. The only difference is how the relationship manifests itself in code. Any class that implements the IShape interface can be said to be ***'a special type of IShape.'***

Revisiting the Square Class

The Square class was probably the most appropriate candidate in our entire class model to take advantage of inheritance. There is no reason for the Square not to inherit all of the properties and behavior defined in the Rectangle class. To do this, we simply extend Rectangle with the Square class.

```
/*There are no changes needed to the Square class to take
advantage of the functionality it is already inheriting
from Rectangle.*/

public class Square extends Rectangle {
 public Square() {
  height = 0;
  width = 0;
 }
 public Square(double h) {
  height = h;
  width = h;
 }
}
```

Revisiting the Triangle Class

Like the Square class, the Triangle class also requires a height and a width, which makes the idea of inheritance tempting, but a Triangle certainly doesn't fulfill the ***'is-a'*** requirement with relation to a Square, and even though a Triangle shares common properties with a Square or Rectangle, the calculation of the area is certainly different. Once again, the proper solution is to use an interface, and avoid using inheritance.

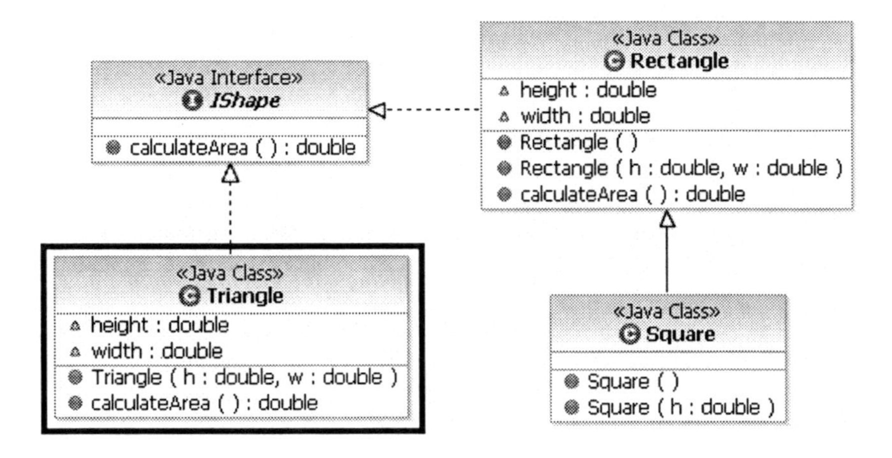


```
public class Triangle implements IShape {

/*instance variables must be added, as they are no
longer inherited from an ancestor class.*/

  double height;
  double width;

  public Triangle(double h, double w) {
    this.height = h;
    this.width = w;
  }

/*This method has not changed, although it no longer
overrides the incorrect implementation in the abstract
Shape class.*/

  public double calculateArea() {
    double area = (height * width) / 2;
    return area;
  }
}
```

Rethinking the Circle Class

A circle can be defined solely by its radius, so inheriting properties for both height and width is simply wasteful. And not only did the Circle not effectively share the properties defined in the abstract shape class, but it did not share the same behavior either. Using inheritance for the Circle class was all around, a bad idea. Once again, using an interface is the correct approach to demonstrate commonality, but allow for a custom implementation.

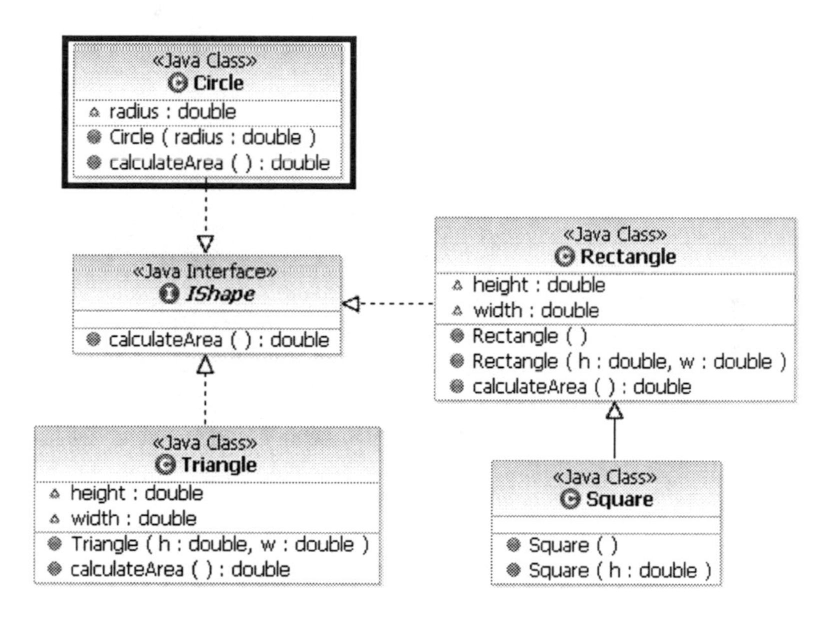


```
public class Circle implements IShape {
    double radius;
  public Circle(double r) {
    radius=r;
  }
  public double calculateArea() {
    //double radius = height / 2; not needed
    double area = Math.PI * radius * radius;
    return area;
  }
}
```

Rethinking the Point

Inheriting two properties of type double that represented the height and width of a line and point was simply a huge waste of memory, even if the calculateArea() method did work successfully. However, in this case, the end certainly did not justify the means.

Both the line and the point should express their common behavior by implementing the IShape interface, while expressing their specialization by declaring properties that are pertinent to their existence.

```
public class Point implements IShape {

 int xCoordinate;
 int yCoordinate;

 public Point(int x, int y) {
  this.xCoordinate = x;
  this.yCoordinate = y;
  //this.height = 0; commented out, now irrelevant
  //this.width = 0;  commented out, now irrelevant
 }
 public double calculateArea() {
  /*simply returning zero is sufficient.*/
  return 0;
 }
}
```

The Point class implements the IShape interface, but also provides specialized properties that are pertinent to a two dimensional point, namely the xCoordinate and the yCoordinate.

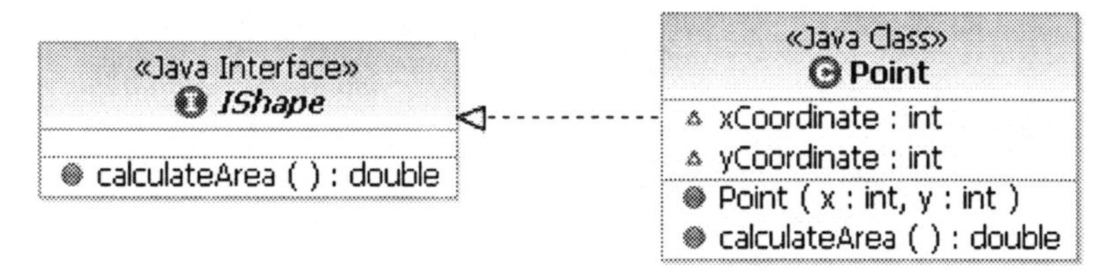

Finally, Rethinking the Line

Again, the Line class has no need for a height and width property. Setting memory aside for properties that are not used is wasteful. Instead, to express common behavior, the Line should extend the IShape interface, return a simple zero for the calculateArea() method, and implement any specialized behavior that makes sense for a line.

```
public class Line implements IShape {

  Point pointA;
  Point pointB;

  public Line(Point a, Point b) {
    this.pointA = a;
    this.pointB = b;
  }

  public double getLength() {
    double height = (this.pointA.xCoordinate -
                              this.pointB.xCoordinate);
    double width = (this.pointA.yCoordinate -
                              this.pointB.yCoordinate);
    double length = Math.sqrt((Math.pow(height, 2) +
                                  Math.pow(width, 2)));
    return length;
  }

  public double calculateArea() {
   return 0;
  }
}
```

Be aware that not all UML diagrams will show parent classes at the top, or multiplicity always on the right hand side. The layout of the UML diagram isn't what's important for the associates exam; what is

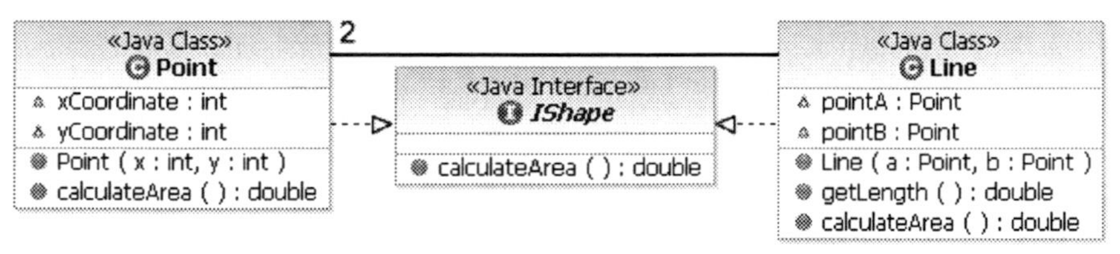

important is that you can understand how to read relationships on a UML diagram, such as ***a Line is associated with two Points,*** or ***the Point and the Line are types of IShape objects.***

The Line Has Two Points

One thing to note about the UML diagram that describes the relationship between a Line and a Point, is the fact that a Line has two points, namely, a startPoint and an endPoint. A Line can't have just a startPoint, and it can't just have an endPoint. A Line really must have both a startPoint and an endPoint. A good object model would try to enforce this rule somehow, and the good place to enforce this type of a rule would be in the constructor.

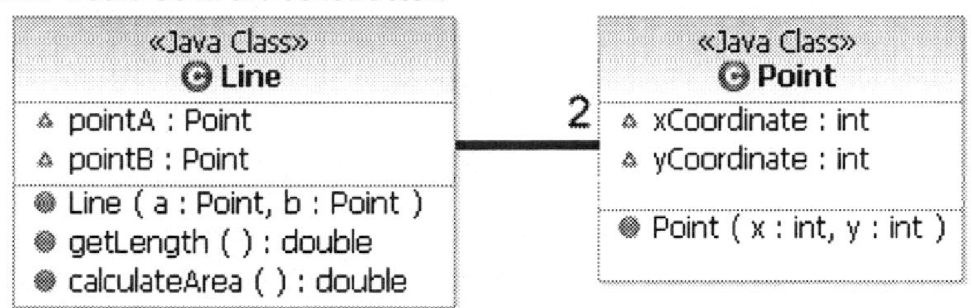

Enforcing the Association

When a Line object is created, it is passed in two Point objects. However, a lazy programmer could potentially pass in two null objects instead of real-life, instantiated Points. In the constructor of the Line, it might be a good idea to check for such a condition.

```
public class Line implements IShape {
  Point pointA; Point pointB;
  public Line(Point a, Point b) {
    /* Check to see if a null Point has been passed in */

    if (a==null || b == null) {
       System.exit(0);   /* kills the JVM */
    }
    this.pointA = a;
    this.pointB = b;
  }
  public double getLength() {
    double height = (this.pointA.xCoordinate -
                                this.pointB.xCoordinate);
    double width = (this.pointA.yCoordinate -
                                this.pointB.yCoordinate);
    double length = Math.sqrt((Math.pow(height, 2) +
                                    Math.pow(width, 2)));
    return length;
  }

  public double calculateArea() {
   return 0;
  }
}
```

Lollipop Notation

Sometimes, when a class implements a number of interfaces, it is slightly easier to document the relationship by simply showing the name of the class, and then simply drawing a lollipop that extends out from the class, towards a circle, with the circular end defining the name of an interface the class is implementing.

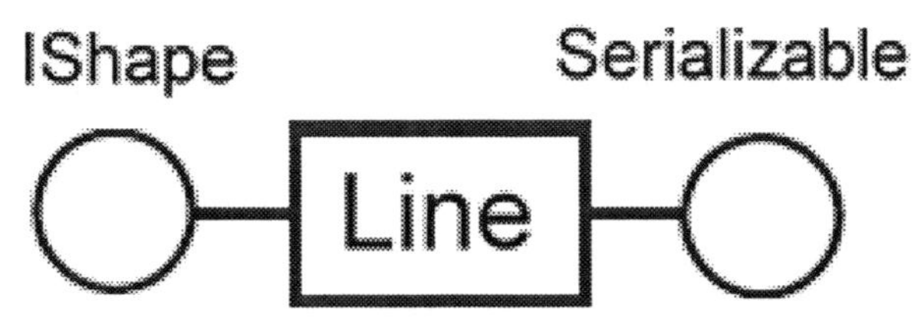

In the Shapes example, the Line class implements the IShape interface, but it might also implement the Serializable interface, after all, all good JavaBeans should be Serializable. If both the IShape and Serializable interfaces were implemented by the Line class, lollipop notation might be an appropriate notation. With the Line class implementing java.io.Serializable and IShape interfaces, we would have the Line class defined in a normal, UML class diagram, and the interfaces IShape and Serializable listed above separate, round ends of a lollipop. Known as lollipop notation, this UML artifact is designed to try and make it easier to express the relationship between classes and interfaces when many interfaces are being implemented.

```
public class Line implements IShape, java.io.Serializable
{}
```

The Enumeration Type (enum)

Java is an object-oriented language, and everything in Java is an object, with the exception of the things that are not objects.☺ Primitive types are not objects, and interfaces are really *types*, not instantiable objects. There's another thing in Java that isn't really an object, which was introduced in Java 1.5, and that non-object thing is called an enum.

Quite often, in just about any program, you need to define a variable that can only take on a certain number of values. For example, perhaps you were painting cars, and car exteriors could only be painted one of three colors: red, green or blue. How could you efficiently represent this tri-valued parameter or property in code?

You couldn't represent this property as a boolean, because there are three potential values, and a boolean can only describe two states, namely true or false. You could use a String variable, taking the values of "RED", "GREEN", and "BLUE", but even then, there wouldn't be anything stopping a user from typing in the String "YELLOW". To use a String, and enforce that the program only accept the three color Strings in which you are interested, you would have to write all sorts of supporting code, which would be a pain to write, and even more of a pain to maintain, especially if someone introduccs a crazy new color, such as "SILVER."

Well, with Java 1.5, the Java Gods introduced the idea of an ***enum*** type. Essentially, an enum, also known as an ***enumeration type***, is used to define a static number of values a *type* can take, all of which is enforced at design-time by a compiler. So, for our car exteriors examples, we could create an enumeration type that has three possible values:

```
public enum ExteriorColor { RED, GREEN, BLUE}
```

After defining an enum, you can then use the enum in code, declaring variables of your custom enumeration type:

```
ExteriorColor myCarColor = ExteriorColor.RED;
```

And once used in code, enums can be used like other standard object types, being incorporated into flow control and conditional logic:

```
if (myCarColor.equals(ExteriorColor.RED)){
   /*do something*/
}
```

Enumeration types, newly introduced in Java 1.5, are fantastic and effective when you need to define a property that can take on only a set of standard, predefined, values.

Question

Interfaces overcome the Java limitation of:
O a) many to many relationships
O b) single inheritance
O c) polymorphism
O d) inheriting from the Object class

Question

Fill in the blank: classes _____ interfaces, while interfaces _____ other interfaces.
O a) extend, extend
O b) extend, implement
O c) implement, implement
O d) implement, extend

Question

Which of the following can be defined in an interface?
☐ a) concrete methods
☐ b) abstract methods
☐ c) instance variables
☐ d) constants

Question

The most flexible argument to use as a method parameter, or the most pluggable property to declare as an instance variable, is:
O a) a concrete class
O b) an abstract class
O c) an interface
O d) a constant

Answer

Interfaces overcome the Java limitation of:
O a) many to many relationships O b) single inheritance O c) polymorphism O d) inheriting from the Object class
Java allows for only single inheritance. A class can only have a single parent class. However, a class can implement an unlimited number of interfaces, and implementing interfaces, like inheriting from a parent class, represents an ***'is-a'*** relationship. Another unique aspect of an interface is that an interface itself can extend another interface; yes, it uses the keyword ***extends***, which is the same keyword that is used for inheritance. So, while you can't have multiple class inheritance in Java, an interface can indeed inherit from multiple interfaces, making a form of multiple inheritance possible. It's crazy stuff, but it's true!

Answer

Fill in the blank: classes _____ interfaces, while interfaces _____ other interfaces.
O a) extend, extend O b) extend, implement O c) implement, implement O d) implement, extend
The keyword *implements* is used when a class indicates that it is going to code all of the abstract methods that are part of a given interface. On the other hand, interfaces themselves do not implement other interfaces, but instead, ***extend*** them, using the keyword extends.

Answer

Which of the following can be defined in an interface?
☐ a) concrete methods ☐ b) abstract methods ☐ c) instance variables ☐ d) constants
An interface cannot have any instance variables defined, or any method implementations. Instead, an interface simply defines methods that sub-types, implementing the interface, commit to coding. An interface can define static final variables, which is just a technical way of saying that you can define constants in an interface. Defining constants in an interface is legal and valid, but not overly common.

Answer

The most flexible argument to use as a method parameter, or the most pluggable property to declare as an instance variable, is:
O a) a concrete class O b) an abstract class O c) an interface O d) a constant
Always use the most flexible and pluggable component when defining instance variables and method arguments. The most flexible artifact in the entire Java programming language is the interface, so when asked for a flexible solution, the one that incorporates interfaces will always be the winner. Abstract classes come a close second, and then concrete classes come in last. Answer d), a constant, doesn't make any sense in this scenario. One of the terms you'll hear bandied about is ***program to an interface.*** This philosophy embodies the idea that when the option is there, you should always use the most general type available, which is typically an interface.

Chapter 11
Arrays and Multiplicities

Implementing Larger Multiplicities

So far, our Shapes example has described a variety of is-a relationships, and for the Line class, a has-a association relationship with the Point class, insomuch as the Line class has two Points. However, in typical enterprise applications, a one to many, zero to many, or *n* to many relationship is very common. For example, a class can have many students, and an exam can have many questions, and in any given scenario, a multiplicity may not have a predictable limit. For example, one class might have five students, while another class might have five hundred students. How can we define, within our Java code, a multiplicity, which at development time, has an unknown upper limit? Well, there are a variety of ways, with perhaps the most simplest, not to mention the way it is used on the SCJA exam, being to use an array.

For example, let's say we re-architected our Shapes solution to have an abstract class called SimplePolygon, that implemented the IShape interface, and simply defined the various Points where the sides, or edges, of a Polygon would meet. By it's definition, a polygon is a any closed shape with three sides or more, which includes our Triangle, Square, Circle, Rectangle and so on. So, a polygon would need to define at least three points, although it may potentially define many points, depending upon how many sides the polygon of interest has. So, the relationship between the SimplePolygon class and the Point class would be three to many.

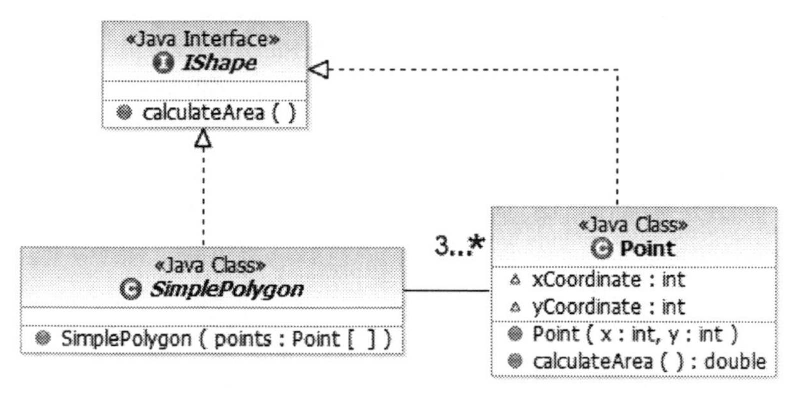

Object Association Through an Array

To express the idea that a SimplePolygon can potentially have many points, an array of Point objects is declared as a property, or instance variable, of the SimplePolygon class. The size of the array is not specified when the property is declared, allowing for the number of Point objects contained by the array to change depending upon the type of SimplePolygon being created.

```
public abstract class SimplePolygon implements IShape{

  Point[] point;

  public SimplePolygon(Point[] points){   }

}
```

Working with Arrays

Arrays are a fundamental component of just about any programming language. In fact, they are so fundamental, programmers often forget that arrays are even objects, assuming that they are simply a fundamental programming construct. But make no mistake about it: arrays are objects in Java.

So, what is an array? Well, an array is a Java component that contains a collection, or assortment, of other types. From the sun tutorials:

"An array is a container object that holds a fixed number of values of a single type. The length of an array is established when the array is created. After creation, its length is fixed. Each item in an array is called an element, and each element is accessed by its numerical index."

http://java.sun.com/docs/books/tutorial/java/nutsandbolts/arrays.html

Declaring, Initializing and Referencing Arrays

Arrays are essentially a collection of similar types. Arrays can be made up a bunch of primitive types, a bunch of object types, and even a bunch of interfaces. Arrays are declared by using the standard type and variable name styntax, with the difference being the presence of square brackets, either next to the type declaration or the variable name:

```
int[] days;
int days [];

String names[];
String[] names;
```

Declaring an array does not determine a size, or allocate any actual memory for storing information. Instead, the size of an array is determined, and memory set aside for the data the array contains, when the array is initialized.

```
String[] name; /*declaration of an array of Strings named name*/

name = new String[5];          /* array is given a size of 5 */
```

Once an array has been declared and its size initialized, individual elements can be referenced. It should be noted, however, that arrays are zero based, so an array with five elements would have indexes of 0,1,2,3 and 4. Referencing index 5 or greater on an array with a size of 5 will end up triggering an IndexOutOfBoundsException, which is a very annoying runtime exception to have to deal with.

```
name[0] = "Ridley";
name[3] = "Bent";

System.out.println(name[0]);/* will print out Ridley */
System.out.println(name[5]);/*IndexOutOfBoundsException!!!*/
```

Back to the SimplePolygon

So, the idea of the abstract class SimplePolygon is that someone might want to define a given shape by simply passing in the various points at which the edges of a shape intersect. So, perhaps a class named Pentagon might subclass SimplyPolygon, with a constructor that takes an array of Point objects as an argument:

```
/*create an array of five Points */
Point[] pentagonPoints = new Point[5];

/*initialize all five elements of the array of Points */
pentagonPoints[0] = new Point(-1, 0);
pentagonPoints[1] = new Point( 1, 0);
pentagonPoints[2] = new Point(-3, 2);
pentagonPoints[3] = new Point( 3, 2);
pentagonPoints[4] = new Point( 0, 5);

/*create a Pentagon object based on the array of five Points*/
Pentagon p = new Pentagon(pentagonPoints);

/* Note: the Pentagon class was never coded. This example simply
demonstrates how a call to the constructor of the hypothetical
Pentagon class might look.*/
```

The length of an Array

In many instances, it is necessary to discover the number of elements contained within an array, and perhaps, loop through each of those elements. To help facilitate this, you can determine the size of an array by referencing the length property:

```
Point[] chiliagonPoints = new Point[100];
System.out.println(chiliagonPoints.length);
/* prints out 100 */
```

One point of confusion is the difference between the length property of an array, and the length() method of the String class. To find the size of an array, you use the length property, which does not have round braces following the word length. Don't confuse this with the length() method of the String class, which tells you how many characters a given String contains.

Enforcing Multiplicities

It was stated that a SimplePolygon had to have at least three valid Points; how could we enforce this multiplicity rule in our SimplePolygon class?

Well, the constructor of the SimplePolygon class takes an array of Point objects as its argument. Using the length property of the array, we can easily loop through each element in the array of points, and check to ensure that at least three points in the array are not null. If the array of Point objects passed into the constructor of the SimplePolygon class does not have at least three, non-null Point objects, then we can terminate execution using System.exit(0). It would look something like this:

```
public abstract class SimplePolygon implements IShape{

  Point[] point;

  public SimplePolygon(Point[] points){

    /* loop through all array elements */
    for (int i = 0; i<points.length; i++ ) {
    /* count the number of non-null array elements */
      int nonNullCount = 0;

      /* check to see if the element is not null */
      if (points[i]!= null) {
        nonNullCount++ ;
      }
  }

  /* if there are not at least three non-null Point objects
in the array, terminate execution. */

  if (nonNullCount < 3) {
    System.exit(0);
    //or throw new Exception();
  }

}
```

Question

What is the best way to determing the number of elements contained in an array?

- O a) call the length() method on the array
- O b) call the length property of the array
- O c) call the size() method on the array
- O d) call the size property of the array

Question

Given the following declaration and initialization of an array:

```
int[] x = int[10];
```

How would you reference the fifth element in the array?

- O a) x[5]
- O b) x[4]
- O c) x(5)
- O d) x(4)

Question

What happens when you reference the fifth element in a four element array?

- O a) the array automatically expands in size to accomodate the newly referenced element
- O b) a null object is returned to the calling program
- O c) a NullPointerException is thrown
- O d) an ArrayIndexOutOfBoundsException is thrown

Answer

What is the best way to determing the number of elements contained in an array?
O a) call the length() method on the array O b) call the length property of the array O c) call the size() method on the array O d) call the size property of the array
Option b) is correct. Properties of well encapsulated objects are ***supposed*** to be accessed through public methods, but the array seems to break that rule by allowing direct access to the length property. I believe this has something to do with making Java close in syntax to C and C++, but I can't be sure. What I am sure of is that people often confuse the length() method of the String class with the length property of an array, much to the detriment of their certification score. The length of an array is a property. Make sure you remember that. Many of the dynamic collection classes, which unlike an array, can dynamically expand and contract when new elements are added or removed, can report the number of elements they contain using the size() method call. Don't confuse the size method of classes such a the java.util.Vector with the length property of an array. Again, the number of elements in an array is accessed through the property named ***length***.

Answer

Given the following declaration and initialization of an array: int[] x = int[10]; How would you reference the fifth element in the array?
O a) x[5] O b) x[4] O c) x(5) O d) x(4)
Option b) is correct. Arrays use zero based counting, so to access the fifth element in an array named x, you would request x[4]. Options c) and d) use an incorrect syntax.

Answer

What happens when you reference the fifth element in a four element array?
O a) the array automatically expands in size to accomodate the newly referenced element O b) a null object is returned to the calling program O c) a NullPointerException is thrown O d) an ArrayIndexOutOfBoundsException is thrown
Option d) is correct. When you try to access an element of an array that is beyond the array's size, you are unpleasantly delivered an ArrayIndexOutOfBoundsException. This is known as an unchecked exception, because the Java compiler does not force you to look for it in your code. Be careful when accessing arrays to ensure you don't go beyond the limit of the array.

Chapter 12
Instance Methods

Objects are interesting because of two things: one, they have properties, and two, they have methods.

The methods an object has represents the type of things an objects can ***do***, which typically involves providing access to, or manipulating, the properties an object maintains. Deep down, properties simply represent the boring old state of an object. Methods are responsible for giving an object its interesting behavior.

The Structure of the Java Method

Methods in Java always follow the same, basic structure:

- access modifier (public, private, protected or <default>)
- a single return type (a type, a class or primitive)
- method name (any valid Java name)
- arguments (types, classes or primitives)

You can optionally add on java.lang.Exceptions at the end of a method, or even add some kewl keywords like final or abstract in along with the access modifier, but for the most part, every method will have an access modifier, return type, method name and argument list. This combination of defining elements is known as the ***method signature.***

Accessors and Mutators

The two most common methods you'll see inside of a Java class are the accessor and mutator methods, also known as setters and getters.

```
/*an example of a setter, aka mutator, method*/

public void setName(String n){
  this.name = n;
}
```

For this *setter*, a String, called n, is passed into the method, with the intention of updating the value of the instance variable *name*. The setter is simply a worker method that doesn't return any value to the calling program. The return type of a setter is always void.

Any value passed into a method is said to have visibility for the entire method. In the case of the setter, the variable n would be described as having ***method scope***.

```
/*an example of a getter, aka accessor, method*/

public String getName(){
  return this.name;
}
```

The above method is a *getter*. A getter method has an empty argument list, and has no data passed into the method. However, the method does *return* a value, specifically in this case, a String representing the name.

Instance Methods and UML

In UML, instance methods are defined by showing the name of the method, followed by the method signature, a colon, and then the return type. The UML class diagram for the Customer class assumes setter and getter methods will be added to the Customer class. You should note that the syntax for UML is not proper Java syntax. Trying to compile getAge():int in a Java program will make the Java compiler Gods very, very angry.

It should also be noted that setter and getter methods are often left off of a UML diagram for a class, especially one that has many properties, as the setters and getters can usually be assumed, and having loads of setter and getter methods on a diagram can be superfluous, taking away from information that is more pertinent to the implementation of the class.

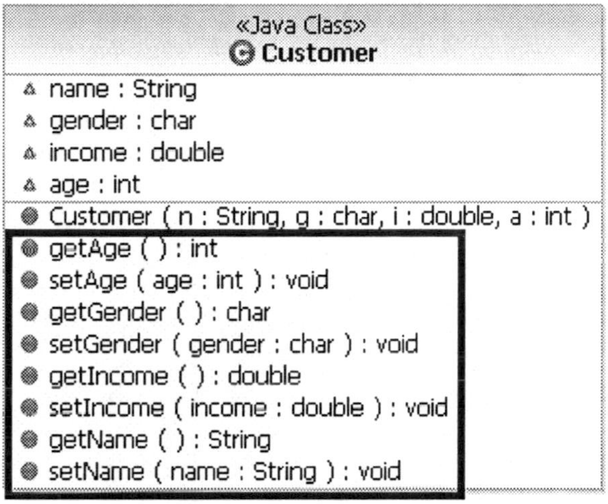

```
«Java Class»
Customer
name : String
gender : char
income : double
age : int
Customer ( n : String, g : char, i : double, a : int )
getAge ( ) : int
setAge ( age : int ) : void
getGender ( ) : char
setGender ( gender : char ) : void
getIncome ( ) : double
setIncome ( income : double ) : void
getName ( ) : String
setName ( name : String ) : void
```

Overloading Methods

The great thing about Java is the fact that a Java class can have any number of methods, those methods can take any number of parameters, and the methods themselves can return any type of object. In fact, in Java, you can have any number of methods with the same name, as long as all of those commonly named methods have a different argument list. Having multiple methods with the same name, but different argument lists, is known as ***method overloading.***

Creative Return Types

One thing to note about Java methods is that only one thing, object or primitive type, can be designated as the return type.

Sometimes you will have a method that takes something as an argument, and then needs to return two values. Perhaps a method takes a zing as a parameter, and needs to return a zong and a zup to the calling program. How could you do that in Java if you can only return one thing from a method?

Well, the answer is to create objects! If you have a method that returns a zong and a zup, you should first check to see if there already exists an object that contains a zong and a zup, and return that object. Alternatively, you could create a new object that encapsulates information about a zong and a zup, perhaps called ZupZong, and return that to the calling program.

Remember, Java is an object oriented programming language. If there are logically related properties, working with those logically related properties is done most efficiently when those properties are congregated into a single, easy to use, Java object.

Methods and Variable Scope

There are alot of different types of scopes you'll hear people talking about when it comes to Java. You'll hear about *local scope, method scope, block scope* and *class scope.* Well, I'm here to make it all very easy for you – there's really only one type of scope in Java, and that's block scope.

A block of code is all of the code placed in between a set of squiggly brackets, {...}, also affectionately known as chicken lips. A variable declared within an open and closed chicken lip has scope for that block, and all sub-blocks within that block. That's how scope works in Java.

Now the reason that people confuse things so much is because there are a couple of fairly special *blocks* in Java. And like every rule in Java, there are exceptions, but that's to be expected. After all, rules are simply coat hangers for exceptions, aren't they?

As you've probably noticed, every class, following its class definition of course, starts with an open brace, and ends with a closed brace. That's the first *special block* in any piece of Java code.

```
public class ScopeCreep extends Object
{

/*anything declared in here is visible to all methods
(although static methods are an exception)*/

}
```

Java and the Different Types of Block Scope

Any instance or static variables declared within ***class defining blocks,*** but not inside any method, is visible in every single instance method of the class. A variable declared at the class level would have scope for every instance method of the class, so I guess you could say that it has instance level, or class block, scope.

So, what is the next type of block scope we can talk about? Well, what does the class block contain? It contains methods, and every method starts and ends with an open and closed squiggly brace. So, any variable declared within a method's opening and closing braces, but not inside any sub block, such as an if statement block or a block associated with a while loop, is visible for the entire method. So, if a variable is declared within a method, but not inside any sub-block of the method, you could say that the variable has ***method scope.***

Finally, there is just plain old ***block scope***, which occurs when a set of squiggly braces appear within a method block, such as the opening and closing braces of a for loop, or an if statement. Any variable declared within a block has scope for that block, and any sub-blocks of the block in which it was declared. This is the essence of block scope.

Going Out of Scope: Taking Out the Garbage

So, why is the scope of a variable so important? Well, there are a couple of reasons.

First of all, when a variable goes out of scope, it becomes available for garbage collection. Every variable we create, be it an int, float, double or String, takes up room in memory, and the more memory the JVM has to manage, the slower the JVM will become. When a variable goes out of scope, it becomes available for garbage collection, which will remove the variable from memory, and that's a good thing.

The other reason variable scope is so important is due to potential variable naming conflicts. For example, you could never have two variables with the same name in the same block. You can't declare a variable named x twice in a common block of code.

However, you can use the same variable over and over again in different places of your code, so long as the variable has gone out of scope. That's why you can use the variable name i for just about every loop in a Java class – when declared in a loop, the variable i is local to the loop block, and that block only. Once the loop has finished all of its iterations, the variable i goes out of scope, is garbage collected, and the name i can be used again by your application code.

Scope is important, and it is important to recognize when a variable is in scope, or when it is out of scope; but no matter what anyone tells you, all scope issues boil down to block scope, which means focusing on the block of code in which a variable has been declared.

Question

You need to code a method that takes two primitive type doubles, calculates a value, and returns an int. What would the method signature look like?

- O a) public int calculate(double a, double b)
- O b) public int x calculate(double, double)
- O c) public (double a double b) calculate (int)
- O d) public int x calculate (double a, double b)

Question

Two methods with the same name in the same class:

- ☐ a) is not allowed in Java
- ☐ b) is not allowed in some languages, but is allowed in Java
- ☐ c) is known as method overloading
- ☐ d) is known as method overriding

Question

Instance methods:

- ☐ a) provide the behavior of an object
- ☐ b) provide the properties of an object
- ☐ c) can manipulate instance variables
- ☐ d) can manipulate variables passed in as parameters

Question

Instance variables:

- ☐ a) have scope within all instance methods of a class
- ☐ b) are not visible in static methods, unless passed in as arguments
- ☐ c) are in scope so long as the instance they are associated with is in scope
- ☐ d) become available for garbage collection when the object they are associated with is no longer in scope

Answer

You need to code a method that takes two primitive type doubles, calculates a value, and returns an int. What would the method signature look like?

- O a) public int calculate(double a, double b)
- O b) public int x calculate(double, double)
- O c) public (double a double b) calculate (int)
- O d) public int x calculate (double a, double b)

Instance methods always take the same form: access modifier, followed by a return type, followed by the method name and arguments.

public int calculate(double a, double b) indicates that this method is called calculate, take two arguments, namely a double to be named a, and a double named b, and when completed, will return to the calling program a value in the form of an int.

Answer

Two methods with the same name in the same class:

- ☐ a) is not allowed in Java
- ☐ b) is not allowed in some languages, but is allowed in Java
- ☐ c) is known as method overloading
- ☐ d) is known as method overriding

Quite often a class will provide a behavior that can be tweaked slightly if extra information is provided. If this is the case, Java allows you to create multiple methods with the same name in a class, so long as each method takes a different set of arguments. This is known as method overloading.

The String class overloads quite a few methods, one of which is indexOf, which can take a String as an argument, or a String and an int. With just a String provided, the indexOf method returns the index at which the String is first encountered. Alternatively, you can provide an int as well, and the search for a matching string will start at the index of the int specified.

Method overloading is a common practice in Java programming.

Answer

Instance methods:
☐ a) provide the behavior of an object ☐ b) provide the properties of an object ☐ c) can manipulate instance variables ☐ d) can manipulate variables passed in as parameters
Answers a) c) and d) are correct. Methods are said to give classes their behavior, which to a large extent, involves manipulating instance variables in a meaningful way. Of course, instance methods not only manipulate instance variables of the class, but they can also work with any types or primitives that are passed into the method as parameters.

Answer

Instance variables:
☐ a) have scope within all instance methods of a class ☐ b) are not visible in static methods, unless passed in as arguments ☐ c) are in scope so long as the instance they are associated with is in scope ☐ d) become available for garbage collection when the object they are associated with is no longer in scope
This is a bit of a trick question, as all four answers are correct. Instance variables are visible in all instance methods of a class, with static methods, which are class methods, as opposed to being instance methods, being the exceptional method where instance variables are not visible unless explicitly passed in as arguments. Instance variables are in scope so long as the instance they are associated with is in scope. When an object goes out of scope, the garbage collector comes around and takes out all of the instance variable trash that is no longer referenced by an in-scope object.

Chapter 13 Exposing Your Privates

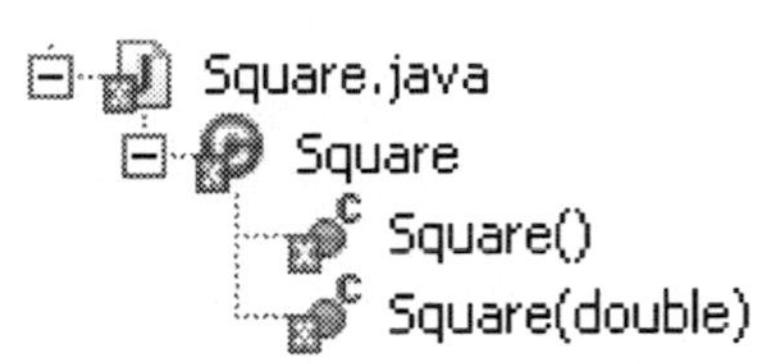

Look at what I've done to my Square!!! Everything is broken, and none of my code works! Why, oh Java Gods, why???

Well, I'll tell you what I did. I put the ***private*** access modifier on the height and width properties defined in the Rectangle class, and because of the sloppy and lazy manner in which I've been accessing my variables, all of my sloppy and lazy code in the Square class doesn't work anymore. Serves me right!

```
public class Rectangle implements IShape {

/*instance variables should be declared as private*/

   private double height;
   private double width;

/*Notice how making these properties private in the
parent class, Rectangle, makes them no longer
accessible in even the subclass, Square.*/
   ✂✂✂
   ...
   ✂✂✂
}
```

Data Encapsulation in Java

When developing applications, we like our Java objects to ***encapsulate*** and ***protect*** their data. Data is important, and we must protect it. When a Java class declares an instance variable, nobody should be able to directly access that variable using standard dot notation, with the exception of instances of that particular class itself.

The idea of protecting data, in the form of instance variables, by making them private, is known as ***data encapsulation***. When we mark a variable as being private, no other class, regardless of whether that other class is on the same class hierarchy or not, can directly access that private variable. Nobody can directly access a private variable, and nobody, with the exception of the class itself, can directly modify a private variable. When a variable is made private, it is simply no longer exposed. As we like to say, we don't expose our privates in Java.

As a general rule, that applies to life, not just Java, it isn't polite to expose your privates.

As we can see from the number of errors in my code, encapsulation certainly works in Java, but for our Rectangle and Square example, it has almost worked too well: a rectangle can't even see its inherited height and width properties! What can we do?

Accessors and Mutators (Setters and Getters)

Well, in Java, we encapsulate instance variables by marking them with the **private** keyword, and if we so chose, we can expose those variables by coding *setters* and *getters* for them, or as they're referred to in more polite circles, accessors and mutators.

Accessors and mutators always take the same form:

```
public *returnType* get*PropertyName*(){
  return propertyName;
}
public void set*PropertyName*( *type* propertyName){
  this.propertyName = propertyName;
}
```

Once setters and getters are coded, other instances or objects that need to access the private property can gain access through the getter. Any instances that want to update the property can do it through the setter. Mitigating access through setters and getters gives the class control over who and how private data is accessed and manipulated.

For our Rectangle class, after making the height and width properties private, we need to provide the corresponding setters and getters.

```
✂✂✂
public double getHeight() {
  return height;
}
public void setHeight(double height) {
  this.height = height;
}
public double getWidth() {
  return width;
}
public void setWidth(double width) {
  this.width = width;
}
✂✂✂
```

Using Setters and Getters

Once our setters and getters have been added, we should eliminate all direct references to the instance variables, and instead, use the setter and getter methods. Even within the Rectangle class, where directly accessing instance variable data is technically allowed, we should still access properties by using setters and getters.

You should always access instance variables through setters and getters. This ensures a great level of control over access and changes to instance level properties. If everyone updates a property through a setter, and if an upper limit or lower limit ever needs to be set for that property, the setter could be changed, and the behavior would be updated and ensured universally for all objects that access that property through the adjusted mutator, including places within the class itself.

Even classes should access their own properties through their own setters and getters. Always using setters and getters is an important habit to adopt.

Fixing the Square Class

Just because an instance variable is made private doesn't mean that property isn't inherited by subclasses. Private instance variables are inherited just as easily as public instance variables; but while the properties are inherited, they are not *visible* to the subclass. If the subclass wants to call upon the inherited, private instance variables, it must go through the inherited, public setters and getters. Using the public setters and getters of the Rectangle class is how the Square class will be able to set its own height and width properties.

```
public class Square extends Rectangle {

  public Square() {
    this.setHeight(0);
    this.setWidth(0);
  }
  public Square(double h) {
    this.setHeight(h);
    this.setWidth(h);
  }
}
```

Data Encapsulation and UML

For the associates exam, you need to know the difference between a private and public instance variable or method, and you need to know how to distinguish between public and private methods on a class diagram. This process is pretty easy: public methods have a plus sign next to them (+), and private methods have a minus sign (-) next to them.

For the Rectangle class, the height and width properties are private, and the methods, including the constructors, accessors and mutators, and the calculateArea() method, are all public, as is demonstrated in the UML diagram.

```
«Java Class»
Rectangle
— height : double
— width : double
+ Rectangle ( )
+ Rectangle ( h : double, w : double )
+ calculateArea ( ) : double
+ getHeight ( ) : double
+ setHeight ( height : double ) : void
+ getWidth ( ) : double
+ setWidth ( width : double ) : void
```

The JavaBean Specification

If you've been working in a Java based environment, you've probably heard plenty of talk about JavaBeans. The question often arises, *"what the heck is a JavaBean?"*

Defining a JavaBean is actually a pretty daunting task. Technically, there is a whole JavaBean specification that describes what a JavaBean is, and how it is supposed to be used. That specification is pretty huge, and I doubt reading it would make defining a JavaBean any easier.

Technically, a JavaBean is a reusable component, written in Java, *that can be manipulated in an application builder tool.*

Java provides a cross platform runtime environment. It was thought, many years ago, that Java should also be a cross-platform development language, insomuch as people using J++, JBuilder, VisualAge for Java or Rational Application Developer should be able to develop Java code and swap that code back and forth, and the different development tools wouldn't have any problems understanding how to manipulate the code. To make this possible, a specification standardized how JavaBeans should be created, and described a number of mechanisms that would allow visual development tools to manipulate JavaBeans most effectively.

Naming Conventions and Default Constructors

The thing is, nowadays, the term JavaBean has more to do with how we develop reusable components, as opposed to how development tools consume our code. The JavaBean specification has a number of important rules with regards to developing Java code, such as encapsulating data by making instance variables private, and only making them readable or writable by exposing private instance variables through public setters and getters. Naming conventions are an important part of the JavaBean specification, as is the fact that every JavaBean should define a default constructor, although many developers would think of their Java components as JavaBeans, even if a default constructor was left out of the mix.

Serializable: The Breakfast Interface

Another interesting aspect of a JavaBean, which is just generally a best practice for all reusable component development, is the requirement that all JavaBeans implement the java.io.Serializable interface. All JavaBeans must be Serializable: you must be able to pour milk over them and have them for breakfast.

A JavaBean is Serializable when it implements the java.io.Serializable interface. However, the crazy thing about the Serializable interface is the fact that it doesn't define any methods which implementing classes must implement, which after all, is the whole point of an interface! Because it doesn't define any methods to implement, java.io.Serializable is known as a marker interface. By implementing the java.io.Serializable interface, you are marking your JavaBean as being Serializable, and you are subsequently making a very, very important commitment to the Java Virtual Machine.

When you define a class as being Serializable, you are telling the JVM that all of the instance variables that make up the class are of the basic Java data types, and if you do have a more complex object as an instance variable in your class, then that class must be able to be broken down into the eight basic Java data types as well. Basically, when you implement the java.io.Serializable interface, you are telling the JVM that if you flatten your Java class out like a pancake, all you would see are basic, Java, primitive types.

Now why is this so important? Why is it so important for all JavaBeans to be Serializable? Well, it has to do with storing the state of a JavaBean, or delivering the state of a JavaBean across a network.

The JVM is very smart when it comes to the basic, Java, primitive types. A JVM knows how to store ints and double data types to the hard drive, and it knows how to send floats and chars across a network connection. If your JavaBeans are all Serializable, and then, perhaps your application gets deployed to a clustered, workload managed environment, or, if the JVM goes to sleep for a while, and wants to temporarily store the state of your JavaBean on the hard drive, then if your JavaBeans are Serializable, then the JVM will know exactly how to passivate or cluster your data.

Marker Interfaces and Annotations (Advanced Stuff!)

One thing to note about marker interfaces is the fact that they are going out of fashion. Java 5 introduces a new concept, called annotations, that allow you to document information about a class, like the fact that it is Serializable, outside of the Java code. Annotations are not covered on the SCJA exam, and it will be a bit of time before you start seeing annotations being used heavily, or for that matter, correctly, in Java applications. But it's worth mentioning that, as earlier Java implementations get phased out, annotations will slowly get phased in.

```
/* Using an interface to mark a class as Serializable*/

public class OldMarker implements Serializable
{...}

/* Using an annotation to mark a class as Serializable*/

@Serializable
public class NewMarker {...}
```

Defining a JavaBean

So, what is a JavaBean? Well, technically, a JavaBean is a reusable component, written in Java, that can be edited in a visual builder tool, and complies to the rigorous standards set out in the JavaBean specification.

From a more everyday definition, a JavaBean is a reusable component, written in Java, that should comply to the various Java naming conventions, encapsulate data by making instance variables private, and allowing access only through public setters and getters. And unless you have extremely compelling reasons to do otherwise, a

JavaBean should have a default constructor, and should implement the java.io.Serializable interface.

Of course, there are no Java cops forcing you to code this way, but then again, fear of prosecution should never be the most compelling reason to do the right thing. Writing code that conforms to the JavaBeans specification is definitely the right thing to do.

Question

Given a property called ageLimit, what would be the correctly named accessor for this property?

- O a) public void ageLimit()
- O b) public int getAgeLimit()
- O c) public int getAgelimit()
- O d) public int getAgelimit(int age)

Question

Private variables:

- ☐ a) are read only if only an accessor is provided
- ☐ b) are write only if only a mutator is provided
- ☐ c) cannot be directly accessed by parent classes
- ☐ d) cannot be directly accessed by subclasses

Question

Internal methods of a class should:

- ☐ a) be marked as private, so only the class can access them
- ☐ b) be marked as private, so external classes cannot see them
- ☐ c) have instance properties passed as arguments to the method
- ☐ d) be able to access all instance methods of the class

Question

Which symbol denotes a public method or variable?

- O a) #
- O b) *
- O c) -
- O d) +

Answer

Given an int property called agelimit, what would be the correctly named accessor for this property?
○ a) public void ageLimit() ○ b) public int getAgeLimit() ○ c) public int getAgelimit() ○ d) public int getAgelimit(int age)
With a int property named ageLimit, the getter will return an int, and be called getAgeLimit(). Notice that the first letter of the property name is made upper case in the method name, although it is lower cased in the property name. The rule with methods is that they always start with a lower case letter, and each new word in the name is given an upper casing. Also, you should note that getters are typically public, they do not take any arguments, and define a return type that is consistent with the variable they are returning to the calling program, which in this case, is an int ***(an int property called ageLimit).***

Answer

Private variables:
☐ a) are read only if only an accessor is provided ☐ b) are write only if only a mutator is provided ☐ c) cannot be directly accessed by parent classes ☐ d) cannot be directly accessed by subclasses
This is sort of a trick question, because all four options are correct. A private variable can only be directly accessed from within the class in which it is defined. A subclass cannot directly access a private variable defined in a parent class, and a parent class certainly can't access private variables defined in a sibling class. If an instance variable is marked as private, and only has a getter method associated with it, the property is referred to as being read-only. If only a setter is made available to a private property, the property is said to be write-only. If both setters and getters are provided, the instance variable is said to be readable and writable.

Answer

Internal methods of a class should:
☐ a) be marked as private, so only the class can access them ☐ b) be marked as private, so external classes cannot see them ☐ c) have instance properties passed as arguments to the method ☐ d) be able to access all instance methods of the class
Answers a) b) and d) are correct. Answer c) is incorrect because internal methods of a class can access all instance variables of that class. That's just a rule of instance variable scope in Java. However, the other three options are correct. Internal methods, that have no real meaning or application to external programs, should be marked as being private. Private methods can be invoked ad nauseum from within the class, but like private variables, external classes and instances can't see them.

Answer

Which symbol denotes a public method or variable?
○ a) # ○ b) * ○ c) - ○ d) +
The two symbols you need to know for the associates exam are the plus and minus signs. The plus sign denotes a public method, while the minus sign denotes a private method. Instance variables should be marked as private (-) and setters and getters are generally marked as being public (+).

Chapter 14 Polymorphism

Polymorphism: a big word that I think means 'many-forms'; it is a combination of the two Greek words poly (many) and morph (forms).

I've seen some really awful definitions of polymorphism in my time, most of which, for some reason or another, deal with printing data to a printer or something. Polymorphism is a fairly simple concept. I'm not sure why so many people see the need to complicate it with print spoolers?

Taking it to the Bank

Let's use a little example. Imagine you just started a new job, and you take your first paycheck to the bank. Because it's a big check, you want a cute, young, brunette teller to cash it for you. That way, all the girls working at the bank will know what a big shot you are. Only, instead of being impressed with your big check, the teller informs you that there's going to be a hold on your check, and you won't be able to take any money out because your current balance is too low. So, what would you do? You would do what any normal human being would do. You'd pull out a gun and you'd rob the bank.

Now, as you exit the bank with a boatload of money in your pockets, you quickly realize that running away on foot simply isn't going to cut it. You're going to need a getaway vehicle. So, what type of getaway vehicle are you going to choose? Well, you could steal a kid's bike and cycle away; That'd work, and it'd be faster than running on foot. Still, you'd probably prefer something faster than a bike. You could jump on the bus? Or you could jump a senior citizen as they step out of their Cadillac, steal their keys, and make a stylish getaway in a pimpin' white Caddy.

The point is, when you exit the bank, the getaway vehicle you choose can take on many different forms, and each form has its own set of benefits and drawbacks. A bike, car, bus, motorcycle and helicopter all make possible choices for escaping from the scene of your crime. All of those options provide the ability to move you or help you travel to your new destination, and each of these getaway vehicles implements the getaway *behavior* in its own unique way.

A getaway vehicle can take on many different forms, and the benefits and drawbacks of each option depends on how that option implements the behavior of taking you away from the scene of the crime.

From the standpoint of polymorphism, cars, trucks, bikes and feet all share the common behavior of being able to move you. If you need to get away, all of those methods of getting away will work. Many different types of objects can be used to help you achieve your goals. The generic idea of a 'getaway vehicle' is a very, very polymorphic concept.

Polymorphism in Java

Polymorphism is everywhere in Java. The use of inheritance and abstraction creates innumerable ***'is-a'*** types of relationships. Essentially, polymorphism is a big word that embraces the idea that ***'any time I need an object, any type or sub-type of that object will do.'*** As long as the object I receive implements the behavior I'm interested in, then that object is as good a choice as any.

GUI Components and Polymorphism

Applets are little Java programs that run inside of a web page. They can display all sorts of different components, from textfields, to buttons to scrollable lists.

In Java, textfields, buttons and lists all inherit from a common ancestor, the ancestor class being appropriately named java.awt.Component. Since any of these components can be added to the viewable area of an applet, the applet class has a special method called add, that takes an instance of a java.awt.Component as a parameter. You can pass any component you want to the add method, just so long as what you pass does indeed inherit from the class java.awt.Component. A Component is an abstract idea, and true instances of a component can take many different forms. An applet that displays a textfield, a checkbox and button is a perfect example of polymorphism.

The Unidirectional Nature of Polymorphism

Polymorphism works in one direction and one direction only. Polymorphism is unidirectional, not bi-directional *(not that there's anything wrong with that.)*

For example, say it's your birthday, and you want your parents to buy you a German Engineered sports car. Then your birthday comes, and all of a sudden, sitting in the driveway, is a rusty old winter beater that looks like it was towed out of Al Bundy's garage. You wanted a very specific, German Engineered sports car, but what you got was a very generic type of car that does little more than run. You wanted a BMW or a Mercedes, but instead, you got something much more generic.

On the other hand, if you've just pulled a robbery, and you need a car, any car, to help you get away, and all of a sudden you see a rusty old Dodge with the doors unlocked, the key in the ignition, and the engine running, you're going to be more than happy to jack that car and make a speedy getaway. In this case, you need something generic, a getaway vehicle, and a specific instance of a getaway vehicle, the rusty old Dodge, will more than suffice. Polymorphism is unidirectional. With polymorphism, you ask for something very general and generic, and you are happy when you get any object that satisfies your generic description.

Polymorphism and Coding to an Interface

When developing code, it's important to make your code as flexible as possible. One way to make your code incredibly flexible and pluggable is to define instance variables and method parameters using the least specific, or most general, type of object you could imagine.

If you define method parameters that take a very general interface or abstract class as an argument, other developers have the flexibility to pass into your method any class that functionally implements the requirements of that interface or abstract class.

The same thing goes for instance variables as well. Defining instance variables at a very general level, and then allowing those instance variables to be initialized with more specific, concrete objects at runtime, makes your code, and your applications, much more flexible.

When defining instance variables, or figuring out what types of objects to pass as arguments to a method, always choose the most generic type you can, so long as that generic object provides the functionality your application requires.

Polymorphism Questions

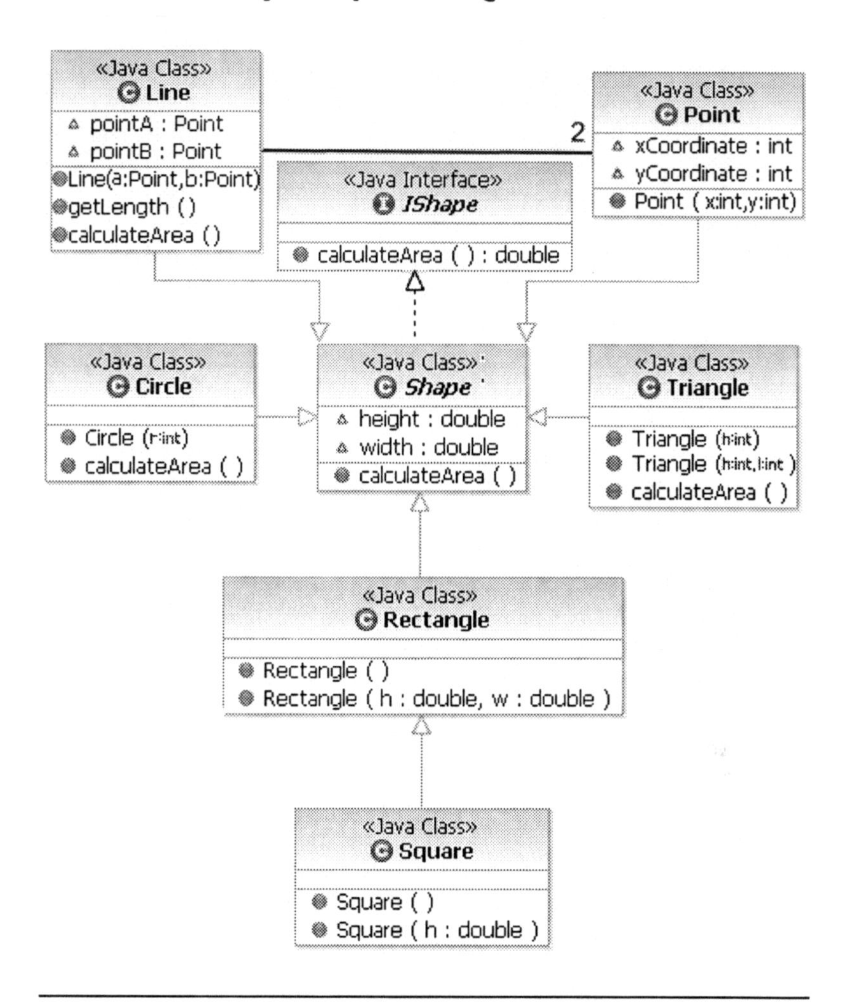

The questions in this section will be based upon the above diagram, assuming that all calculateArea methods have been coded in a manner that would make my grade 8 geometry teacher happy.

*Note that in this example, Shape is an abstract class, not an interface, and the calculateArea method in the Shape class is coded as return height*width;*

For the following questions, assume any constructors used are implemented properly, even if they do not appear on the diagram, or, appear really, really, really small (sorry about that - Cameron).

Question

Which of the following are valid lines of code, according to the given class diagram?

- ☐ a) Square s1 = new Square( );
- ☐ b) Rectangle r1 = new Rectangle( ) ;
- ☐ c) Rectangle r2d2 = new Square(5);
- ☐ d) Square estew = new Rectangle(4,4);

Question

Which of the following lines of code are valid?

- ☐ a) IShape shape = new IShape();
- ☐ b) Shape abstractShape = new Shape();
- ☐ c) Shape sq = new Square(10);
- ☐ d) IShape rect = new Rectangle(4,5);

Question

A method needs to be coded that evaluates whether the area of a Square and a Rectangle are the same. A boolean value is returned, depending upon whether the evaluation is true or not. What would be the most appropriate method signature for this method?

- O a) public boolean compare(Rectangle rect, Square sq) { }
- O b) public boolean compare(Rectangle aRect, Rectangle eRect) { }
- O c) public boolean compare(Shape s1, Shape s2) { }
- O d) public boolean compare(IShape s1, IShape s2) { }

Question

Assuming that a Triangle codes the calculate area method correctly as:

return(.5)*height*width;

and the calculateArea method is defined in the abstract class as:

return height* width;

what would be the output of the following code:

```
Shape shapeUp = new Triangle(10,10);
System.out.println(shapeUp.calculateArea());
```

- O a) 100
- O b) 50
- O c) 10
- O d) 0

Question

Which of the following are valid lines of code, given the following:
/*assume all constructors used in the example exist, and are implemented correctly*/

```
Shape shape = new Rectangle(4,4);
IShape tri = new Triangle(5,3);
Square square = new Square(5);
Rectangle rect = new Rectangle(3,5);
Line line = new Line (new Point(0,0), new Point(1,1));
```

- ☐ a) shape = tri;
- ☐ b) tri = shape;
- ☐ c) rect = square;
- ☐ d) square = rect;

Answer

Which of the following are valid lines of code, according to the given class diagram?
☐ a) Square s1 = new Square( ); ☐ b) Rectangle r1 = new Rectangle( ) ; ☐ c) Rectangle r2d2 = new Square(5); ☐ d) Square estew = new Rectangle(4,4);
Answers a) b) and c) are all valid.

Look at what the left hand side of the assignment is saying. When you see the code Sqaure s1, what is being said is that **we need a Square**. When someone provides a new Square(), everything is good.

Option b) needs Rectangle r1, so a new Rectangle() is provided, so everyone is happy.

Option c) is a little more confusing, but if you think about it, it makes sense. If we need a Rectangle r2d2, and someone writes code that says new Square(5); will we be happy? We wanted a Rectangle and we got a Square? Is a Square a special type of rectangle? Of course it is. If you need a car, and someone gives you the keys to a BMW, you're not going to complain, are you?

This is polymorphism in action. A Rectangle can take many forms, and one form of a Rectangle is a Square. If we need a Rectangle, and we are provided a special type of Rectangle called a Square, then life is good.

Option d) won't work though. We have said that we need a very special object, a Sqaure named *estew*. If we need a Square, and someone creates a new Rectangle(4,4); even if the sides are the same length, according to our class diagram, a Rectangle is not a special type of Square, and our code would be very unhappy. Polymorphism is unidirectional, and if we want something special like a Square, and get something more generic, like a Rectangle, our code will be very unhappy, and require counseling.

Answer

Which of the following lines of code are valid?
☐ a) IShape shape = new IShape();   ☐ b) Shape abstractShape = new Shape();   ☐ c) Shape sq = new Square(10);   ☐ d) IShape rect = new Rectangle(4,5);
Options a) and b) are not valid and incorrect because you cannot, under any circumstance, create a concrete instance of an abstract class (Shape) or an interface (IShape).   Now, having said that, options c) and d) will compile fine. Now doesn't that contradict the reason given for options a) and b) being ***incorrect***? Well, not really.   Think about it. Option c) says "I need a Shape that I want to call sq." Someone comes along and provides a new Square(10); The code asked for a Shape and got a Square, which ***is a*** special type of Shape. Everyone is happy.   Furthermore, option d) says "give me an instance of a class that implements the IShape interface." A new Rectangle(4,5); which does indeed implement the IShape interface, is provided. An object type that implements the IShape interface is requested, and an object type that implements the IShape interface is provided. How could life get any better?

Answer

A method needs to be coded that evaluates whether the area of a Square and a Rectangle are the same. A boolean value is returned, depending upon whether the evaluation is true or not. What would be the most appropriate method signature for this method?
O a) public boolean compare(Rectangle rect, Square sq) { } O b) public boolean compare(Rectangle aRect, Rectangle eRect) { } O c) public boolean compare(Shape s1, Shape s2) { } O d) public boolean compare(IShape s1, IShape s2) { }
Answer d) is correct. All of the methods stated would work, but option d) is the most flexible. To compare a rectangle and a square, all you need to do is call the calculateArea method on each object. But, if you're looking long-term and for potentially pluggable and flexible solutions, you'll realize that any instance that implements the IShape interface could be passed into the method, because the calculateArea method is defined abstractly in the IShape interface. Coding a method signature that passes in two IShape interface objects is the most flexible, and the most appropriate way to code a solution for this problem.

Answer

Assuming that a Triangle codes the calculate area method correctly as:

return(.5)*height*width;

and the calculateArea method is defined in the abstract class as:

return height* width;

what would be the output of the following code:

```
Shape shapeUp = new Triangle(10,10);
System.out.println(shapeUp.calculateArea());
```

O a) 100
O b) 50
O c) 10
O d) 0

Okay, the object is being held as a Shape, but was created as a Triangle. Will the calculation of the area return 10*10, as it is coded in the Shape class, or will it be calculated as (.5)*10*10 as it is defined in the Triangle class? The answer is the latter, making option b) correct.

The rule with polymorphism is that an object can be held as any general parent type, but regardless of how it is being held, it will behave as the object it was created as. In this example, the Triangle is being held as a Shape, but the Triangle will never stop behaving as a Triangle. If you ask a Triangle to calculate its area, it will calculate it as length times width divided by two, even if the Triangle is being held as an object of type Shape, as in this example.

An object will always behave as the type that it was created, regardless of how it is being referenced in code. This is another important aspect of polymorphism.

It should be noted that this ***looking up of which method to call on an object*** is closely related to something called ***late binding,*** which says when a method is called on an object, the compiler looks at how the object was created, and begins looking at the bottom of the class hierarchy for a matching method to call. The JVM works up the hierarchy until it finds a match, and when it does, it invokes the method. The fact that all of this gets done at runtime, as opposed to compile time, is why it is referred to as ***late binding.***

Answer

Which of the following are valid lines of code, given the following:
/*assume all constructors used in the example exist, and are implemented correctly*/

```
Shape shape = new Rectangle(4,4);
IShape tri = new Triangle(5,3);
Square square = new Square(5);
Rectangle rect = new Rectangle(3,5);
Line line = new Line (new Point(0,0), new Point(1,1));
```

☐ a) shape = tri;

☐ b) tri = shape;

☐ c) rect = square;

☐ d) square = rect;

Option a) will work. If you need a Shape, and are given a Triangle, life is good.

Option b) will work. If you have an IShape, and get a Rectangle, life is good.

Option c) will work, as if you need a Rectangle, and are given a Square, life is good.

Option d) will not work. A Rectangle is not a special type of Square.

Chapter 15
Static Variables and Methods

Static Variables and Methods...The methods and variables that stick to your clothes when you take them out of the dryer.

Static variables and methods are an important part of the Java programming language, but in their use, they seem to break a few of the rules regarding method and variable use, and as such, they are sometimes one of the more confusing concepts for Java neophytes to understand. Static variables and methods do not play a huge part in the Sun Certified Java Associates exam, so don't spend too much time mentally fighting over static methods and variables. However, a little background on the topic will go a long way; and I assure you, the keyword static won't be entirely absent on the SCJA exam.

Java Classes and Instances

In Java, we create classes, and from those classes, we create instances. So, for example, if we had a SavingsAccount class, that class would likely have a number of properties and methods, including a customerName, a balance, and methods for depositing and withdrawing money.

«Java Class»
SavingsAccount
- customerName : String
- balance : double
+ getBalance ( )
- setBalance ( )
+ getCustomerName ( )
- setCustomerName ( )
+ SavingsAccount ( )
+ deposit ( )
+ withdraw ( )
+ accrueInterest ( )

From this particular class, you could easily create instances:

```
SavingsAccount camsAccount =
                    new SavingsAccount("Cam", 100.01);
SavingsAccount jimsAccount =
                    new SavingsAccount("Jim", 500.50);
SavingsAccount kimsAccount =
                    new SavingsAccount("Kim", 500.50);
```

When we create instances, the JVM is simply putting memory aside to store the information provided when the constructor is called. So, the variableName camsAccount points to a memory location that stores the name "Cam" and the int value 100.01. The variable name kimsAccount points to a memory location that stores the String "Kim" and the int value 500.50.

Calling Instance Methods: A Review

So, what happens when Kim takes a c-note ($100) out of her bank account? Well, the memory location that the variable kimsAccount points to doesn't change - that stays constant. The place where the String "Kim" is stored never changes. However, the bytes that were formerly used to store the balance of 500.50 are changed to reflect the fact that after withdrawing $100, the balance is reduced to $400.50.

```
/*take 100 bucks out of kims account.*/
kimsAccount.balance = 500.50 - 100;

/*this is the instance method for doing a withdraw.*/
public void withdraw(double amount) {
  this.balance = this.balance-amount;
}
```

Of course, reducing Kim's bank balance by $100 doesn't reduce anyone else's bank balance. Every instance of a SavingsAccount has its own, separate memory location where the account holder's name, and the account holder's balance, are stored. This is the whole idea behind object-oriented programming - we can create an infinite number of objects, and the JVM keeps all of the various properties and values associated with those objects organized for us.

Variables Common to All Instances

But what if there was a property, a.k.a. variable, that was common to EVERY instance of the SavingsAccount class.

Lets say, for example, that every savings account gets the same interest rate. Banks usually do that. They usually have some crappy, basic SavingsAccount that accrues interest at some insultingly low rate. The rate then applies to everyone that uses that basic SavingsAccount.

So, for our example, we'll say that every SavingsAccount accrues interest at a rate of 1%. It doesn't matter if you're Bob, Joe, Kim or

Cam, if you have a SavingsAccount at this bank, you get an interest rate of 1%.

Using the Keyword Static

As you can see, this interest rate applies to every SavingsAccount. The interest rate is not associated with a particular account or person, but with EVERY instance of the class. Since it is common to all instances of the class, we refer to it as a class level variable. Of course, the word class already has a very special meaning in Java, so the word we actually use to identify a class level variable is the word static, indicating that the value is the same for every instance of the class.

```
public static double interestRate = .01;
```

Note, that static doesn't mean constant or final. A static variable can change, the only difference is that when it changes, it changes for EVERY member of the class, not any one instance in particular.

Local variables, such as variables declared inside of a method or flow control block, can never be static. Only variables declared inside of the class declaration, but outside of any methods, can be called static. Static variable declarations are usually found right alongside instance variable declarations; Actually, they usually go towards the top of the class where variables are declared.

```
public class SavingsAccount {

  public static double interestRate = .01;
  private String customerName;
  private double balance;

  /*...methods would go here...*/

}
```

Referencing Static Variables

Since static variables are associated with the class, and not any particular instance, you reference a static variable by using dot notation, referencing the name of the class on the left of the dot, and the name of the static variable on the right: SavingsAccount.interestRate

```
/*create a new savings account for cam.*/
SavingsAccount camsAccount =
                     new SavingsAccount("Cam", 100.01);

/*use the static variable to apply interest*/
camsAccount.balance =
   camsAccount.balance * SavingsAccount.interestRate;
```

From the perspective of the JVM, a static variable is stored in one, single location, and every class instance points to that location. Of course, a static variable isn't constant. If anyone changes the value of the static variable, that single memory location gets updated, and as a result, every object, which means ***every instance of the class***, that references that memory location, has the value they reference updated simultaneously.

Notice that you could never say SavingsAccount.balance. The variable balance is an *instance* variable, and when you reference it, you need an actual instance. If you wrote SavingsAccount.balance, the compiler would give you a fairly cryptic error message about not being able to make a static call to an instance variable.

```
//what would this line print out?
System.out.println(SavingsAccount.interestRate);

//why would this cause a compile error?
System.out.println(SavingsAccount.customerName);
```

Initializing Static Variables

Since static variables apply to every instance of a class, they are usually initialized as soon as they are declared. Since a static variable isn't tied to any one member or instance of a class, but is instead associated with *every* instance of a class, you do not typically initialize or update a static variable inside of a constructor, although there can be exceptions to that rule, and it is possible.

To help address the question of *'when'* to initialize static variables, Java provides something called a static method block that is run the first time any instance of a particular class is created. You can use this block to initialize static variables, with faith in the fact that the method will only ever be called once.

Thinking about Static *Methods*

So, a static variable is a variable that is common to every instance of a class, and is not associated with any particular instance. So, what do you think a static ***method*** is?

A method can also be declared as being static. Static methods are just worker methods. Static methods cannot directly reference any instance (non-static) variables or instance (non-static) methods within the same class. A static method can only use static variables. Any other data you wish a static method to work on must be passed into the method through its method signature. A static method can work with instances, but only if those instances are explicitly passed into the static method.

So, static methods in a class can only see that class' static variables. Static methods in a class cannot access instance variables directly. In order to work with instances in a static method, those instances must be passed in explicitly.

Constant *Variables* in Java

When you want to declare a constant in java, you use the words final and static together.

Basically, the keyword final indicates that a value cannot change once it is given its initial value. A final variable is just that - final. However, if the value is constant, it wouldn't make sense for every instance of a class to make a copy of it, would it? If a variable isn't static, every instance that is created gets its own copy of the data.

It wouldn't make sense to have a million Java objects all keeping their own, separate copies of that same number or String - that would be a massive waste of memory. To indicate that a variable never changes, we use the keyword final. To ensure that every instance points to the same copy of that data, and does not make separate copies of the final variable, we also mark it as static. This is why, in Java, to indicate that a variable is constant, we use the keywords static and final in combination.

```
public class SavingsAccount {

  /*where is this static variable visible?*/
  public static double interestRate = .01;

  /*the following are non-static, instance variables*/
  private String customerName;
  private double balance;

  public static void doSomething(){
     System.out.println(interestRate); /*legal*/
     //System.out.println(balance);    /*illegal*/
  }

  public void doSomethingElse() {
    /*legal - but not good naming*/
    System.out.println(interestRate);
    /*legal - an instance is calling this method*/
    System.out.println(balance);
  }

  public static double
           doSomethingCrazy(SavingsAccount account){

      double interestAccrued = account.balance *
                          SavingsAccount.interestRate;

      return interestAccrued;
/*legal reference because the account object was passed
into the method. The instance variable is never referenced
without a using the name of the instance.*/
  }
}
```

Note that while instance methods can see both instance variables and static variables that are defined for the class, static methods can only see static variables. A static method does not have automatic access to instance variables or instance methods defined for the class.

Notes and Naming

Also notice the naming convention for constants in Java. Whenever you have a constant, you use all upper case letters. Words should be separated by an underscore. All constants should be pronounced using all upper case letters.

*Note: the keyword **final** can be used on methods as well as instance variables, although the meaning is a fair bit different depending upon how the keyword final is used. final **methods** are final in so much as they cannot be overridden by any child class - just so you know.*

Question

The Math class is a static class. How would the static variable PI of the Math class be referenced in code?

- O a) Math.PI;
- O b) Math m = new Math(); m.PI;
- O c) Math.PI( );
- O d) PI;

Question

What would be the result of making an instance variable final, but not static, as in the following code:

```
public class Softener{
 final int rate = 4;
}
```

- O a) the variable **rate** would not be constant
- O b) each instance of the class Softener would have its own copy of the same data
- O c) each instance could have a different value for **rate**
- O d) code will not compile if an instance variable is final but not static

Question

What happens when you change the value of a static variable for just one instance of a class?

- ☐ a) the one instance has a new value, but all other instances share the old value of the static variable
- ☐ b) a single memory location shared by all instances is updated
- ☐ c) a compile error occurs because static variables must also be final
- ☐ d) the value changes for all instance of the class

Answer

The Math class is a static class. How would the static variable PI of the Math class be referenced in code?
O a) Math.PI;
With a static class, all methods and properties are referenced simply by using the name of the class, followed by a dot, followed by the name of the variable or method. Since PI is a constant, no parenthesis are placed after the variable name, as would be required with a method.

Answer

What would be the result of making an instance variable final, but not static, as in the following code:

```
public class Softener{
 final int rate = 4;
}
```

O b) each instance of the class Softener would have its own copy of the same data

This code will compile, and all instances of the Softener class will get a rate of 4. However, each instance will keep their own copy of the data, and if there are lots of Softener classes created, that's going to end up in a lot of wasted memory space.

Answer

What happens when you change the value of a static variable for just one instance of a class?
☐ b) a single memory location shared by all instances is updated ☐ d) the value changes for all instance of the class
Answers b) and d) are correct. All instances of a class point to the same memory location for a static variable. If this one memory location is changed, the value changes for all instances of the class, as all instances are pointing to the same, static, memory location.

15 Questions: Object Oriented Concepts

Question 1

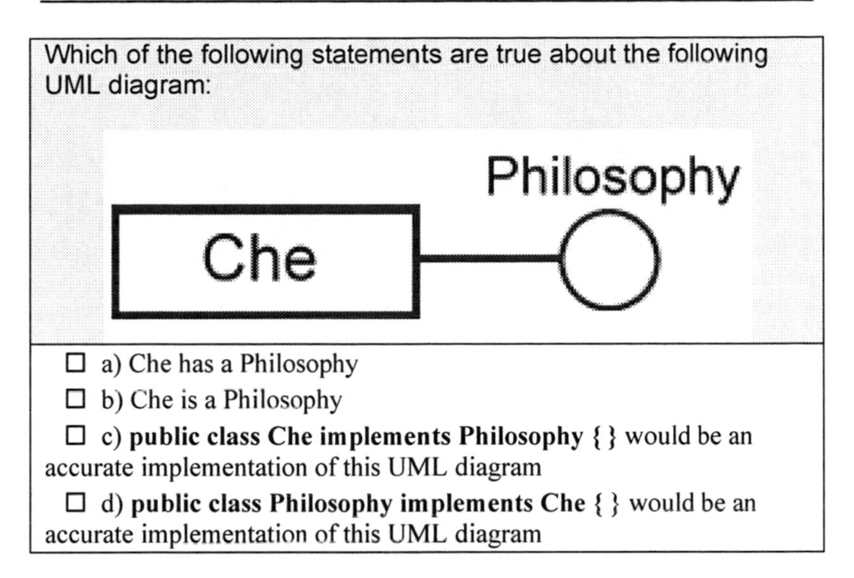

Which of the following statements are true about the following UML diagram:

☐ a) Che has a Philosophy

☐ b) Che is a Philosophy

☐ c) **public class Che implements Philosophy { }** would be an accurate implementation of this UML diagram

☐ d) **public class Philosophy implements Che { }** would be an accurate implementation of this UML diagram

Question 2

Given the following class, which of the following statements are true:

Totally
− foo : Foo
+ bar ( )

☐ a) the class is named Totally, has an operation named foo, and an attribute named bar

☐ b) the class is named Totally, has an operation named bar, and an attribute named foo

☐ c) the class is named Totally, has a method named foo, and a property named bar

☐ d) the class is named Totally, has a method named bar, and a property named foo

Question 3

Given the following diagram, which of the following statements must be true?

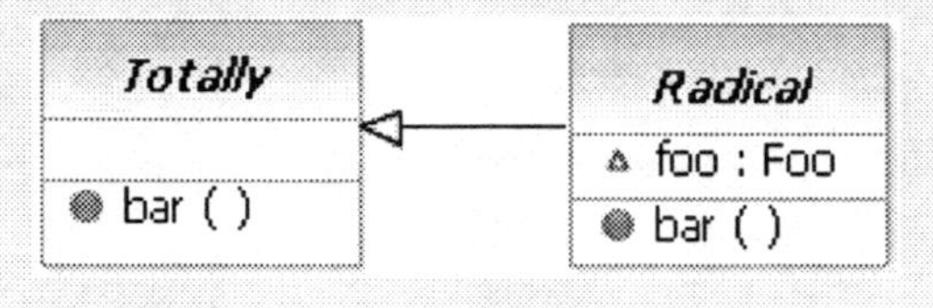

- ☐ a) Radical implements Totally
- ☐ b) Radical inherits from Totally
- ☐ c) Totally is an abstract class
- ☐ d) Radical is an abstract class

Question 4

What is true about the component represented on the following diagram?

- O a) this is an abstract class
- O b) this is a Java 1.5 enumeration
- O c) this is an interface
- O d) this is a concrete class

Question 5

Which class on this diagram is successfully implementing the Gradeable interface?

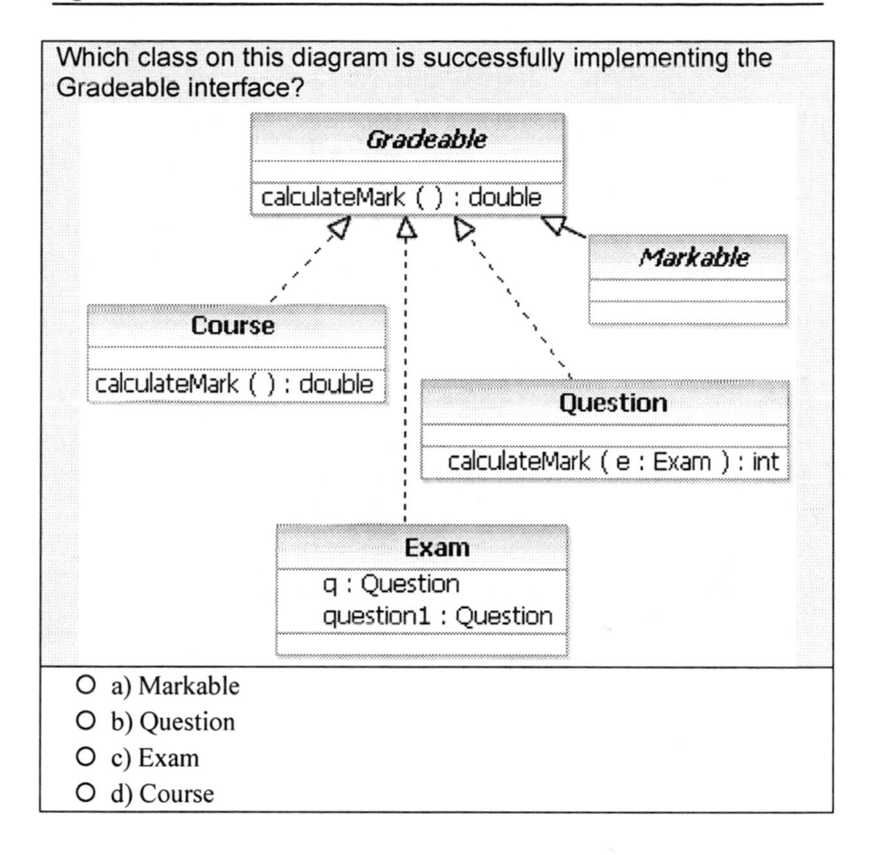

- a) Markable
- b) Question
- c) Exam
- d) Course

Question 6

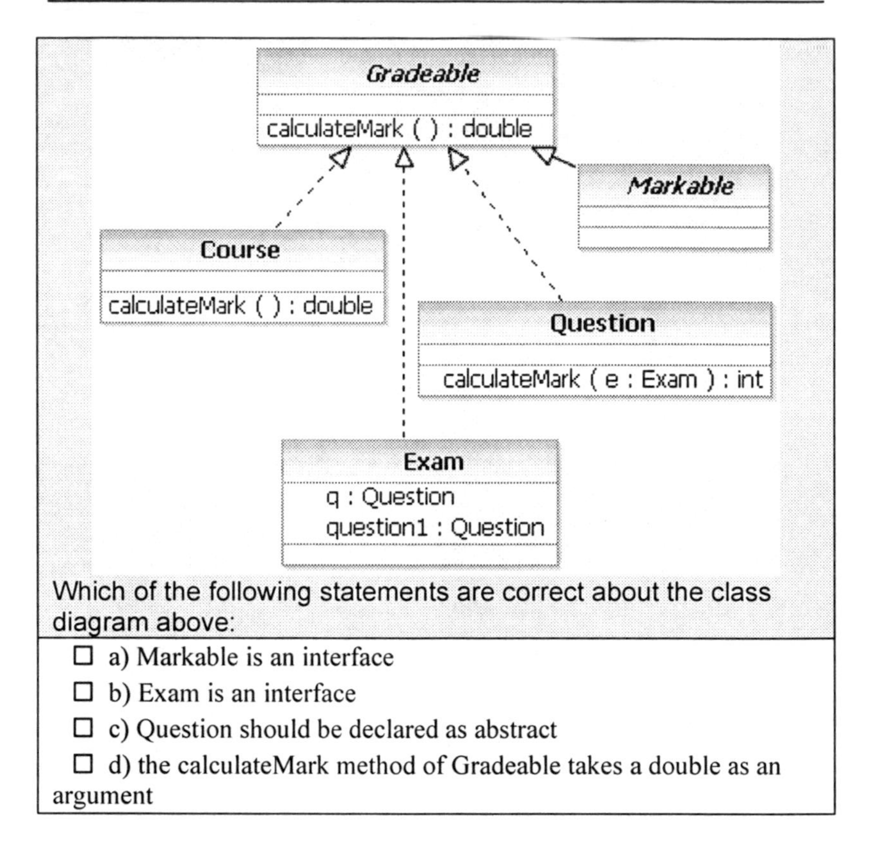

Which of the following statements are correct about the class diagram above:

☐ a) Markable is an interface

☐ b) Exam is an interface

☐ c) Question should be declared as abstract

☐ d) the calculateMark method of Gradeable takes a double as an argument

Question 7

What is the relation between a bank and its savings accounts?

O a) association

O b) composition

O c) inheritance

O d) polymorphism

Question 8

```
public class Top {

 public void doIt(int i){}
 public void doIt(String s) {}
 public void doSomething(){}

}


public class Bottom {

 public void doSomething(){}

}
```

Which of the following statements are true?

- O a) the doIt() method is overloaded
- O b) the doIt() method is overridden
- O c) the doSomething() method is overloaded
- O d) the doSomething() method is overridden

Question 9

```
public class Jay {
 private Dee salinger

 public Jay(Dee sal) {
  if (sal == null){
   System.exit(0); //error!!!
  }
  salinger = sal;
 }
}


public class Dee {

}
```

Which of the following statements are true?

O a) A Jay is associated with 0..1 Dee objects
O b) A Jay is associated with 1..* Dee objects
O c) A Jay is associated with 1 Dee objects
O d) A Jay is associated with 0..* Dee objects

Question 10

```
public interface Corruptable {
  String doIt();
}

public class Youth implements Corruptable {

//line xxx

}
```

Which of the following pieces of code, placed on line xxx, would allow this class to successfully compile?

O a) private String doIt(){}
O b) int doIt(){}
O c) Object doIt(){}
O d) public String doIt(){}

Question 11

```
public interface Corruptable {
  Object doIt();
}

public class Youth implements Corruptable {

//line xxx

}
```

Which of the following pieces of code, placed on line xxx, would allow this class to successfully compile?

- ☐ a) private String doIt(){}
- ☐ b) Object doIt(int i){}
- ☐ c) Object doIt(){}
- ☐ d) public String doIt(){}

Questions 12 through 15 will be based upon the following Class Diagram:

Figure 12-15

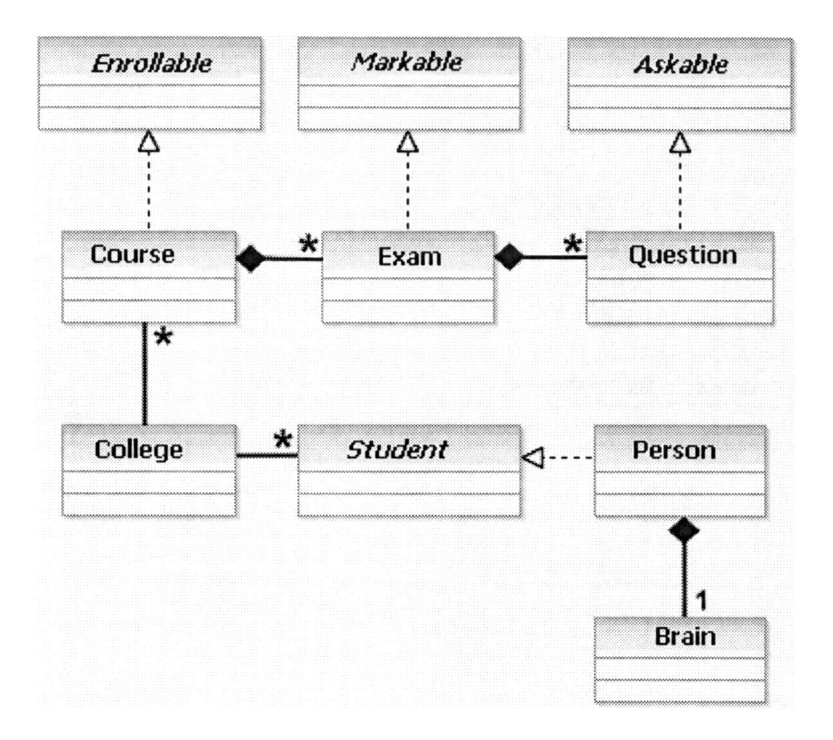

Question 12

Which of the following are true about the class diagram in Figure 12-15?
☐ a) if a Question is destroyed, its associated Exam is destroyed ☐ b) if an Exam is destroyed, its associated Questions are destroyed ☐ c) if a Course is destroyed, its associated Exams are destroyed ☐ d) if a Course is destroyed, its associated Questions are destroyed

Question 13

What is the ratio of interfaces to concrete classes to abstract classes in class diagram in Figure 12-15?
O a) 4:5:1 O b) 4:6:0 O c) 4:1:5 O d) 5:0:4

Question 14

Which of the following statements are correct about the class diagram in Figure 12-15?
☐ a) A college is associated with many students ☐ b) A course can have many exams ☐ c) A Student has one brain ☐ d) A Question is associated with one and only one Exam

Question 15

What type of relationship exists between a College and its Students, according to Figure 12-15?
O a) association O b) polymorphism O c) composition O d) inheritance

Answer 1

Options b) and c) are correct.

A lolipop diagram defines an interfact where the circular part of the popsicle is. In this case, Philosophy is the interface, and the class Che implements the Philosophy interface, making options b) and c) correct.

Answer 2

Options b) and d) are correct. In Java terms, an ***operation*** and a method are the same thing, and the terms ***attribute*** and a ***property*** can be used interchangeably. Furthermore, in a three-tier class diagram, the name of the ***class*** appears in the top tier, the ***properties*** appear in the second tier, and the ***methods*** appear in the third tier.

Answer 3

Options b) c) and d) are all correct. Radical has an instance variable, which means it must be a class. Furthermore, the solid line with a closed headed arrow means inheritance, and classes can only inherit from other classes, as opposed to implementing an interface. Since the class names are italicized, and both must be classes, we can say that both Totally and Radical are abstract classes, with Radical inheriting from Totally.

Answer 4

The only revealing piece of information on this diagram is the fact that the name of the class is italicized. When a class name is italicized, the class is abstract. Interfaces will also have their names italicized, but interfaces cannot have instance variables. This Totally class has an instance variable of type Foo, named foo. An interface cannot have an instance variable, so this must be an abstract class. Option a) is correct.

Answer 5

Option d) is the correct answer, as only Course is both pointing to Gradeable with a closed headed arrow and a dotted line, while also expressly stating in the UML that it is overriding the methods defined in the Gradeable interface.

Question looks like it is overriding the calculateMark method properly, but the method defined in the interface does not take any parameters, and the calculateMark method in the Question class takes an Exam as an argument. To properly implement an interface, the methods in the implementing class must match in both name and method signature with the method in the interface being overridden.

Answer 6

Options a) and c) are correct. Not only is the class named *Markable* in italics, which means it is either an interface or an abstract class, but it also has a solid line with a closed headed arrow pointing at the Gradeable interface. If Markable were a class, the arrow pointing towards the Gradeable interface would not be solid. Classes implement interfaces, whereas interfaces *extend* other interfaces. According to the closed headed arrow with the solid line, Markable is ***extending*** the Gradeable interface, not implementing it.

Also, Question should be declared as abstract, as it is not properly implementing the calculateMark() method defined in the Gradeable interface. If a class implements an interface, but does not properly override all of the methods defined in the interface, the class must be declared as being abstract in order for it to compile. For that matter, Exam should be declared as abstract as well.

Option d) is incorrect, as the calculateMark method of the Gradeable class returns a double, and takes no arguments.

Answer 7

Option b) is correct.

A bank is associated with bank accounts, but the relationship goes beyond simple association, as a bank is likely heavily involved in the lifecycle of its bankaccounts. A bank would take part in opening, closing, and managing the bankaccounts that it maintains. More to the point, if a bank closes, so would all of its associated bank accounts, confirming that the relationship between a bank and its accounts is indeed a ***composition*** relationship.

Answer 8

Option a) is correct.

When a class has multiple methods with the same name, but ***different method signatures***, aka argument lists, the like named methods are considered to be ***overloaded***. Overloading is associated with multiple methods with the ***same name*** being in the ***same class.*** ***Overriding*** is when a subclass contains a method with the exact same method name ***and*** method signature. The doSomething() method would be considered to be overloading the doSomething() method in the Top class if Bottom inherited from Top. However, **Bottom does not inherit from Top**, so we can't say that the doSomething() method is being overridden.

Answer 9

Option c) is the correct answer. Since there is only one constructor for the Jay class, and that constructor requires a real, instantiated Dee object, not to mention the fact that there is a single instance variable of type Dee defined in the Jay class, we can say that a Jay is associated with one and only one Dee object.

Notice how a Jay can't be created without a Dee. This very much enforces the idea that a Jay is strongly associated with one Dee.

Answer 10

Only option d) is correct. When overriding, the sub-type must use the exact same method name, return type, and argument list. Furthermore, **an overridden method cannot be more restrictive with regards to its access modifier than the method being overridden.** In this case, the doIt() method in the Youth class cannot be private, making option a) incorrect. Option b) has an incorrect return type, and option c) does not return a String, but instead, a generic object.

Answer 11

Options c) and d), as they have the same method name, same argument signature, and are not more restrictive with their access modifier. Option d) returns a String, not an Object, but a String is-an object, so polymorphically, this is completely valid.

Answer 12

This is a tricky one, but options b) c) and d) are correct. A course is composed of Exams, and an Exam is composed of Questions. Since composition implies that if the composing object is destroyed, then all composed objects are destroyed as well, we can say if a Course is deleted, then so are all of its Exams, and if an Exam is deleted, so are all of its Questions. However, the relationship will also link down the chain, so if a Course is destroyed, so will all of the Questions associated with all of the associated exams, making d) correct as well.

Answer 13

Option b) is correct. Enrollable, Markable, Askable and Student are all interfaces. The rest of the classes are indeed concrete, and can be instantiated with the new keyword.

When defining roles, roles should always be interfaces. That's a general rule of OO design. Even though a role, such as Manager or Student might seem to make sense as an abstract class to inherit from, it makes for a more rigid design for the future. Flexible designs are best. Roles should almost always be defined as interfaces. Embrace the idea of programming to an interface!

Answer 14

All of the options are true with the exception of c). While a Person is-a student according to the class diagram, a Student isn't necessarily a Person. I'm not sure what else a student might be, but those Honda people are making some pretty clever robots these days, so maybe we've got an android in the class. According to our diagram, a Person has a brain, and a Person is-a Student, but we have no evidence suggesting that all Students are Person objects, and as a result, cannot conclude that all Students have brains.

Option d) is interesting. There is no multiplicity specified from the Question to the Exam; the only explicit multiplicity is the asterisk that shows that an Exam can have many questions. But in fact, a composition relationship implies that the composed object is associated with only one composing object – this is just part of the definition of a composition relationship.

Answer 15

Option a) is correct. A solid line connecting two classes on a class diagram represents an association relationship. In this example, a College can be associated with many students.

Part Three:
Java Coding Basics

Chapter 16
Getting Jiggy with the SDK

One of the fundamental requirements of the Sun Certified Java Associates exam is the ability to compile and run Java code using the ***java*** *and* ***javac*** *utilities that are distributed with the Standard Development toolKit (SDK). Working with the java and javac utilities is the focus of this chapter.*

However, it should be noted that finding and downloading the SDK from the Sun Microsystems website can be a challenge for a Java neophyte. It's very easy to become confused with the many options, and accidentally download the wrong thing. Furthermore, there are a million little, annoying mistakes you can easily make when attempting to compile and run your very first Java program. If you're struggling with the installation of the SDK, or the compiling and running of your first piece of Java code, call out for help, and get an experienced Java programmer to bail you out. You'll find that once you've got everything installed and running, learning Java will become easy and fun!

There Comes a Time to Run

To run a Java program, you need a Java Runtime Environment, or as it's affectionately known in polite circles, a JRE. A JRE allows you to run basic Java programs that use the standard Java libraries, such as java.io and java.lang. The JRE is not a J2EE (Enterprise Edition) runtime, or a J2ME (Micro Edition) runtime. The JRE is just a standard, vanilla, Java Runtime Environment that you can download, free of charge from Sun Microsystems, and install on your personal computer at home.

Of course, if you want to become a Sun Certified Java Associate, you'll want to go way beyond the simple *running* of code. To go beyond simply running Java programs, and to instead, make the leap into the world of writing, compiling, *and* running Java code, you need, at the very least, the Standard Development toolKit (SDK) from Sun, which can be found, waiting for you, somewhere on the javasoft.com website.

Hacking Out Java Code

In its most simple, scaled down, bare naked form, a Java program can be developed as a single text file, coded according to the Java syntax, and compiled using a special utility that is distributed as part of the Standard Java Development toolKit (SDK). The special utility provided by the SDK for compiling Java source files is called javac, which as you probably guessed, is an abbreviation for ***Java*** compiler. The javac utility can be found in a subfolder of the SDK installation directory called bin.

If you've downloaded and installed the Standard Development Kit from Sun Microsystems, you can write a little Java program using your favorite text editor, such as Notepad or Editpad, save your Java source file in the SDK's bin directory, and then use the javac utility to compile your Java source file into *executable* Java byte code.

The Requisite Hello World

For example, I could write the following program in notepad, and save it to the bin directory of the SDK with the name HelloWorld.java. I could then compile this HelloWorld.java file using the javac utility.

```
/*This file must be saved as HelloWorld.java .*/
public class HelloWorld extends Object
{
  /*The main method is the entry point for Java programs.*/
  public static void main(String args[])
  {
    /*System.out.print sends output to the user.*/
    System.out.println("Hello World");
  }
}
```

From the command prompt, in the bin directory of the SDK, I could run the command **javac HelloWorld.java**, and the HelloWorld.java file would be compiled.

Once a .java source file is successfully compiled, a new .class file will magically appear in the bin directory alongside your source file. In our case, the compiled class file will be named **HelloWorld.class**.

When you compile a .java source file, if compilation succeeds, a corresponding class file is created. This .class file is the bytecode embodiment of your Java source code, and it is this compiled byte-code that is run by the Java Virtual Machine (JVM). In Java, we don't generate executable files, but instead, we create lots of .class files. If an application is comprised of multiple class files working together, we package those class files together in a single, compressed file known as a Java Application aRchive, or as they're affectionately known, a JAR.

Common Compiling Mistake #1: *Java is case sensitive. If anything is cAseD incorrectly, you will get compile errors. Like my stepmother about her massive girth, Java is equally sensitive about its case.*

Common Compiling Mistake #2: *The name you use to save the file must be the case sensitive class name, plus the .java extension. Make sure your silly text editor does not add a .txt extension as well.*

Running from the Law

To run the class file that was created based upon your Java source code, you use another utility found in the bin directory of the SDK, named java.exe (or java.**sh** on unix). At the command prompt, you just need to type java.exe, and then the name of your compiled class file, without the .class extension, and your compiled Java class will run. That's how easy it is to create, compile, and run classes with the Standard Java Development toolKit.

```
C:\jdk1.5.0_07\bin>javac HelloWorld.java
C:\jdk1.5.0_07\bin>java HelloWorld
Hello World
C:\jdk1.5.0_07\bin>
```

Because "SubFolder" Wasn't Good Enough

Now, a typical Java application isn't just one Java file with lots of code in it. Java applications are made up of many, organized, compiled, Java files working together to create an object oriented experience for the user. Because code organization is penultimately important, you'll want to organize your code into sub directories or subfolders; after all, placing everything in the bin directory of the SDK is just nutty. So, for our little HelloWorld application, we might want to create a subfolder, off the bin directory, such as \com\examscam\intro. Although it is really nothing more than a folder on the file system, Java gives subdirectories the cute name 'package.' So, if we placed our HelloWorld.java file in the \com\examscam\intro subfolder, we could say that our code has been placed in the com.examscam.intro package.

When choosing subfolder names, or more Java appropriately, package names, companies usually use their domain name backwards as the first couple of subfolders. This ensures that a company's custom code won't conflict with code brought in from other organizations. Also, folder names should always be written in lower case letters. Lower case package names is an important Java convention.

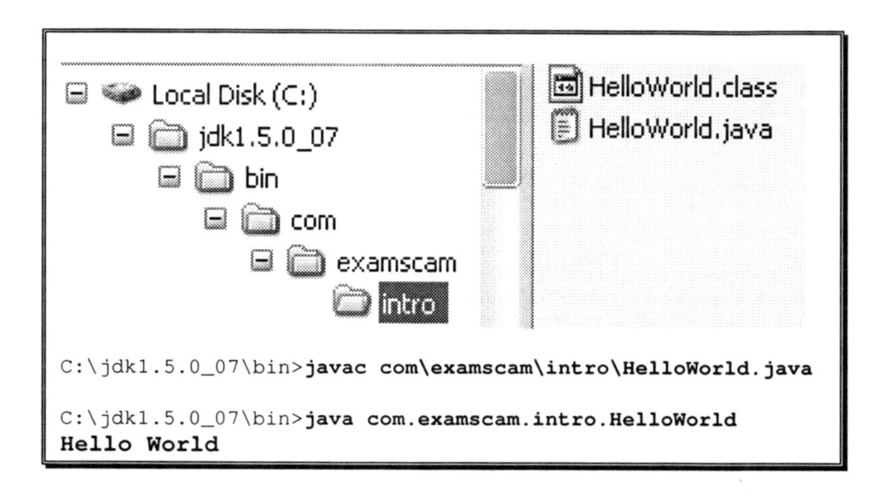

Sure, a Java application isn't just one single Java file with lots of code in it, but I do pine for that monolithic Java program that is just one big source file, with one method called ***go()****, that does everything, and is stored right there in the bin directory of the SDK. Wouldn't that be heaven?*

The Package Declaration

Now, if we place our Java code in a sub-folder, we must inform the JVM. The way this is done is by placing a ***package statement*** on the top line of a Java source file.

```
/*tell the complier our code is in the
com/examscam/intro subfolder, off the classpath*/
package com.examscam.intro;
```

Also, since a Java program might run on both a Unix and a Windows platform, the folder names are separated by dots, or periods, as opposed to folder slashes. After all, a Unix platform slash (/) is different from a Windows platform slash (\), and we don't want any platform *dependent* artifacts or symbols in our platform *independent* programs.

If you add this package statement to your HelloWorld.java file, and move the HelloWorld.java file to the com\examscam\intro folder, you compile the class by specifying:

```
javac com\examscam\intro\HelloWorld.java
```

The javac utility will compile your packaged code. To run the compiled code, from the bin directory, you specify:

```
java com.examscam.intro.HelloWorld
```

Notice how when you switch to the java command, you use a dot delimitated package name, and there is no .class or .java extension at the end.

*Remember, Java is case sensitive. If you have a class declaration that says public class Helloworld, and you run javac Hello**W**orld.java, your code won't compile because your class name is a different CaSE from the name you are using to compile your code.*

Finding Java Class Files

Java class libraries are typically packaged as jar files, and depending upon how your applications are deployed, important jar files and required class files may end up in a variety of different places on your file system. To have the java runtime find files that might not be, and probably won't be, found directly off the bin directory of the SDK, you can specify a –classpath option. To use the classpath command line option, you specify the java utility, use the –classpath switch, and then specify a number of file folders and jar files, separated by a semi-colon, for which the java runtime utility should search for class files and resources.

```
/*This would be entered as a single line in the
command window.*/

java -classpath C:\app\stuff.jar; C:\other\scam.jar
com.examscam.HelloWorld
```

Setting System Properties

A JVM runs with a number of system properties. You can configure system properties by using the –D option for the JVM. All you have to do is use the –D flag, and provide the system property name immediately following the D, an equals sign, and then the value to be assigned to the property. For example to set the file.encoding property of the Java runtime to utf-8, you could set the system property as so:

```
java -Dfile.encoding = utf-8 HelloWorld
```

Differentiating Between *java –D* and *javac –d*

The ***java runtime utility*** uses the big D switch to allow the setting of system properties. Alternatively, the Java ***compiler***, javac, uses the –d command to specify an output directory for generated class files. For example, if you specified **–d C:\myclassfiles** while running the javac utility, your class files will end up being placed in their package relative folders under C:\myclassfiles.

Discovering the Runtime Environment *-version*

Another useful option of the java utility is the –version switch. Using this option with the java runtime utility will tell you version information about the JVM on which you are running.

```
C:\jdk1.5.0_07\bin>java -version
java version "1.5.0_07"
Java(TM) 2 Runtime Environment, Standard Edition
(build 1.5.0_07-b03)
Java HotSpot(TM) Client VM (build 1.5.0_07-b03, mixed
mode, sharing)
```

How to Partition Your Code Correctly

As was mentioned, code should be organized both physically and logically into packages. The question that always arises is "how best to do this?" Whenever I'm asked how to do something in Java, I always look to see how the Java Gods at Sun Microsystems do it. If you want to learn about organizing code into Java packages, you should look at the structure and organization of the standard Java class libraries, which is exactly what we are going to do here:

Fundamental Java Packages: Beyond java.lang

All of the basic objects you use in your Java programs reside in a very important package called **java.lang**. The java.lang package defines the uber class **Object**, from which every class in Java inherits. The java.lang package also defines wrapper classes for the primitive types, namely **Long, Double**, **Integer** and **Character**. It also includes the character **String** class, which is absolutely essential for pretty much every Java program in existence, along with the static **Math** class that provides a variety of math related constants like PI, and methods for doing moderately complex, yet common, mathematical functions.

How can you tell that Double, Integer and Character are ***wrapper*** *classes? Just look at them. They're the ones wearing the baggy clothes and the bulky gold chains around their necks.*

One thing to note for the exam is that all the classes in java.lang are, by default, available to your Java programs. You can conjure up an object in the java.lang package directly by name, and the Java compiler will know exactly what you're talking about. Other important packages include: **java.util, java.net, java.io, java.awt and javax.swing.**

I/O, I/O, It's Off To Work I Go

As you could probably guess, java.io contains all sorts of classes for reading from, or writing to, a variety of file types and output streams. The java.io package also defines a bunch of exception classes associated with writing and reading from input or output streams, such as the FileNotFoundException.

Networking with the java.net Package

The java.net package has a variety of classes dedicated to network communication. Java was born at the beginning of the information age, and as a result, it has the best set of classes and libraries available for working with network connections. The java.net package is the foundation of all good networking applications in Java.

GUI Development with java.awt and javax.swing

The java.awt and javax.swing packages contain a variety of classes associated with GUI based programming. To create a standalone Java application that contains buttons and textfields, and runs outside of an Internet browser, the java.awt, and javax.swing packages are the ones to use.

Package names can't start with the name java, as that package name is reserved for standard java packages. However, this caused a problem when Sun released a new set of packages to upgrade the Java 1.1 libraries. Sun couldn't call their classes ***java****.swing, because the java word would mess up old compilers. To get around this problem, Sun put an x at the end of the word java, creating the javax (pronounced javex, or java-ecks) packages.*

The java.awt (awt = abstract windowing toolkit) package was the original package provided by Java to create programs with a graphical user interface (GUI). However, the button and list and textfield classes weren't the most robust in the world, and people found them to be a little kludgy to work with. When Sun released Java 1.2, they provided a new set of windowing packages called Swing, and they put them in a package called javax.swing The swing package provided all of the same basic functionality of the awt package, but was implemented with a much more architecturally pleasing model-view-controller (MVC) type of philosophy. Developers find Swing to be much more flexible and fun to work with, but still, older applications may not support Java 1.2, so quite often, for backwards compatibility, java.awt is chosen as a windowing environment over the newer, and much sleeker, swing components.

Of course, while Swing is much hipper and sexier than its awt cousin, it should be noted that all of the Swing components are actually based upon objects defined in the awt package. While Swing components have replaced awt components in many end user applications, the implementation of Swing relies quite heavily on the awt package, especially the ***java.awt.Component*** class.

Utilizing java.util

The basic utility classes are found in the java.util package. This package is one of the most heavily used packages in the java platform, as it contains all of the basic collection classes, such as Vector, ArrayList, List, Iterator, HashMap and Enumeration. These classes are absolutely essential when implementing one to many relationships between objects. Along with the basic collection classes, the java.util package includes the GregorianDate and Date classes, and the Random class for generating random numbers.

Importing Packages

One thing about working with classes in packages outside of java.lang is the fact that you must place an ***import*** statement at the top of your class file to make those classes available. Well, you either do that, or put the whole package and class name in your code when you make a reference.

```
java.util.Random r = new java.util.Random();
System.out.println(r.next());

/* or */

import java.util.Random;
✂✂✂
Random r = new Random();
✂✂✂
```

If your applications rely heavily on a large number of classes in a particular package, you can just use the splat symbol, *, after the package name to make all of the classes in that specific package available to your programs.

```
import java.util.*;
```

Placing a java.util.*; import statement at the top of your source code file allows you to use any class in this package. Note, the splat, *, does not import anything in potential sub packages of java.util.

How many different ways can you say asterix (*)? My manager Denise called it a 'splat' the other day. I liked that, although it took me a while to figure out what she was talking about. The Star? The Wildcard? The Wildman? The squished bug? If you have any good ones of your own, email them to me.

*** Discouraging the WildMan ***

Using a star, *, for a package import is easily done, but it is discouraged. It is also a sign of a lazy programmer. One of the nice things about import statements that use ***actual class names*** is the fact that a new developer can look at a Java source file, and get an instant impression of the types of classes used to implement the solution.

```
/*The package statement, always at the top. */

package com.examscam.intro;

/*Demonstrating two types of imports.*/
import java.util.Random;
import java.io.*;          /*using the WildMan.*/

public class HelloWorld extends Object
{

/*The main method is the start point of an application*/
  public static void main(String args[])
  {
    System.out.println("HelloWorld");

    /*Using an object in the imported package.*/
    Random r = new Random();

  }
}
```

Get a Real Development Tool

If you have never written a Java source file using a simple text editor, and compiled and run that code using javac.exe (or javac.sh on Unix) and java.exe (or java.sh on Unix), then you simply don't deserve to get Java certified. At the most basic level, you absolutely must know how to compile and run basic Java code. You'd be surprised how often something in your system isn't working, and rather than running a program from a shell script or a development tool, you need to verify your environment by running some code directly using the java.exe utility. Having a basic understanding about how to use the important tools in the bin directory of the SDK is a necessity.

But having said that, you shouldn't toil through the learning process armed with nothing more than a text editor and the javac utility. There are a number of fantastic tools out there for writing, compiling, testing and debugging Java programs, such as IBM's Rational Application Developer and Borland's JBuilder. There's even the open source Eclipse tool, found at www.eclipse.org, that is a fantastic and highly recommended tool for developing Java code. I recommend it, and if need be, I am quite willing to sell you licenses to use it, all at a very reasonable price.

But the point is, you should get yourself a builder tool that will help you write and debug your Java code, as opposed to building all of your examples with a text editor and the SDK. Trust me, you'll save yourself a boatload of grief.

Question

Given a file named HelloWorld.java in the bin directory, which of the following commands would properly compile this code?

- O a) java HelloWorld
- O b) javac HelloWorld
- O c) java HelloWorld.java
- O d) javac HelloWorld.java
- O e) java HelloWorld.class
- O f) javac HelloWorld.class

Question

Given a successfully compiled class named HelloWorld.java, and assuming the HelloWorld.java source file contains an executable main method, which of the following would be the proper way to run that file?

- O a) java HelloWorld
- O b) javac HelloWorld
- O c) java HelloWorld.java
- O d) javacHelloWorld.java
- O e) java HelloWorld.class
- O f) javac HelloWorld.class

Question

Which of the following errors would stop a compiled Java source file named HelloWorld.java from running properly?

- ☐ a) main method was spelled Main in the source code
- ☐ b) command used to run the program was java HelloWorld
- ☐ c) command used to run the program was java Helloworld
- ☐ d) the HelloWorld.java file does not include a package statement

Question

Which of the following mistakes would stop a Java source file, with a class declaration of:
public class HelloWorld extends Object { ...}
from compiling into a Java class file?

- ☐ a) the file was saved as HeloWorld.java
- ☐ b) the file was compiled using javac HelloWorld.java
- ☐ c) the text editor appended a .txt extension to the file name
- ☐ d) the file was compiled using javac HelloWorld

Question

When a Java source file is saved in a subdirectory off of the classpath named com.mcnz.util, which package statement would correctly be placed at the top of the source file?

- O a) package com.mcnz.util.*;
- O b) package com.mcnz.util;
- O c) package "com.mcnz.util.*";
- O d) package com\mcnz\util;

Question

Which of the following packages need explicit import statements if your Java source code uses classes contained within them?

- ☐ a) java.lang
- ☐ b) java.util
- ☐ c) java.io
- ☐ d) java.net

Answer

Given a file named HelloWorld.java in the bin directory, which of the following commands would properly compile this code?
O a) java HelloWorld O b) javac HelloWorld O c) java HelloWorld.java O d) javac HelloWorld.java O e) java HelloWorld.class O f) javac HelloWorld.class
The utility used to ***compile*** Java code is the javac utility, as opposed to the java utility that is used to ***run*** code. When compiling code, you need to specify the case sensitive name of the class, along with the .java extension. If you leave out the extension, the compilation won't work. And don't try to compile any files with a .class extension, as .class files are the result of compilation, and cannot be further compiled.

Answer

Given a successfully compiled class named HelloWorld.java, and assuming the HelloWorld.java source file contains an executable main method, which of the following would be the proper way to run that file?
O a) java HelloWorld O b) javac HelloWorld O c) java HelloWorld.java O d) javacHelloWorld.java O e) java HelloWorld.class O f) javac HelloWorld.class
The java utility, the one that doesn't have the c at the end, is used to run Java code. The code that is run exists on the file system as a .class file, so in this case, a file named HelloWorld.class is being run with the java utility. However, unlike the javac command, the extension is not referenced by the utility. If you run java HelloWorld.class, you'll end up having a problem.

Answer

Which of the following errors would stop a compiled Java source file named HelloWorld.java from running properly?
☐ a) main method was spelled Main in the source code ☐ b) command used to run the program was java HelloWorld ☐ c) command used to run the program was java Helloworld ☐ d) the HelloWorld.java file does not include a package statement
Java is case sensitive. The main method is pronounced with a lower case m, not an upper case M. Also, a java file named HelloWorld.java would compile into HelloWorld.class. Any attempt to run this class will fail if you use a lower case w in the command ***java HelloWorld***

Answer

Which of the following mistakes would stop a Java source file, with a class declaration of: **public class HelloWorld extends Object { ...}** from compiling into a Java class file?
☐ a) the file was saved as HeloWorld.java ☐ b) the file was compiled using javac HelloWorld.java ☐ c) the text editor appended a .txt extension to the file name ☐ d) the file was compiled using javac HelloWorld
Always be aware of what your text editor is doing. Some nasty text editors append a .txt extension to files, even though it looks like you've specified a .java extension. Also, the javac utility requires you to specify the full name of the file, including the extension. If you try to compile HelloWorld, you'll have problems, although compiling HelloWorld**.java** should work just fine. Option a) would be problematic, as the file is spelled incorrectly, as HeloWorld.java is missing an important letter. Options a) c) and d) are correct, because they are all incorrect. ☺

Answer

When a Java source file is saved in a subdirectory off of the classpath named com.mcnz.util, which package statement would correctly be placed at the top of the source file?
O a) package com.mcnz.util.*; O b) package com.mcnz.util; O c) package "com.mcnz.util.*"; O d) package com\mcnz\util;
The wildman is used for import statements, not package statements, and folder names are separated by dots, not slashes, to ensure code runs properly on all platforms. Quotes are just bad. The package com.mcnz.util; is the right statement to have at the top of this class file.

Answer

Which of the following packages need explicit import statements if your Java source code uses classes contained within them?
☐ a) java.lang ☐ b) java.util ☐ c) java.io ☐ d) java.net
The only classes you get free of charge in a Java program are those classes defined in java.lang, such as String and Integer. If you wish to use classes in any other package than java.lang, you need to explicitly import those packages, or reference the class using the full package name.

Chapter 17
Manipulating Data

So, computer programs are all about manipulating data, right? Computer programs ingest all sorts of data, they manipulate and transform that data, and then they do something with that data, be it provide information to a user, write data to a database, or display some type of graphic on a computer screen.

Java has eight primitive data types: long, int, short, byte, double, float, char and boolean. These are the basic Java constructs upon which data transitions are performed. Sure, Java allows you to create objects that can do all sorts of wonderful things, but deep down inside, when a Java object does something, underneath the covers, it's actually a bunch of primitive data types that are having their contents manipulated.

To become Java certified, you have to know the basic operators that can work on primitive data types. Probably the first, most straight forward operator, is the assignment operator, =, also known as the single equals sign.

Note: it is important to emphasize that a single equals sign is the assignment operator, as a double equals sign, ==, is used to compare the value of primitive types, or the memory locations of Java objects.

```
int i = 10;
boolean blackFlag = false;
float sum = 19.99f;/*the f is needed for this float*/
double yourFun = 18.67;
char broiled = 'w';
```

Variable Assignment with the Single Equals Sign

The easiest way to manipulate data is to simply assign a new value to a variable. To give a new value to a previously initialized variable, you simply use the assignment operator and supply a new value.

```
int x = 10;/*declare and initialize a variable named x*/
x = 20;     /*assign a new value to the variable x*/
x = 30;     /*no need to specify the data type again*/
x = 40;     /*x is an int until it goes out of scope*/
```

Revisiting Strong Typing

Notice how the data *type* is only specified once for any given variable that is declared. After a variable has been 'typed', it forever behaves as that data type. If x is declared as an int, you can forever use that variable as an int without having to explicitly state that your x is an int; just don't try to assign a floating point value to it!

```
int x = 10; /*x is typed as an int*/
x = 5;      /*no need to specify the type anymore*/
int x = 10; /*if you try to specify the type again,
               you'll get an error*/
boolean x = false; /*oh, just try changing the
                     variable type. The compiler will
                     hate you for it!*/
```

Data Manipulation: The Mathematical Operators

Of course, simply assigning a variable a new value is pretty boring. Most data assignments include addition, subtraction, multiplication, division, and yes, even modulus calculation, also known as *'figuring out the remainder from a division operation.'*

The Basic Mathematical Operators

addition	+	subtraction	-
multiplication	*	division	/
The Dreaded Modulus		**%**	

```
int x = 10;
int y = 20;

int addition       = x + y;  /* 10 + 20 = 30  */
int subtraction    = y - x;  /* 20 - 10 = 10  */
int multiplication = x * y;  /* 10 * 20 = 200 */
int division       = y / x;  /* 20 / 10 = 2   */
int modulus        = x % 3;  /* 10 % 3  = 1   */
```

Mathematical Shortcuts

Quite often you will have a situation where a number must be manipulated, and the result stored using the original variable name, such as:

```
int x = 10; /* type, name and initialize to 10 */
x = x + 1;  /* increment x by one */
x = x - 1;  /* decremement x by one */
```

Because these types of operations are so common, a special operator exists to optimize these statements, both with regards to the amount of code that needs to be written, and the amount of bytecode the compilation generates.

```
int x = 0;
x = x + 1;   /* is the same as */  x += 1;
x = x - 1;   /* is the same as */  x -= 1;
x = x / 1;   /* is the same as */  x /= 1;
x = x % 1;   /* is the same as */  x %= 1;

int m = 10;
m += 10;
System.out.println(m);   /* prints out 20 */
m -= 20;
System.out.println(m);   /* prints out 0 */
```

The Unary Operators

Another cute couple of shortcuts are the unary operators, ++ and --.

*++ (two consecutive plus signs) instructs the JVM to take a variable and **add** one.*
*-- (two consecutive minus signs) instructs the JVM to take a variable and **subtract** one.*

```
int x = 10;
x++;        /* is the same as */    x = x+1;
x--;        /* is the same as */    x = x-1;
```

Question

When performing the modulus operation:
int remainder = x % 99;
Which of the following statements are true, assuming x is a valid int?

- O a) The remainder will never be less than 99.
- O b) The remainder will never exceed 98.
- O c) The remainder will never be 0.
- O d) The remainder will never be negative.

Question

Given the following variable declarations, which of the following will print out the number 5?
int x = 6; int y = 4; int z = 1;

- ☐ a) System.out.println(--x);
- ☐ b) System.out.println(x--);
- ☐ c) System.out.println(y+1);
- ☐ d) System.out.println(3 + x % 4);
- ☐ e) System.out.println(x % 4 + 3);

Question

Given the initialization

int x = 10;

x+=5; is the equivalent of:

- O a) 15
- O b) x = x + 5;
- O c) x = = x + 5;
- O d) x = 5;

Question

What is the problem with the following code?

```
int x;
int y = x ++;
```

- O a) y has not been initialized
- O b) x has not been initialized
- O c) x has not been declared
- O d) x has not been typed

Answer

When performing the modulus operation: **int remainder = x % 99;** Which of the following statements are true, assuming x is a valid int?
○ a) The remainder will never be less than 99. ○ b) The remainder will never exceed 98. ○ c) The remainder will never be 0. ○ d) The remainder will never be negative.
If the variable x is 99, the remainder will be zero, and if x is 98, the remainder will take its maximum value of 98, as 99 will never be reached. Also, the remainder can take on a negative value if x is negative.

Answer

Given the following variable declarations, which of the following will print out the number 5? **int x = 6; int y = 4; int z = 1;**
☐ a) System.out.println(--x); ☐ b) System.out.println(x--); ☐ c) System.out.println(y+1); ☐ d) System.out.println(3 + x % 4); ☐ e) System.out.println(x % 4 + 3);
--x tells the compiler to first subtract one, and then print out the number, so a) is correct. Alternatively, b would print out 6, as x-- tells the compiler to print out the value of x, which is 6, and then subtract one from it. Answers c) d) and e) will also print out a value of 5.

Answer

Given the initialization
int x = 10;
x+=5; is the equivalent of:

- O a) 15
- O b) x = x + 5;
- O c) x == x + 5;
- O d) x = 5;

The code x+=5; is equivalent to x = x +5; although under the covers, the JVM apparently does a few shortcuts when it sees an operator like this, helping to speed your code up in the most insignificant of manners. Remember, a double equals sign is for comparison.

Answer

What is the problem with the following code?
int x;
int y = x ++;

- O a) y has not been initialized
- O b) x has not been initialized
- O c) x has not been declared
- O d) x has not been typed

Before a variable can be used in an expression, it must be initialized. If you wrote code that declared an int variable named x, but never assigned a value to x, the compiler would cough up a lung if you tried to add to the uninitialized variable. If x was given a value, such as int x = 10; then the code would not have a problem compiling.

Chapter 18
Conditional Logic

Computer programs are all about manipulating data, but knowing when to manipulate data, or what type of data to transform, all requires logic. That's where conditional processing comes in.

Conditional logic in Java is achieved through the use of **if ( ) { }** statements, or potentially, **if ( ){ } else { }** statements.

```
int x = 7;
if (x<7){
 System.out.println("value is less than seven");
}
else{
 System.out.println("value is greater or equal to seven");
}
```

The if( ) { } else { } Block

The structure of an if...else statement goes like this:

Start of with the word **if**, followed by a conditional statement placed within round brackets, **( )**. The conditional statement must evaluate to true or false.

Following the round brackets, you have a matching set of open and closed curly braces. When the conditional statement is true, the code within the curly brackets are executed.

If the conditional statement does not evaluate to true, the JVM looks for an else statement. When an else statement exists, the code contained in the curly brackets, **{ }**, following the word **else,** will be executed, so long as the conditional statement following the if is false.

```
/*an if statement without a corresponding else.*/

if (age >= 65) {
   System.out.println("You get a seniors discount");
}
```

Peculiarities of the if Statement

A peculiar rule applies to the if statement, that says when there is only one line to be executed after the if, you do not need curly braces. If there are no curly braces after the condition, the first statement, and the first statement only, following the condition will be executed when the condition is true. While this is a valid programming construct, your developers should never do it. Always place the statements to be executed after a condition within a block, aka curly braces. Developers who don't should be scolded.

Note: conditional statements must evaluate to true or false. Some languages allow the content of a conditional statement to evaluate to the number 1 or zero, indicating true or false. This is not valid in Java. Make sure your expressions evaluate to either the boolean value true, or the boolean value false.

Conditional Operators

The conditional segment contained in the round braces of an if statement will contain some combination of conditional operators that work with data to generate a boolean result of *true* or *false*. To do this, some combination of relational and logical operators must be involved. The relational and logical operators include:

greater than	>	less than	<
greater than or equal to	>=	less than or equal to	<=
and	&&	or	||

Getting Tied in Nots

An interesting, and much loved operator in the Java programming language is the ***'bang'*** or ***'not'*** operator. The ***exclamation point*** negates any boolean or conditional statement of which it sits in front, turning a true into a false, or a false into a true.

```
int x =10;
if (!(x==10)){
   System.out.println("BANG!!! x is NOT ten.");
}
else {
   System.out.println("x is ten.");
}
```

Dropping the Bang

So, if you had a statement that said:

if (x = =10) { }

you could drop a bang on that expression and create the opposite expression:

if (! (x = =10)) { }

Of course, the expression (!(x==10)) isn't all that handsome. The BANG can be combined with the equal sign to create an operator, != , that means ***not equal to.***

!(x==10) is the same as (x!=10)

```
int x = 10;
if ((x!=10)){
  System.out.println("BANG!!! x is NOT ten.");
}else {
  System.out.println("x is ten.");
}
```

When I was in grade 1, my teacher told me to think of the greater than or less than operator as a Pac Man with an open mouth. A Pac man would always want to eat the value that was the greatest. I still think of a Pac Man when trying to figure out which way a less than or greater than sign goes.

The Unloved Switch Statement

Along with the if(){}else{} statement, another, less used conditional statement is the switch statement. The switch statement looks at an whole number, and then matches that number with a special case:

```
int day = 5;
switch (day) {
  case 1: System.out.println("Monday"); break;
  case 2: System.out.println("Tuesday"); break;
  case 3: System.out.println("Wednesday"); break;
  case 4: System.out.println("Thursday"); break;
  case 5: System.out.println("Friday"); break;
  case 6: System.out.println("Saturday"); break;
  case 7: System.out.println("Sunday"); break;
  default: System.out.println("Not valid!");break;
}
```

Opening the Flood Gates

The idea here, is that the switch looks at the value passed in, and then matches the value to a case. Based on the input, the appropriate condition is executed.

One thing to note about the switch statement is that it is cascading. So, in our example, if someone provided a day of 5, if there was no break statement, *Friday Saturday Sunday*, would be printed out to the user. Once a matching condition is met, the flood gates are opened, and every following case is executed, unless a break statement is encountered.

The default is executed if the value passed in does not match any of the existing cases.

Passing Judgment on the Switch

I don't like the switch statement. A switch statement is like crack to a programmer addicted to procedural programs. In Java, we like to be more object oriented. Rather than doing something based on a value, we should be able to pass a value to an object, and the object should know implicitly what to do with that value. It's a philosophical argument, but an application loaded down with lots of switch statements is probably not taking full advantage of the object oriented approach to programming.

Question

What would be the result of running the following code:

```
int x = 10;
int y = x;
if ((x > 20) && (y > 0)){
  System.out.print("Hello World");
} else {
  if ((x > 20) || (y > 0)) {
    System.out.print("Goodbye World");
  }
}
```

- O a) Hello World
- O b) Goodbye World
- O c) Hello WorldGoodbye World
- O d) HelloWorld Goodbye World

Question

Which of the following are valid conditional operators?

- ☐ a) !
- ☐ b) =
- ☐ c) >=
- ☐ d) =>

Question

Which of the following answers would produce the output "Hello World", if it was placed on the blanked out line?

```
int x = 10;
int y = x;
█████████
{
  System.out.print("Hello World");
}
```

- ☐ a) if (x = = y)
- ☐ b) if (x!=y)
- ☐ c) if (x = y)
- ☐ d) if (x <= y)
- ☐ e) if (x >= y)

Answer

What would be the result of running the following code:

```
int x = 10;
int y = x;
if ((x > 20) && (y > 0)){
  System.out.print("Hello World");
} else {
  if ((x > 20) || (y > 0)) {
    System.out.print("Goodbye World");
  }
}
```

○ a) Hello World

○ b) Goodbye World

○ c) Hello WorldGoodbye World

○ d) HelloWorld Goodbye World

For the condition in the first if to be true, both x must be greater than 20, and y must be greater than zero. Since x is 10, the condition is false, taking us into the else block. With the double pipelines, only one condition must be true, and since y is greater than 0, the block is entered, printing out the words Goodbye World to the console.

Answer

Which of the following are valid conditional operators?

☐ **a) !**

☐ b) = NOT A CONDITIONAL OPERATOR

☐ **c) >=**

☐ d) => NOT A CONDITIONAL OPERATOR

Answers a) and c) are correct. A single equals sign, as with b), is an assignment operator, and does not evaluate to true or false, as is required with a conditional operator. Answer d) has the equals sign and greater than sign in the wrong order; it should be in the order used for c). The exclamation point is the bang, or not operator, and toggles any true statement to false, or false statement to true.

Answer

Which of the following answers would produce the output "Hello World", if it was placed on the blanked out line?

```
int x = 10;
int y = x;
██████████
{
  System.out.print("Hello World");
}
```

- ☐ a) if (x = = y)
- ☐ b) if (x!=y)
- ☐ c) if (x = y)
- ☐ d) if (x <= y)
- ☐ e) if (x >= y)

Answers a) d) and e) are correct.

Be careful not to fall into the trap of the single equals sign. A single equals sign does not evaluate to true or false, but is instead, simply an assignment operator, and will cause compiler errors if you use it as a conditional statement. Since x and y are the same value, both of the 'less or greater than and equals to' equations will evaluate to true, causing Hello World to be printed out.

Chapter 19
Iterative Loops

Computer programs manipulate data. That's what they do. Of course, computer programs follow certain logical operations, and make decisions about how and when to manipulate the data they are given, but at the most basic level, computer programs are simply responsible for intelligently manipulating data.

Now where do computer programs get their intelligence from? From those clever sausages known as *'application developers,'* of course. Developers write computer programs, and insert their own logic, or intelligence, into computer programs, largely through conditional if(){}else{} statements, and to a lesser extent, switch statements. The uber important, conditional if(){}else{} statement is typically where you find the majority of a computer program's application logic.

But the reason we use computers is the great speed and efficiency with which computer programs can manipulate data, not just the ability to evaluate a conditional if statement. Computers can do repetitive tasksg incredibly quickly and efficiently, and to take advantage of the massive processing power today's computers provide us, we use iterative loops.

There are several types of looping statements in Java, namely the *for loop, while loop* and the *do while loop,* but far and away, the *for loop* is the most common.

The *Four* Loop

The for loop is so named because there are ***four*** important aspects to it: the variable assignment, the conditional statement, the incrementor, and the block of code that is designated to run during each iteration. Okay, maybe it's called a for loop because it starts with the word for, but nevertheless, it is kinda funny how there are four important parts to it.

```
for (int i=0; i<10; i++){
 System.out.println(i);
}
```

Nuances of the For Loop

The looping structures in Java are similar to the looping structures found in just about every other programming language in existence. For loops and conditional statements aren't the sexy, salacious part of the Java programming language, but it is important to familiarize yourself with some of the nuances of Java's looping syntax if you plan on becoming both competent with the language, and certified by Sun Microsystems.

Like its if(){}else{} brethren, a for loop declaration does not necessarily need to be followed by open and closed, curly braces, although as part of a good programming strategy, it should be. If the curly braces are missing, the first statement following the loop declaration is executed on each iteration of the loop

Also, each part of the for loop declaration is optional. For example, you can leave out the variable initialization, so long as the variable is initialized somewhere else in your code. Also, the iterator is also optional. In fact, you can create an infinite loop by not putting any real values in the for loop declaration.

Really Messed Up, But Valid, for Loops

```
/*no initializer*/

int i = 10;
for ( ; i<10; i++){
  ++i;
}
```

```
/*no iterator*/

int i = 10;
for ( ; i<10; ){
  i++;
}
```

```
/*no nothing!!!*/

for ( ; ; ){
  i++;
  if (i>10){break;}
}
```

Continue and Break

Notice how in the /***no nothing***/ example, we used the ***break;*** command to exit the for loop. If you ever want to short circuit a for loop during its execution, you can use the keyword *break*. This will exit the loop and move the flow of execution to the first statement following the for loop code block.

Also, sometimes you want to short circuit a for loop, but instead of completely exiting the for loop, you want execution to return to the beginning of the loop, without executing the remaining lines of code in the loop. If this is the behavior you need, you can use the ***continue;*** keyword. The continue keyword tells execution to exit out of the ***current*** loop iteration, but return to the top of the loop for ***further*** iterations.

While We're At It

Less common than the for loop, but equally important, is the while loop.

The while( ){} loop simply takes a conditional statement, evaluates that conditional statement, and then executes code in the corresponding block until the conditional statement becomes ***false***.

```
int i = 0;
while (i!=10){
  System.out.println(++i);
}
```

One thing you always need to note about a while loop is the fact that you must have some code within the iteration block that, under some circumstance, changes the evaluated conditional statement to false. If you do not, you will have created an infinite loop, which is valid, but can be egregiously annoying.

To Infinity and Beyond! Infinite While Loops

Of course, sometimes you do wish to create an infinite loop, especially when you're kicking off a new thread of execution or something. To create an infinite loop, you can simply set the conditional statement of the while loop to true.

```
while (true) {
/*do something in this infinite loop*/
}
```

Also, break and continue statements can be used within a while loop, just as they are used within a for loop.

A Do, Run, Run, Run; a Do Run While

The last type of flow control statement we'll deal with here is the do{}while() loop.

The do{}while() loop is like an upside down while loop. Whereas a while loop will only ever execute if the conditional statement it evaluates before an iteration is true, a do{}while() loop will always execute ***at least once,*** regardless of the boolean value of the conditional statement with which it is associated. Along with always executing at least once, the do{}while()loop will iterate continually until the conditional statement with which it is associated becomes false.

The do{}while() loop is a great choice if you want to be assured that the code associated with a loop will always be executed at least once, and potentially more than once if the conditional statement at the end of the do{}while() is true.

```
do{
/*do something in this loop*/
}while(true)
```

Generics and Java 1.5

One of the historically annoying aspects of the java.util collection classes is the fact that you can throw any old type of object into them. If you have a Vector, or a Hashtable, you can toss in Strings, StringBuffers, Integers, Sockets, and even other Vectors and Hashtables. You can throw anything into the standard Java collection classes, which can cause all sorts of problems when it comes time to pull things out.

So, say I have a Vector, and I want that vector to contain nothing but Shapes. Sure, it can hold Squares, or Circles, or Triangles, but I don't want anyone to throw anything into the Vector that isn't a shape.

However, the add method of the Vector class takes an Object as an argument, so even if you code your applications to throw nothing but a Shape into your vector, someone can always come along and toss in a String or a Socket. This can end up triggering all sorts of ClassCastExceptions at runtime. Well, in version 1.5, the Java Gods have introduced a new concept called generics that will make all of your collection classes a little bit more type-safe.

Now, when creating a Vector or a Set, or any other type of Collection, you can throw a class name inside of less-than and greater-than signs to indicate the type of objects that will be allowed to be placed in the collection class. So, to create a Vector than can contain nothing but objects that implement the Shape interface, you could use syntax that looks something like this:

```
Vector<Shape> shapes = new Vector<Shape>();
```

The Vector<Shape> declaration is to be read as "a vector containing types of Shapes." Once you have declared a Vector containing types of Shapes, the compiler will make sure that nobody throws anything inside of your Vector that isn't a Shape, or sub-type of Shape. Any attempts to do so will result in a compile time error, meaning invalid code will never even make it into production, something that couldn't be said before generics were introduced into the Java language.

```
/* Declare a Vector that only contains types of Shapes */

Vector<Shape> shapes = new Vector<Shape> ();

shapes.add(new Circle()); /* this will work */
shapes.add(new Square()); /* this will work */
shapes.add(new Rectangle()); /* this will work */
//shapes.add(new String()); /*COMPILE TIME ERROR!!!*/
shapes.add(new Square()); /* This will work */
```

The For-Each Loop

The concept of the generic, which was introduced in version 1.5, addresses the common problem of type checking objects that have been placed into a collection class. Complimenting the idea of generics is the for-each loop, which ensures that when a program pulls objects **out** of a collection class, only objects of a particular type are retrieved.

As was stated before, you can add just about any piece of junk to a java.util collection class. In previous versions of Java, we might create a collection class that is *intended* to only hold Shape objects, or Button objects, but *intention* isn't validated by a Java compiler, so when you pull objects out of a collection, the potential for ClassCastExceptions hangs over your programs like the *Sword of Damocles*.

To avoid the potential of ClassCastExceptions, not to mention the extra code required to cast an Object into your intended type, Java 1.5 introduced the for-each loop, which allows you to confidently loop through a collection of known types, without having to do annoying and needless casts. So, for example, to loop through a Vector of Shape objects, created using the generic syntax Vector<Shape>, you could code a for-each loop that looks like this:

```
for (Shape s : shapes){
 System.out.println(s.toString());
}
```

Reading the For-Each Loop

A big step in understanding how a for-each loop works is to understand how to verbalize the syntax. The syntax:

```
for (Shape s : shapes){/*do something iterative here*/}
```

can be read as "loop through all of the *Shape* objects ***in the collection class named shapes***. As you iterate through this collection class, pull one Shape out of the collection at a time, give that Shape the name s, and allow that Shape named s to be accessed in the corresponding code block."

Here's a full code snippet that creates a Vector of Shape objects, using the generics syntax, along with the code needed to loop through that Vector using the for-each loop construct:

```
Vector<Shape> shapes = new Vector<Shape>();

shapes.add(new Circle());
shapes.add(new Square());
shapes.add(new Rectangle());
//shapes.add(new String());
shapes.add(new Square());

for (Shape s : shapes){
System.out.println(s.toString());
}
```

For-Each and Generics on the SCJA Exam

On the SCJA exam, you won't be asked any extremely in depth questions about generics and the for-each loop. For the exam, you must be familiar with the basic syntax of the for-each loop, and the basic syntax for declaring a collection class that is of a designated type.

The important thing to know for the SCJA exam is ***why*** you might use generics, or a for-each loop. Generics make design-time, type-checking of objects being placed in a collection class, possible. The for-each loop makes it possible to confidently extract objects of a particular type out of a collection class, without having to perform a cast, or worry about the potential for ClassCastExceptions.

Question

You are accepting input from a user, until they provide the String "quit." What is the best iterative structure to use to implement this functionality?

- O a) a for loop
- O b) a while loop
- O c) a do..while loop
- O d) an if statement

Question

What would be the best description of the output of the following code?

```
for (int i=0; i<10; i++)
  System.out.print("Hello World");
  System.out.println("Goodbye World);
```

- O a) *Hello World Goodbye World* ten times
- O b) *Hello World* ten times, then *Goodbye World* ten times
- O c) *Hello World Goodbye World* once
- O d) *Hello World* ten times, and *Goodbye World* once

Question

Which of the following is true about the following loop:

```
while (true) {/*do something*/}
```

- O a) it could broken by a continue statement
- O b) it could broken with a break statement
- O c) it would not compile, because it creates an endless loop
- O d) the loop will be exited when the condition becomes false

Answer

You are accepting input from a user until they provide the String "quit." What is the best iterative structure to use to implement this functionality?

- O a) a for loop
- O b) a while loop
- O c) a do..while loop
- O d) an if statement

As my friends at PETA say, "there's more than one way to skin a cat," and for this question, the solution could probably be implemented with just about any looping structure. However, a do..while loop is intended to be entered once, and then iterated through until a given condition is met. The do…while loop is a perfect solution for this scenario.

Answer

What would be the best description of the output of the following code?

```
for (int i=0; i<10; i++)
  System.out.print("Hello World");
  System.out.println("Goodbye World);
```

- O a) *Hello World Goodbye World* ten times
- O b) *Hello World* ten times, then *Goodbye World* ten times
- O c) *Hello World Goodbye World* once
- O d) *Hello World* ten times, and *Goodbye World* once

This is a dirty little question. The indenting makes it appear that both the hello and goodbye statements are part of the for loops code block, but they are not. If no chicken lips, { } , follow a for loop declaration, only the first line after the declaration is considered to be part of the iterative block. As a result, Hello World gets printed out ten times, and then when the loop is complete, execution goes to the next line of code after the loop, resulting in Goodbye World being printed out once.

Answer

Which of the following is true about the following loop: while (true) {/*do something*/}
O a) it could broken by a continue statement O b) it could broken with a break statement O c) it would not compile, because it creates an endless loop O d) the loop will be exited when the condition becomes false
Since the condition is set to the value true, the loop will be infinite, which is somewhat strange, but completely valid. The only way to break out of this loop is to code some condition inside of the loop that triggers a break, which would take execution out of the loop, and to the first statement that follows the code block.

Chapter 20
Working with Strings

There are eight primitive types in Java, and *Strings aren't one of them.* That surprises a good number of people, because a character String is just about as important as anything you'll ever find in a computer program; but for good reason, a String is not a primitive type in Java.

Stringing You Along

Now, what are objects? Objects are really just an organized assortment of underlying data, which in Java, is represented by the eight, basic, primitive types. And what is a String? Well, a String is just an organized collection of characters, or, more accurately in Java, a collection of *primitives* of type char.

Now, one of the problems with primitive types is that you can't call methods on them. An int doesn't have any methods; similarly, a char doesn't have any methods. Primitive types simply represent data, and as a result, they don't have methods you can invoke. Primitive types just represent data, and that's it. But *objects* can have as many salacious methods as you want them ot have, and the String class is no exception.

Nothing *new* About Strings

Now I call Strings *the messed-up object type,* because they break a whole bunch of important rules about using objects. For example, when you create an object in Java, you create the object by using the ***new*** keyword. The ***new*** keyword instructs the JVM to put aside a whole bunch of memory space to store the new object you're about to create and initialize. But this isn't so with Strings. When you create a String, you don't use the new keyword. Well, you can, but you're not really supposed to.

```
/*You can use new with Strings, but you're not supposed to.*/
String hi = new String("hi");

/*String can be created easily without using the new keyword.*/
String bye = "bye";
```

Overloading the Addition Operator, +

Also, the other *messed-up* thing about Strings is the fact that you can use the + operator to perform String concatenation, (which is just a big word for addition.) Using the + operator for Strings is a form of operator overloading, if you ask me. Operator overloading is basically when you take an operator, in this case, the plus sign, and allow it to work in different situations. A plus sign already works for adding primitive types. Java has overloaded the + operator to make it work for concatenating Strings as well. You're not supposed to be able to overload operators in Java, but someone's gone ahead and done it for Strings. I don't like it!

So, when you have two Strings you want to join together, you can easily use the + operator:

```
String hello = "Hello";
String world = "World";
String space = " ";

String output = hello+space+world;
System.out.println(output);
/* This prints out Hello World */
```

An interesting peculiarity of String concatenation, is the fact that Strings are concatenated from left to right, but if the value used for concatenation is numeric, the JVM will actually do a calculation until the very first character is encountered, after which, String concatenation takes place. Take a look at the following example:

```
String sum = 1 + 2 + " is " + 1 + 2;
System.out.print(sum);
```

What do you think gets printed out? Well, the JVM treats the 1 and the 2 to the left of the word equals numerically, so it adds them together. The result of the addition is concatenated to the String *is,* and then the numbers 1 and 2 to the right are concatenated to the word *is*. As a result, the code snippet ends up printing out *3 is 12,* which doesn't really make sense to you or me, but it makes perfect sense to the compiler. Be careful when using numbers during String concatenation. It can get confusing.

Important Methods of the String Class

Now, since the String class is not a primitive type, it can have methods, and boy, does it ever have some helpful and interesting methods. There are a few methods you need to know, not just for the certification exam, but for your good health, and Java programming benefit as well. According to the SCJA Exam objectives, you must be prepared to recognize the appropriate use of the following methods of the String class: charAt, indexOf, trim, substring, replace, startsWith and endsWith.

Finding a char at a Given Index: charAt(int)

First of all, given a String, you can use the charAt method, and provide a number, and the String class will tell you the value of the char that resides at that index. You should note that this is zero based counting, so charAt(***1***) will actually give you the value of the ***second*** char in the string.

```
String hello = "Hello";
System.out.println(hello.charAt(1));

/* This will print out the letter e */
```

To compliment the charAt(int) method, there is the indexOf(String) method that, given a String, will tell you the index of where the provided String occurs in the instance on which the method is invoked.

```
String hello = "Hello";

System.out.println(hello.indexOf("H"));/*returns 0;*/

System.out.println(hello.indexOf("l"));/*returns 2;*/

System.out.println(hello.indexOf("o"));/*returns 4;*/

System.out.println(hello.indexOf("q"));/*returns -1*/
```

Nuances of the indexOf Method

A few, finer points to notice about the indexOf method, includes the fact that the indexOf method is zero based, so the first letter in a String will be at the indexOf zero.

Furthermore, if a letter occurs more than once in a String, as with the letter 'l' in the word "Hello", the index of the first occurrence will be returned.

Finally, if the argument for the indexOf method is a letter that simply does not exist in the String, then a value of minus one (-1), is returned. These are the nuances of the indexOf method that you will be quizzed on in the SCJA certification exam.

Trimming the Length of a String

Two other methods that sorta compliment each other are the no argument, trim() and length(), methods.

When invoked on a String, the trim() method returns a ***new*** String that is devoid of any trailing or leading whitespace. There's really no point in keeping ten or twenty meaningless, empty blanks, at the end of a String, especially if you're storing that String in a database, or manipulating that String in memory. Most String manipulations start off with a trimming of the String.

```
String blanks = "    Hello World        ";

System.out.println(blanks.length());   /* prints 20 */

String blanksTrimmed = blanks.trim();

System.out.println(blanksTrimmed.length());
                                        /* prints 11 */
```

With the trim() method, it is vitally important to stress the fact that the original String on which the method is invoked is not altered. Only the String returned from the method has whitespace removed – the origially String object remains untouched.

Nuances of the length() Method

The length() method of the String class will tell you how many characters exist in your String. The length() method starts counting at the number one, so a String containing a single character, will return a value of one (1), not zero. New Java developers get used to the zero based counting paradigm, and expect a String with one character to have a length of zero, which is understandable. But the length method starts counting at the first character, so a String with one character in it will indeed return a length count of 1.

Also, you should note that the length method includes blank characters when calculating the length of String. If you don't use a trimmed String, the number returned from invoking the length() method will include any empty spaces that trail the content of your String.

The Overloaded substring Method

Also, if you're doing some String manipulation in your Java programs, the *substring* and *replace* methods might come in handy.

The String class has two, overloaded substring methods, one taking a single int as an argument, the other taking two int values as arguments:

- substring(int beginIndex)
- substring(int beginIndex, int endIndex)

The substring(int beginIndex) method looks at a String, and returns a new String containing all of the characters between the index provided as a parameter, and the end of the String. Note that the substring method is zero based, which means the first character in a given String has an index of zero.

```
String numbers = "123456789";
System.out.println(numbers.substring(5));
/*prints out 6789, as substring is zero based*/
```

There is also a helpful substring method that takes *two* arguments of type int, with the first int indicating a starting index, and the second int indicating an ending index position. This substring method returns all of the characters between and including the first index provided, and ending at, but not including, the last index position. And remember, this is zero based counting. So, on the word Hello, substring(2,4) would return *ll*, not *el.* Sometimes Java neophytes get a little confused as to how many characters will be generated by the call to this substring method. Subtracting the second argument from the first argument tells you how many characters will be returned from this method. From there, you just have to remember that the first parameter, int beginIndex, is the indcx of the first character returned, keeping in mind that the first character in the String is at index position zero.

```
String numbers = "123456789";
System.out.println(numbers.substring(3,7));
/* prints out 4567 due to zero based counting */
```

The Overloaded replace Methods

Data manipulation often involves searching for a given sequence of characters in a String, and then replacing the sequence of interest with a new sequence of characters. To help facilitate this process, the String class provides two, very helpful, overloaded, replace methods:

- replace(char oldChar, char newChar)
- replace(CharSequence target, CharSequence replacement)

The replace methods are fairly straight forward.

The replace method that takes two char values as arguments simply creates a copy of the String of interest, inspects the new String, looks for a given char value in the String of interest, and replaces it with a different char, namely the one provided as the second parameter to this method. It is worthwhile noting that this method will replace *every* matching char, not just the first match that is encountered. Also, this method returns a new String with the appropriate characters replaced – it does not effect the String on which it is invoked.

Along with the replace method that takes two char values as arguments, there is also a replace method that takes two CharSequence types as parameters. Now, don't let the reference to a CharSequence scare you. A CharSequence is simply an interface that is implemented by the String class, so for that sake of simplicity, and the SCJA exam, you can think of this method as taking two String objects as parameters. Basically, this method will look for a given String, or CharSequence, as specified by the first argument, and when that sequence of characters is found, will replace that sequence with the String, or CharSequence, specified by the second argument.

One thing to note is that the replace method either takes two char values as parameters, or two CharSequence objects as parameters. You cannot invoke the replace method with one argument being a char, and the other argument being a String, and vice-versa. Doing so would create a compile error, which is something you want to aviod, and recognize on the SCJA exam.

Another thing to note about the replace method is that it generates a new String object with the appropriate characters replaced, as opposed to simply affecting the String on which it was invoked. The String on which the replace method is invoked is not changed by the method call, but instead, a new String with the appropriate CharSequence replaced, is returned.

beginsWith and endsWith Methods

The final two methods that are explicity referenced in the SCJA exam objectives are the beginsWith and endsWith methods, both of which take a single String as an argument, and return a boolean value of either true or false.

The startsWith method basically tells you if a given String starts with the same String passed in as an argument. The endsWith method basically tells you if a given String ends with the same String that has been passed in as an argument. It's fairly straight forward.

```
String pal = "sit on a pan otis";
System.out.println(pal.startsWith("sit")); /*true*/
System.out.println(pal.startsWith("tis")); /*false*/
System.out.println(pal.endsWith("sit"));   /*false*/
System.out.println(pal.endsWith("tis"));   /*true*/
```

There are a couple of things you need to know about the startsWith and endsWith methods:

First, the methods take String objects as parameters, not char primitive types. Sometimes the SCJA exam will pass in a char as an argument to throw you off. Passing a char as an argument to the startsWith or endsWith method will cause a compile time error.

Secondly, if you pass in an empty String, such as "", the method will return the boolean value of true. That's a bit counter-intuitive, and they may try to trick you up on this fact on the exam.

Third and finally, the startsWith method is overloaded. There is another startsWith method that takes a String and an int as a parameter. This incarnation of the startWith method begins the comparison at the zero-based offset specified by the int argument passed to the method. The endsWith method on the other hand, is not overloaded.

```
/*                  01234567890123456               /*
String pal = "sit on a pan otis";

System.out.println(pal.startsWith("sit"));      //true
System.out.println(pal.startsWith("tis", 14)); //true
```

String Comparisons

I consider the String class to be one of the messed up primitive types, because it breaks a few of the standard rules associated with Java development. One of the rules that the String class breaks, is the one that says instance are created by using the new keyword. With a String, it is very rare to see an instance created with the new keyword.

```
/*You can use new with Strings, but you're not supposed to.*/
String newKeyword = new String("new");

/*String can be created easily without using the new keyword.*/
String noNewKeyword = "not new";
```

There's actually a few interesting things going on behind the scenes when you create an instance of a String, especially when you chose not to use the new keyword. You see, Strings are used constantly in Java programs, and in typical applications, there are usually common character strings that get used over and over and over again. Imagine a busy, web based application, that needs to work with dates and times: how many times do you think the names of the months, or the days of the week, get repeated on a per user basis? What if there were thousands of users hitting the site at the same time? If each String, representing a day or a month, was given a separate memory space, there'd be a massive amount of duplication, and an immense amount of memory going to waste.

However, with Java, when a String is created, the value of the instance is put into something called a String pool. If a new String is needed that matches a value of a String in the String pool, rather than setting side a new chunk of memory, the JVM just points the new instance to the existing String in the String pool – that way, if the month *March* occurs 2000 times in a Java application, rather than having the word *March* duplicated 2000 times, there will only be one actual instance, with each of the 2000 String references simply pointing to this single String. It's all very efficient, and managed for you, behind the scenes, by the very helpful Java Virtual Maching (JVM).

Equality Comparisons

Comparing values for equality is a very common practice in any, standard, computer application. From working with primitive types, we know that int and char and boolean values are compared by using the double equals sign, ==. Furthermore, we know that when we compare objects for equality, we need to use the .equals method, becuase when you use the double equals sign, ==, with objects, you end up comparing the memory locations of the objects, as opposed to the actual objects themselves.

Take a look at the following code block, that compares two java.awt.Color objects:

```
java.awt.Color c1 = new java.awt.Color(225,225,225);
java.awt.Color c2 = new java.awt.Color(225,225,225);

System.out.println(c1==c2);          /* prints false */
System.out.println(c1.equals(c2)); /* prints true  */
```

Notice how a result of false is generated when the two Color objects are compared using the double equals sign, ==, but result of true is generated when the two Color objects are compared using the .equals method. This is the type of result that we would expect, as the two objects are indeed the same colour, with all the same RGB (Red Green Blue) values.

Because the two objects were created individually using the new keyword, each instance stores its information in a separate and isolated memory location. So, when you use the double equals sign to compare objects, you end up comparing memory locations, so two objects that are created separately, such as the Color objects c1 and c2 in the code block, will return a double equals sign comparison of false.

However, the two Color objects, c1 and c2, represent the same colour, so logically, the two colours are the same. A proper comparison of two objects should be done using the .equals method. When colours c1 and c2 are compared using the .equals method, we get a result of true, indicating that the two colours are indeed the same.

So, to get a proper comparison with primitive types, you use the double equals sign, but with objects, the double equals sign compares memory locations, so to get a proper evaluation of the equality of objects, you must use the .equals method. However, the String pool creates a bit of an exception to this rule.

Comparing Strings

By optmizing the use of a String pool, the JVM ends up storing setting aside a single memory location that can be pointed at by references to the same character String. The use of the String pool helps optimize memory use, but it also results in the double equals sign, ==, generating accurate results when String objects are compared.

```
String oneEh = "one";
String oneBee = "one";

System.out.println(oneEh==oneBee);         /* prints true */
System.out.println(oneEh.equals(oneBee)); /* prints true */
```

So, we have worked hard to establish a rule that says objects should be compared using the .equals method, and primitive types must be compared using the double equals sign, ==, but all of a sudden, it appears that String objects can be accurately compared using the double equals sign. Well, the double equals sign will generally generate an accurate comparison of String objects, but sometimes it won't, and it's that lack of dependability that tells you that you should never compare String objects using the double equals sign.

New String Objects

For the most part, the String pool is used for efficiently managing String objects in memory. However, when the *new* keyword is used in conjuction with String object creation, the String that gets created is actually given a separate, isolated, memory location which is not shared with any other String objects in the application. When the new keyword is used in conjunction with String object creation, comparisons of String that share a common character sequence, will generate a false value when a double equals sign is used.

```
String oneEh =  new String("one");
String oneBee = new String("one");

System.out.println(oneEh==oneBee);        /* prints false */
System.out.println(oneEh.equals(oneBee)); /* prints true */
```

Since String objects are typically created without using the new keyword, comparisons using a double equals sign will typically work – but when programming, we don't like solutions that typically work; we like solutions that *always* work. The lesson to be learned is that when comparing objects, whether it is a String or a Color object, to get a true representation of the equality of the objects, use the .equals method, and only use the double equals sign, ==, when you are interested in comparing memory locations.

Heavy String Manipulation in Java

Now the String class makes working with Strings incredibly easy, but because of the way Java manages memory for Strings, heavy String manipulation with the String class isn't recommended. Instead, the StringBuffer class allows you to manipulate a String without the JVM re-writing memory locations all of the time. If you're doing alot of String manipulations in your code, you'd be better off using the StringBuffer class. Actually, if you're doing a whole lot of String manipulation, you'd be really better off kicking off a PERL script and feeding the results back to the Java program, but that's way, way beyond the scope of the certification exam.

It should also be noted that the String class, like the wrapper classes Double, Integer, Boolean and Long, are marked with the final keyword, and as such, cannot be extended. This is to ensure the integrity of application data, and make sure nobody does any tricky or fancy stuff to your data by extending these foundation classes of the SDK.

Question

Given dates in the format dd-mm-yyyy, how would you parse out the numbers, while ignoring the dashes?
O a) day: substring(1,3) month: substring(4,6) year: substring(7,11)
O b) day: substring(0,3) month: substring(3,6) year: substring(6,11)
O c) day: substring(1,2) month: substring(4,5) year: substring(7,10)
O d) day: substring(0,2) month: substring(3,5) year: substring(6,10)

Question

Given dates in the format dd-mm-yyyy, what would the method indexOf("-") return?
O a) the number 2
O b) the number 3
O c) the numbers 2 and 5
O d) the numbers 3 and 6

Question

A web based application receives a String from a textfield. Before saving the String to the database, which method should be called on the String?
O a) validate()
O b) length()
O c) trim()
O d) append()

Question

To loop through a name String, one character at a time, to ensure that none of the characters are numeric, which methods of the String class would be most useful?
☐ a) length
☐ b) charAt
☐ c) trim
☐ d) append

Answer

Given dates in the format dd-mm-yyyy, how would you parse out the numbers, while ignoring the dashes?
O a) day: substring(1,3) month: substring(4,6) year: substring(7,11) O b) day: substring(0,3) month: substring(3,6) year: substring(6,11) O c) day: substring(1,2) month: substring(4,5) year: substring(7,10) O d) day: substring(0,2) month: substring(3,5) year: substring(6,10)

Answer d) is correct. The substring method uses a zero based counting method, inclusive of the first number, and incremental on the last number, meaning if you wanted the first and second characters in a string, you would need to specify 0,2 as the parameters to the substring method.

```
String date = "31-02-1999";
String day = date.substring(0,2);
String month = date.substring(3,5);
String year = date.substring(6,10);
```

Answer

Given dates in the format dd-mm-yyyy, what would the method indexOf("-") return?
O a) the number 2 O b) the number 3 O c) the numbers 2 and 5 O d) the numbers 3 and 6

Again, the indexOf method is a zero based counting method, so the third character in the String is given the index number of two. Note that only one number is returned, even though there are multiple dashes in the String; regardless, only the index of the first encountered match is returned.

Answer

A web based application receives a String from a textfield. Before saving the String to the database, which method should be called on the String?

○ a) validate()
○ b) length()
○ c) trim()
○ d) append()

When character Strings are fed from a user interface, into a programming model, the Strings are often filled with all sorts of trailing whitespace, also known as blank characters, that serve no purpose, and only take up space in memory and on the hard drive if physically stored. The trim() method creates a new String, with all leading and trailing whitespace removed, and getting rid of redundant whitespace will make your programs more efficient.

It is important to note that the trim() method trims off both leading and trailing whitespace, and it ***returns*** a ***new***, trimmed, String, without changing the String on which the method is invoked.

Answer

To loop through a name String, one character at a time, to ensure that none of the characters are numeric, which methods of the String class would be most useful?

☐ a) length
☐ b) charAt
☐ c) trim
☐ d) append

To iterate through each element of a String, and evaluate the current character, the two methods needed would be length, which tells you how many characters are in the String, and charAt, which gets you the character at a particular index.

```
String movement = "26th of July";
for (int i=0; i < movement.length( ); i++) {
  System.out.println(movement.charAt(i));
}
```

Chapter 21
char: The Messed Up Primitive

This section goes extremely in depth on the topic of the char variable, and while you may get questions at this depth on the Sun Certified Java ***Programmer*** exam, you won't deal with anything this intense on the SCJA exam. Nevertheless, it's interesting to examine just how much of a slippery shapeshifter this char primitive type really is. At the very least, for the SCJA exam, you should know the various ways to intialize a char.

Chars are the messed up datatype.

A char is a byte-sized datatype that supposedly represents a character, right? Well, maybe. Let's see what Sun Microsystems has to say about the primitive type *char*.

From Sun: *" Character Data Types: Java language character data is a departure from traditional C. Java's char data type defines a sixteen-bit Unicode character. Unicode characters are unsigned 16-bit values that define character codes in the range 0 through 65,535. If you write a declaration such as:*
char myChar = `Q';
you get a Unicode (16-bit unsigned value) type initialized to the Unicode value of the character Q. By adopting the Unicode character set standard for its character data type, Java language applications are amenable to internationalization and localization, greatly expanding the market for world-wide applications."

So, with standard characters you can find on your keyboard, you can initialize a char fairly easily: **char myChar = 'x';**

With chars, you cannot set them to an empty string. Well, you can, but you can't. You can set them to a blank, but you can't set them to nothing. Well, maybe that makes sense; it confuses me though.

```
char emptyChar = '';/*not allowed...no space*/
char blankChar = ' '; /*allowed...blank, empty space,
but a space nevertheless*/
char emptyUnicodeChar = '\0';
```

Using a Hexadecimal Value

Say you want to print out a copyright symbol. The hex entry for the copyright symbol is 00A9, although I'm sure you already knew that. Here's how you would initialize a char to a hex value:

```
char emptyUnicodeChar = '\u00A9';
System.out.println(emptyUnicodeChar);
```

So, the char data type represents a single character, and one single character *only*. A char can be initialized by actually using the character literal, as in the following line of code:

char myChar = 'c';

A char can also be initialized by specifying the Unicode hex code for the character: ***You will see a Unicode initialization on the exam.***

char theChar = '\u009a';

Initialization of a char requires a single quote, so a double quote will not work.

```
char singleQuoteWorks = 's';
char doubleQuotesWontWork = "s"; /*this line will
                                  cause a compile error*/
```

Char: The Mysterious Integer Type

So, char is a character type, right? Well, maybe; Here's where a char really messes things up. For example, would the following code run?

char c = u;

Of course that won't run, because a char has to be initialized using single quotes around the value to which it is being initialized. So, will the following compile?

char number = 2;

Well, actually, it will. A char can be initialized to any positive, 16-bit number, and it can also be treated as a number in an equation as well. So, the following ***would*** work:

```
char two = 2;
char three = 3;

int result = three * two;

System.out.println(result); //returns 6
```

When a char is initialized to a single digit number without quotes, the char can be treated as a normal number type, and typical mathematical operations, like addition and multiplication, can be applied to the char.

Notice that the result is an int. When two integer types are multiplied, with the exception of a long, the return is an int.

Now, what if we do the same thing with a char, but place single quotes around the single digit integers:

```
char two = '2';
char three = '3';
```

Well, in this case, the chars are treated as Unicode characters, and trying to multiply the char multiplies the Unicode equivalent, which is 50 for the number two, and 51 for the number three. Multiplying two times three results in 2550!

```
int result = three * two;

System.out.println(1*two); //50
System.out.println(1*three);//51

System.out.println(result); //returns 2550
```

Anyways, I can't explain it. All I can say is that a char is a messed up number type. That just about says it all.

15 Questions:
Implementing Java Concepts

Question 1

What Java keyword has been defined to represent an enumeration type?

- O a) enumeration
- O b) Enumeration.
- O c) Enum
- O d) enum

Question 2

Which of the following are valid means of initializing a String?

- ☐ a) String s = "Hello World";
- ☐ b) String s = 'Hello World';
- ☐ c) String s = new String("Hello World");
- ☐ d) String s = new Object("Hello World");

Question 3

Which of the following are valid ways of initializing an Integer?

- ☐ a) Integer x = new Integer(10);
- ☐ b) Integer x = 10;
- ☐ c) Integer x.equals(10);
- ☐ d) Integer x == null;

Question 4

What is the purpose of packages in Java?

- ☐ a) to organize logically related classes together
- ☐ b) to represent a file folder system in a platform independent manner
- ☐ c) to avoid having to separate compiled Java files into subfolders
- ☐ d) to help compress applications into a single file for deployment

Question 5

You are creating a Warning object for various security systems. The Warning object must contain a signal method that subclasses must implement, and each warning object must have a Timer object and Count object associated with them. What Java artifact is best for templating this Warning type?

- O a) interface
- O b) enum
- O c) abstract class
- O d) concrete class

Question 6

Given an interface named Flexible, another interface named Breakable, and a class named Plastic, which of the following would be valid top level declarations?

- ☐ a) class Plastic extends Flexible {}
- ☐ b) class Plastic implements Breakable { }
- ☐ c) interface Flexible implements Breakable { }
- ☐ d) interface Breakable extends Flexible { }

Question 7

A class called Sensor has a method called alarm(). You want to keep track of the number of times the alarm method is called for all instances of the Sensor class. What is the easiest way to implement this functionality?

- O a) create an instance variable named count, and increment the count variable in a static method
- O b) create an instance variable named count, and increment the count variable in the alarm() method
- O c) create a static variable named count, and increment the count variable in a static method
- O d) create a static variable named count, and increment the count variable in the alarm() method

Question 8

A class called Sensor has a method called alarm(). You want each instance of the Sensor class to keep track of the number of times its alarm method goes off. What is the easiest way to implement this functionality?

O a) create an instance variable named count, and increment the count variable in a static method

O b) create an instance variable named count, and increment the count variable in the alarm() method

O c) create a static variable named count, and increment the count variable in a static method

O d) create a static variable named count, and increment the count variable in the alarm() method

Question 9

Which of the following will print out the version of the Java runtime you are using? Assume a file named HelloWorld.java is in the bin directory, and has been compiled.

☐ a) java -version

☐ b) java –version HelloWorld

☐ c) javac -version

☐ d) javac –version HelloWorld.java

☐ e) javac –v HelloWorld.java

☐ f) java –ver

Question 10

Which of the following are valid ways of initializing a char?

☐ a) `char lie = '1';`

☐ b) `char coal = 33333;`

☐ c) `char itable = '\u0057';`

☐ d) `char ming = "x";`

Question 11

Which of the following lines of code will compile without error?

☐ a) `float am = 6.40;`

☐ b) `float cfrb = 10.0 + 10.0;`

☐ c) `float illa = 10.10f;`

☐ d) `float some = (float)(10.10 * 6.40);`

Question 12

What line of code, placed in the blanked out space, would generate the following output:

```
1 5
2 4
3 3
4 2
5 1
```

```
int x = 0;
int y = 5;

for( int i=0; i < 5; i++){
    ████████████████████
}
```

O a) `System.out.println(x++ + " " + y--);`

O b) `System.out.println(++x + " " + --y);`

O c) `System.out.println(x++ + " " + --y);`

O d) `System.out.println(++x + " " + y--);`

Question 13

```
public interface Corruptable {
  Object doIt();
}

public class Youth implements Corruptable {

//line xxx

}
```

Which of the following pieces of code, placed on line xxx, would allow this class to successfully compile?

- ☐ a) private String doIt(){return null;}
- ☐ b) Object doIt(int i){ return null;}
- ☐ c) Object doIt(){return null;}
- ☐ d) public String doIt(){return null;}

Question 14

```
//line xxx

public class PackageTester{

 public static void main (String args[]) {

   Vector v = new Vector();
   v.add(new String("Hello World");
 }
}
```

Assuming that the Vector class is in java.util, which of the following statements added at //line xxx will enable the above code to compile properly?

- O a) package java.util;
- O b) package java.util.*;
- O c) import package java.util.*'
- O d) import java.util.Vector;

Question 15

```
//line xxx

public class PackageTester{

  public static void main (String args[]) {

    System.out.println(Math.pow(2,4));
  }

}
```

Assuming that the Math class is in java.lang, which of the following statements added at //line xxx will enable the above code to compile properly?

- ☐ a) import java.lang.*;
- ☐ b) package java.lang;
- ☐ c) import java.lang.Math;
- ☐ d) no line of code needs to be added

Answer 1

The enum is new to Java 1.5, so if your development environment doesn't support 1.5, you won't be able to test or work with enums. Of course, you can always download the 1.5 JDK from Sun, so you really have no excuse for not compiling a line of code or two that uses an enum.

Option d) is correct, as enum is the special keyword used to designate enumeration types. In code, it would look something like this:

enum Seasons { FALL, WINTER, SPRING, SUMMER;}

Answer 2

Options a) and c) are correct. While it is unusual to use the new keyword when creating a String, it is certainly valid. Option a) is the more traditional way of initializing a String, with double quotes surrounding the String.

String is one of the freak objects, where you can create an instance without the keyword new. Arrays are also included in the freak show.

Answer 3

Both a) and b) are correct. Since big I integer is an object type, and not a primitive type, it is typically initialized using the new keyword.

Before Java 1.5, Integer types had to be initialized using the new keyword. However, with the autoboxing feature of Java 1.5, the code: Integer i = 10; will actually compile. The JVM will 'autobox' or *autowrap* the lower case int of 10 into the upper case, big I, Integer class.

Answer 4

Options a) and b) are the correct answers.

Answer 5

Option c) is the correct answer.

This scenario just shouts out for an abstract class. If there were no instance variables required, such as the Timer and Count objects, an interface would be perfect. But instance variables cannot be defined in an interface, and methods in a concrete class must have an implementation, so for this scenario, only an abstract class, where instance variables and abstract methods can be defined, is appropriate.

Answer 6

☐ b) class Plastic implements Breakable { }

☐ **d) interface Breakable extends Flexible { }**

Options b) and d) are correct. Everyone should be familiar with the fact that classes implement interfaces, making option b) correct. **However, people are often surprised to find out that interfaces EXTEND other interfaces.** You can be guaranteed a question on the SCJA exam to test you on interfaces ***extending*** other interfaces.

Answer 7

Static variables are shared by every instance of a class, so if each instance of a class incremented a static variable each time a particular instance method was invoked, the static variable would be able to keep track of the number of times the given method was called for *all* instances of the class. Option d) is correct. A static variable should be created, and the static variable should be incremented each time the instance method is called.

Answer 8

Notice how this questions is very similar to the previous question, but the answer is quite a bit different. In this scenario, each sensor instance must keep a count of the number of times their alarm method goes off. In this case, an instance variable is needed, not a class level, static variable. For each instance to keep track of the number of times their alarm() method goes off, they would need an instance variable to be incremented in the alarm() method, making option b) correct.

Answer 9

Options a) b) and d) are correct.

The javac command needs a file to compile, even when asking for the version, so option c) will not work, while option d) will. Options a) and b) will both work, although b) will just give you the version of the JRE, and not actually run the HelloWorld class. Options e) and f) are incorrect, as there are no –v or –ver switches with either the javac or java utility.

Answer 10

Believe it or not, but options a) b) and c) are correct.

A char can be initialized to any character, so long as that character is surrounded by single quotes, making option a) correct. An exception to this single quote rule is when a char is initialized to an unsigned (positive) 16 bit whole number. I know, that's a messed up scenario, but it's true. Thirdly, a char can be initialized using the Unicode value of a character, so long as that Unicode character is provided in single quotes with the appropriate syntax.

Option d) is not correct. Even though the char is being initialized to a single character, the x, the fact that the x is in double quotes makes it a String, and this initialization is not valid. *Add char to the freak show.*

Answer 11

If you try to compile a) or b), you will get the following error: Type mismatch: cannot convert from double to float.

Anytime an undecorated decimal is seen in a Java program, if it is to be treated as a floating point or fractional number, the JVM will treat that literal value as a double. This is also true for most mathematical equations that result in a floating point number. As a result, a) and b) both fail to compile. The only way to properly initialize a float is to use option c), where an f is placed at the end of the decimal value, or, option d), which explicitly casts a decimal value into a float.

Option c) is definitely more preferable though. Ever since my movie career ended, I've always had a dislike for casts.

Answer 12

Only option d) is correct.

For the proper output to be displayed, you need the x to be incremented before the printout, and the y to be decremented after the printout. To achieve this, the unary operator must be before the x, and after the y. The other options simply would not produce the desired results.

You can definitely expect a question or two on the unary operators on the SCJA exam. The unary operators, especially when switched between the left and right side of a variable, confuse the very best of us. It's important that you take a code snippet like this and play around with it, and see for yourself how the unary operators behave on the JVM.

Answer 13

In this case, both options c) and d) are correct.

Option a) uses a more restrictive access modifier than the method being overridden in the parent, which is not allowed. Option b) does not have a matching method signature, which means this method overloads the doIt() method, as opposed to overriding it. Options c) and d) are correct.

Answer 14

Only option d) is correct.

The Vector, along with a variety of other collection classes, are found in the java.util package. To use a class from a package other than java.lang, you must explicitly state that you are either importing that class, or importing that entire package. Only option d) properly imports the java.util.Vector class. You could also declare **import java.util.*;** at the top of the class as well.

Answer 15

Options a) c) and d) are correct. You can gain access to all the classes in a package by importing *, or you can import a class directly by name, as in choice c). **However, all of the classes in java.lang, which includes Double, Boolean, String, Integer, Math and Long, to name a few, are automatically available to *all* Java applications, and as a result, an import statement for java.lang.* is not required.**

Part Four:
The Sample Exam

Chapter 23
Sample SCJA Exam

The following exam accurately resembles the actual SCJA exam, both in question content, and the number of questions given.

On the actual exam, you will be asked 51 questions, and given a time limit of 115 minutes.

A passing score is 68%, which means you must get at least 35 questions correct.

Good luck!

Question 1

Which of the following are included in the eight, primitive data types in Java:

- ☐ a) Integer
- ☐ b) Character
- ☐ c) boolean
- ☐ d) double
- ☐ e) String

Question 2

Which of the following techniques are valid for initializing a char?

- O a) char c = “C”;
- O b) char c = C;
- O c) char c = ‘C’;
- O d) char c = ‘see’;

Question 3

Which of the eight primitive types are signed integer types?

- ☐ a) int
- ☐ b) float
- ☐ c) double
- ☐ d) boolean
- ☐ e) char
- ☐ f) byte
- ☐ g) long
- ☐ h) short

Question 4

Which of the following statements are true:

- ☐ a) Implementing an interface relieves the implementing class from having to code methods defined and implemented in the parent
- ☐ b) Extending an abstract class relieves the extending class from having to code methods defined and implemented in the parent
- ☐ c) Abstract classes may contain unimplemented, abstract methods
- ☐ d) Interfaces may contain unimplemented, abstract methods

Question 5

The String class in Java is essentially an organized grouping of char primitive types. Assuming that every char in a String is garbage collected when the String goes out of scope, what could be said about the relationship between a String and the char primitive types that it contains:

- O a) A String is associated with chars
- O b) A String is composed of chars
- O c) A char is associated with Strings
- O d) A char is composed of Strings

Question 6

On a UML diagram, instance variables will typically be decorated with which symbol:

- O a) $
- O b) #
- O c) +
- O d) -

Question 7

What would be the output of the following code:

```
int x = 10;
int y = 5;
System.out.println( x + y  + " = x + y =  "+ x + y);
```

- O a) 15 = 15 = 15
- O b) 15 = x + y = 15
- O c) 15 = x + y = 105
- O d) 105 = x + y = 15

Figure - Q01

```
public interface Zap {
  public abstract String sayIt();
}


abstract class Zep implements Zap{
  public String sayIt(){
    return "Down deep, I am a Zep";
  }
}


class Zip extends Zep{
  public String sayIt(){
    return "Down deep, I am a Zip";
  }
}


class Zop extends Zip{
  public String sayIt(){
    return "Down deep, I am a Zop";
  }
}


class Zup {
  public String sayIt(){
    return "Down deep, I am a Zup";
  }
}
```

Question 8

Given the code in Figure Q01, what code would be valid where the blanked out box appears:

Zap z = ████ ;

- ☐ a) new Zap( );
- ☐ b) new Zep( );
- ☐ c) new Zip( );
- ☐ d) new Zop( );
- ☐ e) new Zup( );

Question 9

Given the code in Figure Q01, what code would be valid where the blanked out box appears:

Zop z = ████ ;

- ○ a) new Zap( );
- ○ b) new Zep( );
- ○ c) new Zip( );
- ○ d) new Zop( );
- ○ e) new Zup( );

Question 10

Given the code in Figure Q01, which of the following statements are true:

- ☐ a) a Zop is a Zap
- ☐ b) a Zop is a Zep
- ☐ c) a Zop is a Zip
- ☐ d) a Zip is a Zop

Question 11

Looking at Fig Q01, and noting which classes explicitly implement the Zap interface, which of the following statements are true:

☐ a) a Zep is a Zap
☐ b) a Zip is a Zap
☐ c) a Zop is a Zap
☐ d) a Zup is a Zap

Question 12

Looking at Figure Q01, what would be the result of attempting to compile and run the following code:

```
Zop z = new Zop();
System.out.println(z.sayIt());
```

O a) the code will not compile
O b) the code will compile but not run
O c) the code will compile, run, and output "Down deep, I am a Zep."
O d) the code will compile, run, and output "Down deep, I am a Zop."

Question 13

Looking at Figure Q01, and noting how the sayIt() method is implemented for both the Zep and the Zop, what would be the result of attempting to compile and run the following code:

```
Zep z = new Zop();
System.out.println(z.sayIt());
```

O a) the code will not compile
O b) the code will compile but not run
O c) the code will compile, run, and output "Down deep, I am a Zep."
O d) the code will compile, run, and say "Down deep, I am a Zop."

Question 14

Given a class that represents a stop-watch, and has a property that represents the start time, what name should be given to the property?

- O a) startTime
- O b) StartTime
- O c) _StartTime
- O d) _startTime

Question 15

Given the following class declaration, which type of UML symbol would be used to connect TypeA with TypeB on a UML diagram?

public abstract class TypeA implements TypeB

- O a) 
- O b)
- O c)
- O d)
- O e)

Question 16

Which of the following symbols represent a composition relationship between two classes?

- O a)
- O b)
- O c)
- O d)
- O e)

Question 17

Which symbol would be used to represent the relationship between TypeA and TypeC, given the following code?

```
public   class   TypeA   extends   TypeB{

  private TypeC sea;

  TypeA (TypeC c)   {
     this.sea = c;
  }

  public   TypeC   getTypeC() {
     return sea;
  }
}
```

- O a) ——————>
- O b) - - - - - - - - - - - - - - -▷
- O c) ——————▷
- O d) ◆——————
- O e) ——————

Question 18

Which option would be a valid implementation of the following pseudo code?

```
if age > 55
  then type := "senior"
  else type := "regular"
endif
```

O a)

```
if (age > 55)
  then type == "senior"
  else type == "regular"
 endif
```

O b)

```
if (age > 55) {
  type = "senior";
}
else {
  type = "regular";
 }
```

O c)

```
if (age > 55) {
  type = "senior";
}
else {
  type = "regular";
 }
endIf
```

O d)

```
if (age > 55)
  var type = {"senior"}
else
  var type = {"regular"}
 endif
```

Question 19

Which option would be a valid implementation of the following pseudo code?

```
evencount := 0
oddcount := 0
for each element in the array
  if element is even
  evencount := evencount + 1
  else
  oddcount := oddcount + 1
  endfor
```

☐ a)

```
for (int i = 0; i<array.length;i++) {
  if (array[i]%2==0){
    evencount++;
  }
  else{
    oddcount++;
  }
}
```

☐ b)

```
for (int i = 0; i<array.length;i++) {
  if (array[i]%2==0)
    evencount++;
  else
    oddcount++;
}
```

☐ c)

```
for (int i = 0; i<array.length;i++)
  if ( i%2==0)
    evencount++;
  else
    oddcount++;
```

Question 20

An application needs to take two floating point numbers as parameters, perform a calculation, and return an integer to the calling program. What would the method signature of this method look like?

- O a) public integer doSomeThing (float a, float b)
- O b) public (float a, float b) doSomeThing (int response)
- O c) public long doSomeThing(double c, double d)
- O d) public double doSomething(double c, double d)

Question 21

According to the JavaBean specification, which of the following options are expected of a compliant JavaBean?

- ☐ a) a JavaBean should have a non-default constructor
- ☐ b) a JavaBean should have a default constructor
- ☐ c) a JavaBean should implement the java.io.Serializable interface
- ☐ d) data should be encapsulated with private instance variables and private setters and getters

Question 22

To loop through a character String, one character at a time, until the character 'x' is encountered, which of the following flow control options would be best to use?

- O a) for loop
- O b) while loop
- O c) do while loop
- O d) if loop

Question 23

Which of the following variable scopes have little meaning in a Java program?
☐ a) instance ☐ b) class ☐ c) method ☐ d) block ☐ e) global ☐ f) program

Question 24

Which of the following is the correct syntax for determining the number of characters in a String? (String string = "abcde";)
O a) string.size; O b) string.size( ); O c) string.length; O d) string.length( );

Question 25

A file named Tester.java, that is the launch point of your J2SE application, is placed in the bin directory of the SDK. Which of the following commands would successfully compile this source file?
O a) java Tester O b) javac Tester O c) java Tester.java O d) javac Tester.java O e) java Tester.class O f) javac Tester.class

Question 26

J2SE applications are deployed as:
O a) JAR files
O b) class files
O c) JavaDoc
O d) packages

Question 27

Objects such as Reader and Writer are found in which package?
O a) java.lang
O b) java.util
O c) java.io
O d) java.net

Question 28

Which option should be used to specify a location for compiled class files to be stored?
O a) -d
O b) -D
O c) -classpath
O d) -output

Question 29

When performing the modulus operation: **int remainder = x % 10;** Which of the following statements are true, assuming x is a valid int?
☐ a) The remainder will never be less than 10.
☐ b) The remainder will never exceed 9.
☐ c) The remainder will never be 0.
☐ d) The remainder could potentially be negative.

Question 30

Given dates in the format dd-mm-yyyy, how would you parse out the numbers, while ignoring the dashes?

- ○ a) day: substring(1,3) month: substring(4,6) year: substring(7,11)
- ○ b) day: substring(0,3) month: substring(3,6) year: substring(6,11)
- ○ c) day: substring(1,2) month: substring(4,5) year: substring(7,10)
- ○ d) day: substring(0,2) month: substring(3,5) year: substring(6,10)

Question 31

Two methods with the same name in the same class:

- ☐ a) is not allowed in Java
- ☐ b) is not allowed in some languages, but is allowed in Java
- ☐ c) is known as method overloading
- ☐ d) is known as method overriding

Question 32

When one object depends upon another for its existence, this is known as:

- ○ a) composition
- ○ b) abstraction
- ○ c) association
- ○ d) inheritance

Question 33

Java Server Pages:

- ☐ a) generate markup, typically html, for display in a client browser
- ☐ b) can generate displays for Microdevices by generating WML
- ☐ c) execute on the client side
- ☐ d) execute on the server side

Question 34

What are the two types of Session Enterprise Java Beans?
☐ a) Stateless Session Bean
☐ b) Stateful Session Bean
☐ c) HttpSession Bean
☐ d) Container Session Bean

Question 35

In web based applications, validation of user input should be performed:
☐ a) On the client side through Java Applets
☐ b) On the client side through JavaScript
☐ c) On the server side through a web container technology such as Servlets or ServletFilters
☐ d) On the EIS/Database tier by the database

Question 36

JMS supports:
☐ a) asynchronous messaging
☐ b) synchronous messaging
☐ c) publish and subscribe messaging
☐ d) point to point messaging

Question 37

A queue is most tightly associated with:
O a) JMS
O b) point to point messaging
O c) subscribe and distribute messaging
O d) publish and subscribe messaging

Question 38

Which technology, available through J2SE, provides facilities for invoking methods on components running on a remote JVM?

- O a) Remote Method Invocation (RMI)
- O b) Enterprise Java Beans
- O c) Remote Invocation of Methods (RIM)
- O d) JMS

Question 39

An application is returning blank characters at the end of a String as dollar signs. How could you most easily delete these dollar signs from the String by using methods of the String class?

- O a) use the method replace("$", " ") followed by a call to trim( )
- O b) use the method replace('$', ' ') followed by a call to trim( )
- O c) use the method replace("$", "")
- O d) call the method replace('$', '')

Question 40

Which conditional statements will evaluate to true, given the following two lines of code:

String one = "Hello";
String two = "Hello";

- ☐ a) (one = two)
- ☐ b) (one = = two)
- ☐ c) (one.equals(two))
- ☐ d) (one != two)

Question 41

When a method is invoked on an object, the JVM looks at the object class for an implementation, and if it does not find one, it moves up the hierarchy chain from the most specific class, to the most generic class until it finds an implementation. The process of performing this method name matching at runtime, as opposed to compile time, is known as:

O a) Late Binding

O b) Just in Time (JIT) Compiling

O c) Early Binding

O d) Just in Time (JIT) Binding

Question 42

Which of the following best describe a switch statement:

☐ a) switch statements are recommended as a best practice for object oriented programming

☐ b) switch statements are discouraged as being un-object oriented

☐ c) after a case condition is met and performed, execution jumps to the end of the switch statement

☐ d) after a case condition is met and performed, each of the following case statements are executed

Question 43

Which of the following statements are true about a setter method:

☐ a) a setter method takes no arguments

☐ b) a setter method takes at least one argument

☐ c) a setter is also known as an accessor

☐ d) a setter is also known as a mutator

Question 44

Given the following class:

```
public class BuyMoreBooks extends ExamScam{
 public static void main(String args[]){
   System.out.println("Discerning Bombs");
 }
}
```

What will be the result of running:

java –version BuyMoreBooks

O a) The version and build of the program, BuyMoreBooks, will display

O b) The version and build of the JVM will display

O c) The version and build of the program, BuyMoreBooks, will display, followed by the words ***Discerning Bombs***

O d) The version and build of the JVM will display, followed by the words ***Discerning Bombs***

Question 45

Given the following class diagram, how would the Customer class be coded:

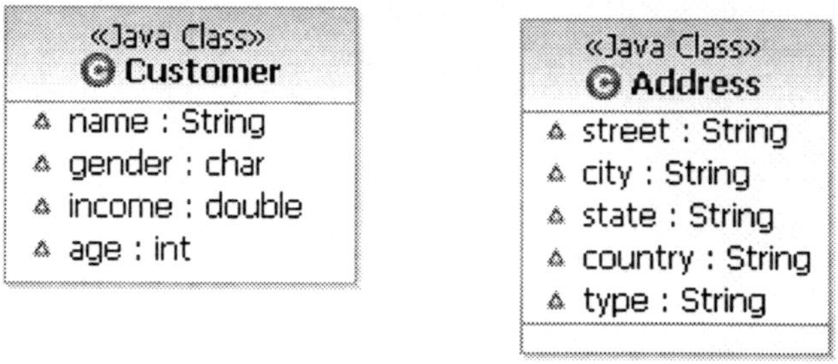

«Java Class» Customer
name : String
gender : char
income : double
age : int

«Java Class» Address
street : String
city : String
state : String
country : String
type : String

O a)

```
public class Customer extends Object {
  String name;  int age;  char gender; double income;
  Address address;

}
```

O b)

```
public class Customer extends Object {
  String name;  int age;  char gender; double income;
  Address address;

  public Address getAddress() {
    return this.address;
  }
}
```

O c)

```
public class Customer extends Object {
  String name;  int age;  char gender; double income;
  Address[] address;
}
```

O d)

```
public class Customer extends Object {
  String name;  int age;  char gender; double income;
}
```

Question 46

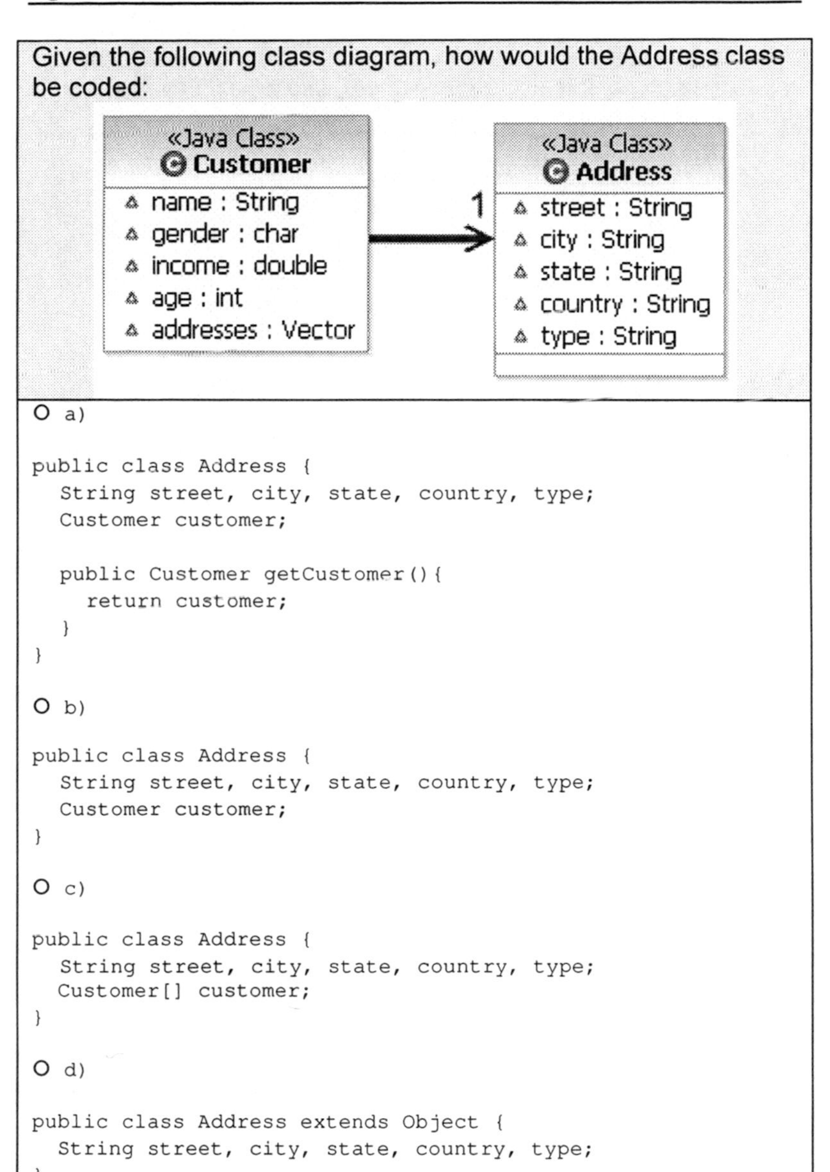

Given the following class diagram, how would the Address class be coded:

O a)

```
public class Address {
  String street, city, state, country, type;
  Customer customer;

  public Customer getCustomer(){
    return customer;
  }
}
```

O b)

```
public class Address {
  String street, city, state, country, type;
  Customer customer;
}
```

O c)

```
public class Address {
  String street, city, state, country, type;
  Customer[] customer;
}
```

O d)

```
public class Address extends Object {
  String street, city, state, country, type;
}
```

Question 47

When declared as instance variables, which of the following types default to false if they are not explicitly initialized by a constructor?

- O a) String
- O b) Boolean
- O c) Double
- O d) boolean

Question 48

Given an instance named joe, with a property named size, how would you reference this property in code?

- O a) joe.size( )
- O b) joe.size
- O c) size.joe
- O d) size.joe( )

Question 49

Which of the following lines of code will ***not*** properly increase the value of the variable x, given the initialization **int x =10;** ?

- O a) x += 10;
- O b) x =+ 10;
- O c) x++;
- O d) ++x;

Question 50

What can be said about the following class, based upon the class diagram:

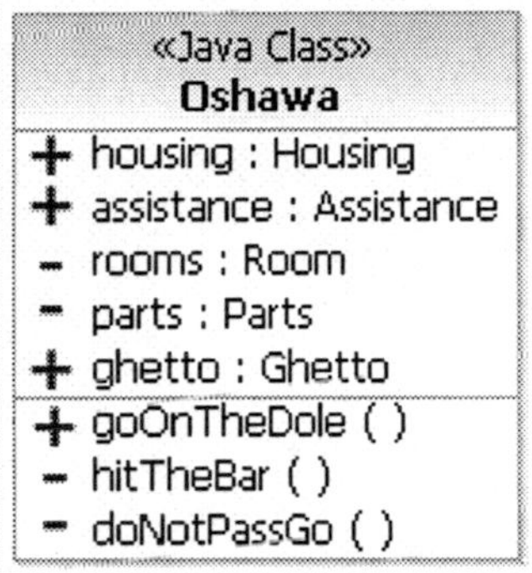

«Java Class»
Oshawa

+ housing : Housing
+ assistance : Assistance
- rooms : Room
- parts : Parts
+ ghetto : Ghetto

+ goOnTheDole ( )
- hitTheBar ( )
- doNotPassGo ( )

☐ a) The class has five properties and three methods
☐ b) The class has five methods and three properties
☐ c) Two methods are private and one property is private
☐ d) Two properties are private and one method is public

Question 51

Which option would be a valid implementation of the following pseudo code?

```
if length > 640
  then size := "too big"
  else size := "acceptable"
endif
```

O a)

```
if (length > 640)
  then type == "too big"
  else type == "acceptable"
 endif
```

O b)

```
if (length > 640) {
  type = "too big";
}
else {
  type = "acceptable";
 }
```

O c)

```
if (length > 640) {
  type = 'too big';
}
else {
  type = 'acceptable';
 }
endIf
```

O d)

```
if (length > 640) {
  type = 'too big';
}
else {
  type = 'acceptable';
 }
```

Chapter 24
Sample SCJA Exam Answers

Answer 1

Which of the following are included in the eight, primitive data types in Java:
☐ a) Integer ☐ b) Character ☐ c) boolean ☐ d) double ☐ e) String
There are eight primitive types: long, int, short, byte, double, float, boolean and char. These eight primitive types are the building blocks of all objects and applications in Java. Notice that the names of primitive types, unlike the class names of Java objects, start with a lower case letter. String, Integer and Character all have leading upper case letters, indicating that they are not primitive types, but are instead, full fledged Java classes.

Answer 2

Which of the following techniques are valid for initializing a char?
O a) char c = "C"; O b) char c = C; O c) char c = 'C'; O d) char c = 'see';
It's easy to get tripped up when initializing a char. A char represents a single character, and unlike a String, the single character must be within single quotes, not double quotes, when performing the initialization.

Answer 3

Which of the eight primitive types are signed integer types?	
☐ a) int	☐ e) char
☐ b) float	☐ f) byte
☐ c) double	☐ g) long
☐ d) boolean	☐ h) short

In polite circles, long, int, short and byte are the whole number, ***integer*** types that cannot contain fractional or decimal values. These primitive types are signed, which means they can take on both positive and negative values.

The char primitive type is also an integer type, as it can use all of its 16 bits to represent an unsigned number, meaning it can only take positive values. Since a char is unsigned, it is an incorrect option to this question.

Answer 4

Which of the following statements are true:

☐ a) Implementing an interface relieves the implementing class from having to code methods defined and implemented in the interface

☐ b) Extending an abstract class relieves the extending class from having to code methods defined and implemented in the parent

☐ c) Abstract classes may contain unimplemented, abstract methods

☐ d) Interfaces may contain unimplemented, abstract methods

Options b) c) and d) are correct. Both abstract classes and interfaces may contain unimplemented, abstract methods. The concrete classes extending the abstract class, or interface, must then implement the abstractly defined methods.

While an abstract class may contain unimplemented methods, it may also provide methods that are indeed implemented. As a result, an extending class gains the functionality of these methods through normal inheritance, making option b) correct.

Option a) is incorrect, as methods defined in an interface are abstract, and implementing classes are forced to add their own method implementations.

Answer 5

The String class in Java is essentially an organized grouping of char primitive types. Assuming that every char in a String is garbage collected when the String goes out of scope, what could be said about the relationship between a String and the char primitive types that it contains:

- O a) A String is associated with chars
- O b) A String is composed of chars
- O c) A char is associated with Strings
- O d) A char is composed of Strings

Answer b) is correct. A String is certainly associated with chars, but in fact, the relationship is stronger than a simple association, as the char associated with a String is deleted when the String is deleted. If we agree that the existence of a char is linked heavily to the existence of the String, it can be said that a String is composed of chars.

By the way, this question has been phrased to force the answer to be option b). I think you'd get a good argument from an experienced programmer that says a String is not technically composed of chars.

Answer 6

On a UML diagram, instance variables will typically be decorated with which symbol:

- O a) $
- O b) #
- O c) +
- O d) -

Part of data encapsulation in Java is keeping instance variables private. On a UML diagram, private variables and methods are denoted with a minus sign, making option d) correct.

Answer 7

What would be the output of the following code:

```
int x = 10;
int y = 5;
System.out.println( x + y  + " = x + y =  "+ x + y);
```

- a) 15 = 15 = 15
- b) 15 = x + y = 15
- c) 15 = x + y = 105
- d) 105 = x + y = 15

The JVM will start doing mathematical operations from left to right, so when x + y is first encountered, the JVM will add them, giving the umber 15. However, once the JVM is asked to add a number to a String, it will do string concatenation, creating a String that says "15 = x + y" When the JVM then adds the x and y values to this string, it continues with String concatenation, as opposed to normal addition, thus appending 105 to the end of the existing String.

The output for this little code snippet ends up being option c):

15 = x + y = 105

Figure - Q01

```
public interface Zap {
  public abstract String sayIt();
}


abstract class Zep implements Zap{
  public String sayIt(){
    return "Down deep, I am a Zep";
  }
}


class Zip extends Zep{
  public String sayIt(){
    return "Down deep, I am a Zip";
  }
}


class Zop extends Zip{
  public String sayIt(){
    return "Down deep, I am a Zop";
  }
}


class Zup {
  public String sayIt(){
    return "Down deep, I am a Zup";
  }
}
```

Answer 8

Given the code in Figure Q01, what code would be valid where the blanked out box appears:

Zap z = ████ ;

- ☐ a) new Zap( );
- ☐ b) new Zep( );
- ☐ c) new Zip( );
- ☐ d) new Zop( );
- ☐ e) new Zup( );

Answers c) and d) are correct.

Zap and Zep cannot be preceded by the new keyword, because they are interfaces and abstract classes respectively, and you cannot create concrete instances of interfaces and abstract classes.

Options c) and d) are correct, because a Zap is being requested, and both a Zip and Zop are special types of Zaps, as they inherit from Zep, which implements the Zap interface.

Option e) is incorrect, as Zup does not inherit from Zep, or is it a subclass of Zep, and Zup does not implement the Zap interface, even though it does define and implement the sayIt( ) method.

Answer 9

Given the code in Figure Q01, what code would be valid where the blanked out box appears:

Zop z = ████ ;

- ○ a) new Zap( );
- ○ b) new Zep( );
- ○ c) new Zip( );
- ○ d) new Zop( );
- ○ e) new Zup( );

Only option d) is correct, as the Zop class is at the bottom of the class hierarchy, and as a result, is the most specific of all of the objects. If you want a Zop, a *less specialized* Zip simply will not do.

Answer 10

Given the code in figure Q01, which of the following statements are true:
☐ a) a Zop is a Zap ☐ b) a Zop is a Zep ☐ c) a Zop is a Zip ☐ d) a Zip is a Zop
Inheritance and interface implementations represent an is-a relationship. Subclasses, and implementing interfaces have an is-a relationship with all ancestor classes and implemented interfaces, making options a) b) and c) correct. However, the is-a relationship only exists for siblings with ancestors, and not the other way around, so we cannot say that a Zip is a Zop, since a Zip is above a Zop on the inheritance hierarchy.

Answer 11

Looking at Fig Q01, and noting which classes explicitly implement the Zap interface, which of the following statements are true:
☐ a) a Zep is a Zap ☐ b) a Zip is a Zap ☐ c) a Zop is a Zap ☐ d) a Zup is a Zap
Options a) b) and c) are correct. Notice that while Zip and Zop do not explicitly state that they implement the Zap interface, we can still consider them to be a type of Zap. This is true, because Zip and Zop inherit from the ancestor class Zep, which does indeed implement the Zap interface, making all siblings of Zep, Zaps as well. Zup does not implement the Zap interface, or extend a class that does implement the Zap interface, so it cannot be considered a Zap.

Answer 12

Looking at Figure Q01, what would be the result of attempting to compile and run the following code:

```
Zop z = new Zop();
System.out.println(z.sayIt());
```

O a) the code will not compile

O b) the code will compile but not run

O c) the code will compile, run, and output "Down deep, I am a Zep."

O d) the code will compile, run, and output "Down deep, I am a Zop."

Answer d) is correct. An instance of the concrete class Zop is required, and an instance of the concrete class Zop is delivered. Furthermore, the behavior of a Zop is to print out "Down deep, I am a Zop" when the sayIt method is invoked, and that is exactly what will happen when we see the method invoked through z.sayIt( );

Answer 13

Looking at Figure Q01, and noting how the sayIt() method is implemented for both the Zep and the Zop, what would be the result of attempting to compile and run the following code:

```
Zep z = new Zop();
System.out.println(z.sayIt());
```

O a) the code will not compile

O b) the code will compile but not run

O c) the code will compile, run, and output "Down deep, I am a Zep."

O d) the code will compile, run, and output "Down deep, I am a Zop."

The answer is d), "Down deep, I am a Zop" This may seem a little counter-intuitive, as the object is being held as a Zep, which returns "Down deep, I am a Zop." However, what is important is not the type the object is being held as. What is important is how the object being held was created. We are holding a Zep, but it was created as a Zop, and a Zop will always behave as a Zop, regardless of how it is being held.

The fact that an object can be held, or referenced, as one type of object, but behave as the object it was created as, combines the ideas of polymorphism and late binding. Polymorphism indicates that an object can take on many different forms, and for us, a Zep can take on the form of a Zip and a Zop.

Late binding implies that when a method is called on an object, not matter which form the object has taken, the JVM will look at how the object was created, and start at that point of the class hierarchy, and work its way up the class hierarchy until it finds a matching method. This is the binding aspect of late binding. The fact that this binding process happens at runtime, rather than compile or build time, is where the word late comes from in the term late binding.

Answer 14

Given a class that represents a stop-watch, and has a property that represents the start time, what name should be given to the property?
O a) startTime O b) StartTime O c) _StartTime O d) _startTime
Option a) is correct. Instance variables should start with a lower case letter, with each new word having an upper case letter. While it would compile and run, instance variables, by the JavaBean convention, should never start with an uppercase letter. Occasionally, you will see instance variables that start with an underscore. Typically, this denotes instance variables or code that has been automatically generated by a builder tool.

Answer 15

Given the following class declaration, which type of UML symbol would be used to connect TypeA with TypeB on a UML diagram? public abstract class TypeA implements TypeB
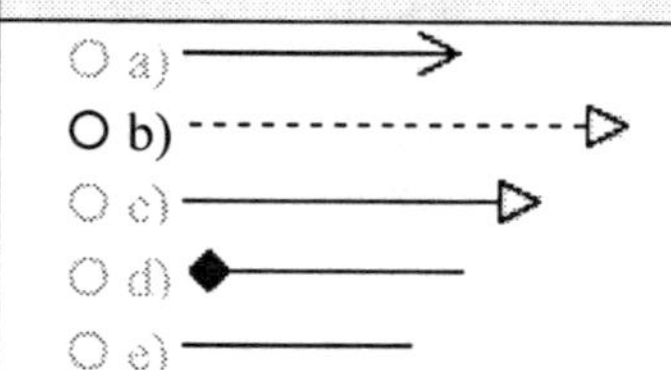
Option b) is correct. When a class implements an interface, a UML diagram will show a dotted line with a closed arrowhead pointing from the implementing class, to the interface being implemented.

Answer 16

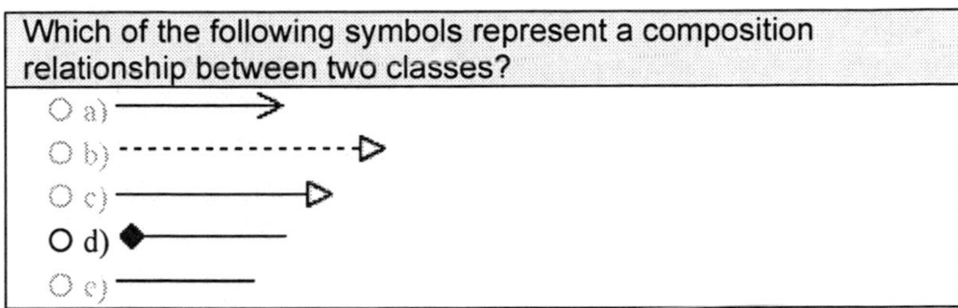

Option d) is correct. A diamond attached to a solid line represents a composition relationship. Containment is a special type of relationship, where one object, the containing object, has significant control over the lifecycle of the contained objects. The diamond is placed adjacent to the containing class, and the solid line goes towards the contained class.

Answer 17

Which symbol would be used to represent the relationship between TypeA and TypeC, given the following code?

```
public class TypeA extends TypeB{

  private TypeC sea;

  TypeA (TypeC c)  { this.sea = c;}

  public TypeC getTypeC() {
    return sea;
  }

}
```

- O a) ————————>
- O b) - - - - - - - - - - - - - - -▷
- O c) ————————▷
- O d) ◆————————
- O e) ————————

Option a) is correct. Since TypeC is an instance property of TypeA, we can say that TypeA has-a TypeC. However, since there is also a getter method, we can say that a TypeC object can be obtained from the TypeA class, which means TypeC is navigable through TypeA. A solid line with an open headed arrow shows a navigable association between two objects, and the class being pointed at with the open headed arrow can be obtained from the associating class.

Answer 18

Which option would be a valid implementation of the following pseudo code?

```
if age > 55
  then type := "senior"
  else type := "regular"
endif
```

○ a)

```
if (age > 55)
  then type == "senior"
  else type == "regular"
 endif
```

○ b)

```
if (age > 55) {
  type = "senior";
}
else {
  type = "regular";
 }
```

○ c)

```
if (age > 55) {
  type = "senior";
}
else {
  type = "regular";
 }
endif
```

○ d)

```
if (age > 55)
  var type = ("senior")
else
  var type = ("regular")
 endif
```

Only option b) is valid Java code. Remember, there is no endif statement in Java.

Answer 19

Which option would be a valid implementation of the following pseudo code?

```
evencount := 0
oddcount := 0
for each element in the array
  if element is even
  evencount := evencount + 1
  else
  oddcount := oddcount + 1
  endfor
```

☐ a)

```
for (int i = 0; i<array.length;i++) {
  if (array[i]%2==0){
    evencount++;
  }
  else{
    oddcount++;
  }
}
```

☐ b)

```
for (int i = 0; i<array.length;i++) {
  if (array[i]%2==0)
    evencount++;
  else
    oddcount++;
}
```

☐ c)

```
for (int i = 0; i<array.length;i++)
  if ( i%2==0)
    evencount++;
  else
    oddcount++;
```

Options a) and b) are valid solutions. If a flow control statement is not followed by braces, the first line after the statement is executed, so both solution a) and b) will work. The for loop in solution c) is missing braces, which it must have to evaluate the full if..else block.

Answer 20

An application needs to take two floating point numbers as parameters, perform a calculation, and return an integer to the calling program. What would the method signature of this method look like?

- ○ a) public integer doSomeThing (float a, float b)
- ○ b) public (float a, float b) doSomeThing (int response)
- ○ c) public long doSomeThing(double c, double d)
- ○ d) public double doSomething(double c, double d)

Option c) is the correct answer. The long is an integer, aka whole number, type, and a double is a decimal, or floating type number. Options a) and b) would simply not compile, and option d) returns a double to the calling program, not an integer type.

Answer 21

According to the JavaBean specification, which of the following options are expected of a compliant JavaBean?

- ☐ a) a JavaBean should have a non-default constructor
- ☐ b) a JavaBean should have a default constructor
- ☐ c) a JavaBean should implement the java.io.Serializable interface
- ☐ d) data should be encapsulated with private instance variables and private setters and getters

A JavaBean should have a default constructor, it should implement the java.io.Serializable interface, and it should encapsulate its data by making instance variables private, and allowing access to those instance variables, when it makes sense, through ***public*** setters and getters. Options b) and c) are correct.

Answer 22

To loop through a character String, one character at a time, until the character 'x' is encountered, which of the following flow control options would be best to use?

- O a) for loop
- O b) while loop
- O c) do while loop
- O d) if loop

Option c) is correct. Since you have to start with the first character in the String, it makes sense that the first character evaluation would happen inside of the loop. When the character in question is encountered, the condition of the do..while loop can be configured to exit.

Answer 23

Which of the following variable scopes have little meaning in a Java program?

- ☐ a) instance
- ☐ b) class
- ☐ c) method
- ☐ d) block
- ☐ e) global
- ☐ f) program

While global and program scope variables may exist in other programming languages, they have very little meaning in Java. In Java, when we talk about variable scope, we talk about instance, class, method or block scope, and to a certain extent, we discuss the access modifier associated with an instance variable, such as whether the variable is public or private. But global and program scopes really don't exist in Java, making options e) and f) correct.

Answer 24

Which of the following is the correct syntax for determining the number of characters in a String? (String string = "abcde";)
O a) string.size; O b) string.size( ); O c) string.length; O d) string.length( );
The size( ) method can be used to figure out the number of elements in a Vector, but it has no meaning with regards to a String. The length ***property*** applies to an array, but not to the String class. To determine the number of characters in a String, you call the method length( );

Answer 25

A file named Tester.java, that is the launch point of your J2SE application is placed in the bin directory of the SDK. Which of the following commands would successfully compile this source file?
O a) java Tester O b) javac Tester O c) java Tester.java O d) javac Tester.java O e) java Tester.class O f) javac Tester.class
Option d) is correct. The utility used to ***compile*** Java code is the javac utility, as opposed to the java utility that is used to ***run*** code. When compiling code, you need to specify the case sensitive name of the class, along with the .java extension. If you leave out the extension, the compilation won't work. And don't try to compile any files with a .class extension, as .class files are the result of compilation, and cannot be further compiled.

Answer 26

J2SE applications are deployed as:
O a) JAR files O b) class files O c) JavaDoc O d) packages
Java applications that run as Applets in a browser, or stand-along applications that run on a JRE are exported as Java Application aRchives, also known as JAR files. Option a) is correct.

Answer 27

Objects such as Reader and Writer are found in which package?
O a) java.lang O b) java.util O c) java.io O d) java.net
Even though the System class, which uses the print method of the PrintWriter, is found in java.lang, the classes that have to do with input and output, such as Reader and Writer, are found in the java.io package. Option c) is correct.

Answer 28

Which option should be used to specify a location for compiled class files to be stored?
O a) -d O b) -D O c) -classpath O d) -output
It's easy to get the two confused, but for the record, the –D switch, pronounced with an upper case D, is used for setting system properties with the java runtime command. The –d switch is used with the compiler to specify a location for compiled code. Option a) is correct.

Answer 29

When performing the modulus operation:
int remainder = x % 10;
Which of the following statements are true, assuming x is a valid int?

- ☐ a) The remainder will never be less than 10.
- ☐ b) The remainder will never exceed 9.
- ☐ c) The remainder will never be 0.
- ☐ d) The remainder could potentially be negative.

Options b) and d) are correct.

If the variable x is 10, then the remainder will be zero, meaning the remainder will never exceed 9, and the remainder can in fact be zero. This makes options a) incorrect, and c) incorrect. If x is negative, the remainder will be negative, and if x is 9, the remainder will be 9, making options b) and d) the correct options.

Answer 30

Given dates in the format dd-mm-yyyy, how would you parse out the numbers, while ignoring the dashes?

- ○ a) day: substring(1,3) month: substring(4,6) year: substring(7,11)
- ○ b) day: substring(0,3) month: substring(3,6) year: substring(6,11)
- ○ c) day: substring(1,2) month: substring(4,5) year: substring(7,10)
- ○ d) day: substring(0,2) month: substring(3,5) year: substring(6,10)

Option d) is correct.

The substring method uses a zero based counting method, inclusive of the first number, and incremental on the last number, meaning if you wanted the first and second characters in a string, you would need to specify 0,2 as the parameters to the substring method.

```
String date = "31-02-1999";
String day = date.substring(0,2);
String month = date.substring(3,5);
String year = date.substring(6,10);
```

Answer 31

Two methods with the same name in the same class:
☐ a) is not allowed in Java ☐ b) is not allowed in some languages, but is allowed in Java ☐ c) is known as method overloading ☐ d) is known as method overriding
Quite often, a class will provide a behavior that can be tweaked slightly if extra information is provided. If this is the case, Java allows you to create multiple methods with the same name in a class, so long as each method takes a different set of arguments. This is known as method overloading. The String class overloads quite a few methods, one of which is indexOf, which can take a String as an argument, or a String and an int. With just a String provided, the indexOf method returns the index at which the String is first encountered. Alternatively, you can provide an int as well, and the search for a matching String will start at the index of the int number specified. Method overloading is a common practice in Java programming.

Answer 32

When one object depends upon another for its existence, this is known as:
O a) composition O b) abstraction O c) association O d) inheritance
Composition is a special type of relationship between objects that involves a 'has-a' relationship, along with strong lifecycle maintenance over the 'had' object. Composition is not a manifestation of inheritance, or extending a parent class. Inheritance represents an is-a relationship, which is quite different from the has-a relationship of composition and association.

Answer 33

Java Server Pages:
☐ a) generate markup, typically html, for display in a client browser ☐ b) can generate displays for Microdevices by generating WML ☐ c) execute on the client side ☐ d) execute on the server side
Options a) b) and d) are correct. JSPs execute on a J2EE application server, and send markup, dynamically, to the client. JSPs are often associated with sending HTML to clients, but any markup language can be generated by a JSP, be it XML, WML or HDML for handheld devices.

Answer 34

What are the two types of Session Enterprise Java Beans?
☐ a) Stateless Session Bean ☐ b) Stateful Session Bean ☐ c) HttpSession Bean ☐ d) Container Session Bean
Options a) and b) are correct. SFSBs and SLSBs are the two type of Enterprise Java Beans that are not associated with persistent data, or associated directly with a messaging infrastructure.

Answer 35

In web based applications, validation of user input should be performed:
☐ a) On the client side through Java Applets ☐ b) On the client side through JavaScript ☐ c) On the server side through a web container technology such as Servlets or ServletFilters ☐ d) On the EIS/Database tier by the database
Options b) and c) are correct. With typical web based applications, validation of user input will be performed by JavaScript on the browser side. However, since JavaScript can easily be turned off by a client, a second round of validation should also be done by your server side components, such as Servlets, Filters, or other technologies used for input validation.

Answer 36

JMS supports:
☐ a) asynchronous messaging ☐ b) synchronous messaging ☐ c) publish and subscribe messaging ☐ d) point to point messaging
JMS is an asynchronous messaging system, which means a message is left by a client, and some time in the future, the message will be handled. The client does not wait for the message to be consumed before going on with its business. JMS supports two types of messages: *publish and subscribe messaging* is the first, and *point to point messaging* is the second.

Answer 37

A queue is most tightly associated with:
O a) JMS O b) point to point messaging O c) subscribe and distribute messaging O d) publish and subscribe messaging
A queue is associated with point to point messaging, whereas a topic is associated with publish an subscribe messaging. Both are valid J2EE destinations.

Answer 38

Which technology, available through J2SE, provides facilities for invoking methods on components running on a remote JVM?
O a) Remote Method Invocation (RMI) O b) Enterprise Java Beans O c) Remote Invocation of Methods (RIM) O d) JMS
RMI, Remote Method Invocation, is a technology that is available to the J2SE environment that provides for the invocation of methods on Java components running in remote JVMs. Stubs, skeletons and an **rmiregistry** are terms and components often heard when talking about J2SE RMI implementations.

Answer 39

An application is returning blank characters at the end of a string as dollar signs. How could you most easily delete these dollar signs from the String by using methods of the String class?

- O a) use the method replace("$", " ") followed by a call to trim( )
- O b) use the method replace('$', ' ') followed by a call to trim( )
- O c) use the method replace("$", "")
- O d) call the method replace('$', '')

The best answer is option c). While both a) and b) work, option c) requires fewer lines of code, and is a better use of the replace method. Of the four solutions, d) would not compile, as '' is not a valid char.

It should be noted that the replace method of the String class in Java 1.5 is overloaded, with one method taking two CharSequence types, and the other taking two primitive char types as arguments.

Answer 40

Which conditional statements will evaluate to true, given the following two lines of code:

```
String one = "Hello";
String two = "Hello";
```

- ☐ a) (one = two)
- ☐ b) (one = = two)
- ☐ c) (one.equals(two))
- ☐ d) (one != two)

You should always use the .equals( ) method to compare two objects, but for a number of reasons that have to do with the efficient management of String data, the double equals sign will usually work when comparing Strings. Nevertheless, you should always compare two String objects using .equals( ), and not the double equals sign.

Answer 41

When a method is invoked on an object, the JVM looks at the object class for an implementation, and if it does not find one, it moves up the hierarchy chain from the most specific class, to the most generic class, until it finds an implementation. The process of performing this method name matching at runtime, as opposed to compile time, is known as:

O a) Late Binding

O b) Just in Time (JIT) Compiling

O c) Early Binding

O d) Just in Time (JIT) Binding

The question itself pretty much defines the idea of late binding. The binding is *late* because it occurs at runtime, as opposed to design time.

Answer 42

Which of the following best describe a switch statement:

☐ a) switch statements are recommended as a best practice for object oriented programming

☐ b) switch statements are discouraged as being un-object oriented

☐ c) after a case condition is met and performed, execution jumps to the end of the switch statement

☐ d) after a case condition is met and performed, each of the following case statements are executed

Options b) and d) are correct.

Finding a true condition in a switch statement opens a flood gate, and each case after the true condition is executed. This is why a break statement is so important when using switches. Switches are also considered un-object oriented, and a heavy reliance on switch statements might be an indication that an object model should be redesigned.

Answer 43

Which of the following statements are true about a setter method:

☐ a) a setter method takes no arguments

☐ b) a setter method takes at least one argument

☐ c) a setter is also known as an accessor

☐ d) a setter is also known as a mutator

Options b) and d) are correct.

A setter takes a value, which is passed into the setter method as an argument, and then updates an instance variable based on the value passed in, making option b) correct. Also, setters are sometimes known as mutator methods.

Answer 44

Given the following class:

```
public class BuyMoreBooks extends ExamScam{
  public static void main(String args[]){
    System.out.println("Discerning Bombs");
 }
}
```

What will be the result of running:

java –version BuyMoreBooks

O a) The version and build of the program, BuyMoreBooks, will display

O b) The version and build of the JVM will display

O c) The version and build of the program, BuyMoreBooks, will display, followed by the words Discerning Bombs

O d) The version and build of the JVM will display, followed by the words Discerning Bombs

Option b) is correct.

The –version switch simply prints out the version and build of the JVM whenever it is used with the java command line utility.

Answer 45

Given the following class diagram, how would the **Customer** class be coded:

«Java Class»
Customer
- name : String
- gender : char
- income : double
- age : int

«Java Class»
Address
- street : String
- city : String
- state : String
- country : String
- type : String

O a)

```
public class Customer extends Object {
  String name;  int age;  char gender; double income;
  Address address;

}
```

O b)

```
public class Customer extends Object {
  String name;  int age;  char gender; double income;
  Address address;

  public Address getAddress() {
    return this.address;
  }
}
```

O c)

```
public class Customer extends Object {
  String name;  int age;  char gender; double income;
  Address[] address;
}
```

O d)

```
public class Customer extends Object {
  String name;  int age;  char gender; double income;
}
```

Option d) is correct. The diagram does not indicate an association between the Customer and the Address, so d) is correct.

Answer 46

Given the following class diagram, how would the **Address** class be coded:

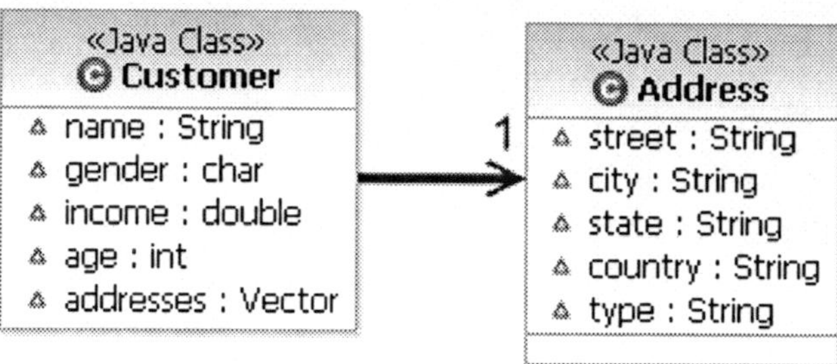

○ a)

```
public class Address {
  String street, city, state, country, type;
  Customer customer;

  public Customer getCustomer(){
    return customer;
  }
}
```

○ b)

```
public class Address {
  String street, city, state, country, type;
  Customer customer;
}
```

○ c)

```
public class Address {
  String street, city, state, country, type;
  Customer[] customer;
}
```

O d)

```
public class Address extends Object {
  String street, city, state, country, type;
}
```

Option d) is correct, as no multiplicity is defined for the Address class, so it does not need a Customer instance.

Answer 47

When declared as instance variables, which of the following types default to false if they are not explicitly initialized by a constructor?
O a) String O b) Boolean O c) Double O d) boolean
Instance variables that are *objects* are initialized to null by default. Primitive types are initialized to zero, with the exception of the boolean, which is initialized by default, to false.

Answer 48

Given an instance named joe, with a property named size, how would you reference this property in code?
O a) joe.size( ) O b) joe.size O c) size.joe O d) size.joe( )
With dot notation, you simply specify the instance, followed by the property name, making option b) correct.

Answer 49

Which of the following lines of code will ***not*** properly increase the value of the variable x, given the initialization **int x = 10;** ?
O a) x += 10; O b) x =+ 10; O c) x++; O d) ++x;
Only b) is correct, because it is incorrect. The plus and equals signs must be transposed for option b) to increment the variable x, otherwise, the value x is simply being assigned the ***positive*** value of 10.

Answer 50

What can be said about the following class, based upon the class diagram:

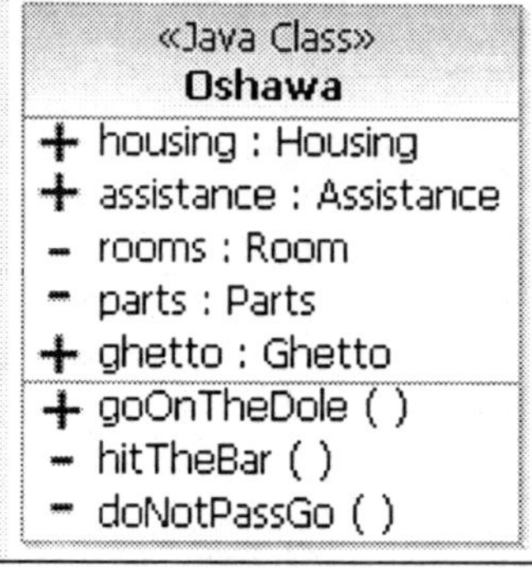

☐ a) The class has five properties and three methods

☐ b) The class has five methods and three properties

☐ c) Two methods are private and one property is private

☐ d) Two properties are private and one method is public

Options a) and d) are correct. In a Class diagram, the first block contains the name of the class, the second block contains properties of the class, and the third block contains methods. Furthermore, the plus sign denotes public properties or methods, and the minus sign denotes private properties or methods. This class has five properties, two of which are private, and three methods, one of which is public.

Answer 51

Which option would be a valid implementation of the following pseudo code?

```
if length > 640
  then size := "too big"
  else size := "acceptable"
endif
```

○ a)

```
if (length > 640)
  then type == "too big"
  else type == "acceptable"
 endif
```

O b)

```
if (length > 640) {
  type = "too big";
}
else {
  type = "acceptable";
 }
```

○ c)

```
if (length > 640) {
  type = 'too big';
}
else {
  type = 'acceptable';
 }
endif
```

O d)

```
if (length > 640) {
  type = 'too big';
}
else {
  type = 'acceptable';
 }
```

Only option b) is valid Java code. Remember, Strings in Java are enclosed in double quotes, not single quotes.

Index

WebSphere, Java, Portal, and J2EE Training

Get Trained by the Expert

Do you need WebSphere, Java, J2EE or Portal training? Come and attend one of the exciting, open enrollment classes in Toronto, Ontario Canada.

Open Enrollment in Toronto, Ottawa and Calgary

Cameron McKenzie, the author of the ExamScam series of books, along with What is WebSphere?, and the *agoodbookon* series of books, uses his unique facilitation techniques, along with his in depth knowledge of Java based technology, to help teach students and inspire them to gain a deeper understanding of the technologies they use.

Custom, Corporate Classes Available

Cameron McKenzie also dedicates two weeks a month to providing custom, corporate training for classes of six students or more. If you can't make it to Toronto, you can always bring Cameron to your own, private, training facilities. Demand is high, so book early, and make sure your education demands will be met in the most efficient, and effective, manner possible.

For more details, email Cameron at mail@cameronmckenzie.com, and check out the www.technicalfacilitation.com website for more details.

More Great Books on Java and J2EE

Always **in stock**, and always **discounted**, when you buy directly from the publisher, either on amazon.com, or directly from the website, **www.pulpjava.com.**

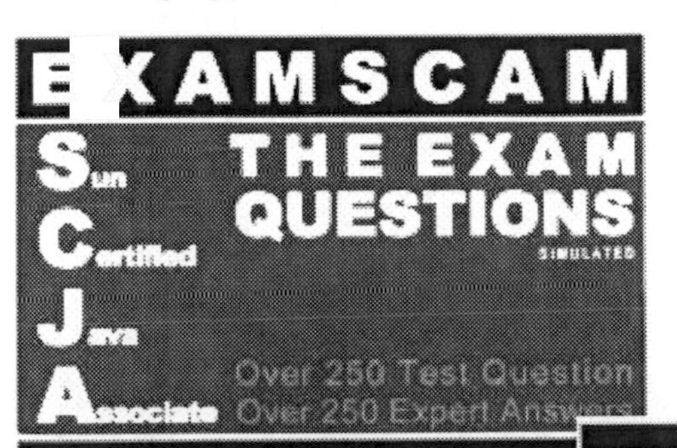

WWW.PULPJAVA.CO
Presents
What is WebSphere?
stifying IBM's Middle-Tier Technology
with content on WebSphere 6.1, Portal, Web Services, and pertinent
ation on versions 4, 5 and 6 of the WebSphere Application Server
w.technicalfacilitation.com

EXAMSCAM
S Certified Java Associate
CERTIFICATION STUDY GUIDE
GET CERTIFIED FAST
The NEW Entry Level Java Certification
Cameron McKenzie
WWW.SCJA.COM

ExamScam
Certification Guide
IBM's Rational Application Developer
IBM Certified Application Developer
Preparing You to Pass Tests 255 and 256